GW01221213

THE NORTHERN COUNTIES RAILWAY

Volume I: Beginnings and Development, 1845–1903

BY THE SAME AUTHOR

The Portstewart Tramway
The Runaway Train: Armagh 1889

Main line train on former Londonderry & Coleraine line at Portvantage Glen about 1875

THE NORTHERN COUNTIES RAILWAY

Volume 1: Beginnings and Development, 1845 - 1903

by

J. R. L. CURRIE

DAVID & CHARLES : NEWTON ABBOT

ISBN 0 7153 5934 7

COPYRIGHT NOTICE

© J. R. L. Currie 1973

All rights reserved. No part of this publication may be reproduced, stored in a retrieval system, or transmitted, in any form or by any means, electronic, mechanical, photocopying, recording or otherwise, without the prior permission of David & Charles (Publishers) Limited

Set in eleven on twelve point Pilgrim
and printed in Great Britain
by Bristol Typesetting Company Limited
for David & Charles (Publishers) Limited
South Devon House Newton Abbot Devon

To the memory of
EDWARD JOHN COTTON
General Manager
Belfast & Northern Counties Railway
1857–1899

Here was a Caesar! when comes such another?

Contents

LIST OF ILLUSTRATIONS		11
FOREWORD		15
1	THE PROVINCE OF ULSTER	17

The northern counties – Belfast – The railway arrives – North of Belfast

2 THE BELFAST AND BALLYMENA RAILWAY   24

In the steps of the Ulster – Rivals – Failure – Proposed again – The prospectus – Related schemes – Towards the Act – Work begins – Land difficulties – Captain Laffan – Opening – Joseph Maunder – The first accounts – To Cookstown and Coleraine – Vicissitudes – Open to Cookstown – Developments at Ballymena – The extension disappoints – A new manager – 'Eagle' – Shortage of capital

3 THE LONDONDERRY AND COLERAINE RAILWAY   64

The twin railways – Work begins – Hard times – To Limavady and Coleraine – The Magilligan branch – The Castledawson extension – The railway in operation – The line is leased – New developments – The B & NC's inheritance – The end of the L & C

4 THE BALLYMENA AND PORTRUSH RAILWAY   88

Early proposals – Portrush – Work progresses – Opening – Dargan – The railway at work – Amalgamation

5 THE MID-VICTORIAN YEARS 1860–1880   107

The new company – Economics – Antrim, Cookstown and Ballycastle – The Belfast Central Railway – Harbour lines – Engineering – The shareholders –

The Londonderry & Coleraine – York Road – Minor mishaps – Further widening – Block working – A loop? – Directors and officials – The golden years

6 THE COUNTY ANTRIM BRANCHES   133
The Carrickfergus and Larne Railway: The 1859 proposal – Work begins – To Stranraer – Delays – Opened on two fronts – Whitehead – Depressed days – The steamer again – Patterns of change – A neighbour at Larne – Ups and downs – Amalgamation
The narrow gauge lines: The Cushendall line – The Larne line – The Ballycastle Railway

7 THE COUNTY LONDONDERRY BRANCHES   166
The Derry Central Railway: Promotion – Difficulties – Work progresses – The line opened – Unprofitable years – The second decade – The end in sight – Protagonists
The Limavady and Dungiven Railway: The Act – Construction – At work – The Board of Works
The Draperstown Railway: Incorporation – Construction – The line opened – The end of the line – *The Portstewart Tramway*

8 THE LATE VICTORIAN COMPANY 1880–1899   207
Hard times – Branches – The Cushendall line – The Larne lines and the steamer – Belfast – Carrickfergus and Coleraine harbours – Engineering – Home Rule – Gill and Wise – Trains and traffic – Magilligan Point – Tragedy at Antrim – Other accidents – Staff relations – Two jubilees

9 TOURISM   240
A Victorian institution – Planning and publicity – Excursions – Special attractions – The hotels – The Holden train

10 INTO THE NEW CENTURY   259
The death of Cotton – The 1899 Act – Road transport experiments – Purchase of the Derry Central – Accidents – Continuing improvements – The Midland in Ulster – The end

| 11 | CONCLUSION | 272 |

Big Nancy Coming Running

APPENDICES
1. Acts of Parliament — 275
2. Directors and officials — 279
3. Dividends paid on ordinary shares — 283
4. Share capital as at 30 June 1902 — 284
5. B & NCR statistics, 1861–1903 — 285
6. Mileage and rolling stock, 1903 — 287

INDEX — 289

List of Illustrations

FRONTISPIECE
Main line train on former Londonderry & Coleraine line at Portvantage Glen about 1875

PLATES

The Rt Hon John Young	33
Edward John Cotton	33
Group of officials, 1868 (*J. H. Houston's Collection*)	34
Bowman Malcolm (*J. H. Houston's Collection*)	34
Walter Bailey	34
Randalstown Viaduct	51
Bann Bridge	51
Londonderry (Waterside) station	52
Castlerock station	52
Whitehead new station (*Lawrence Collection*)	101
Whitehead Promenade (*Lawrence Collection*)	101
Larne Harbour c 1876 (*Lawrence Collection*)	102
Larne Harbour new station (*Lawrence Collection*)	102
Overall view of Larne (*Lawrence Collection*)	119
PS *Princess Beatrice* (*Lawrence Collection*)	119
Portrush new station (*Lawrence Collection*)	120
Northern Counties Hotel	120
York Road station, Belfast: façade (*Lawrence Collection*)	169
York Road station, Belfast: approaches (*Dr E. M. Patterson's Collection*)	169

Coleraine new station	170
Maghera station	170
Trooperslane station	187
Carrickfergus station	187
Narrow gauge train at Ballymena (*Lawrence Collection*)	188
Royal Train, 1897 (*J. H. Houston's Collection*)	188
Parkmore—Cushendall mail car (*Lawrence Collection*)	237
Steam road wagon	237
Ess-na-Larach waterfall, Glenariff (*Lawrence Collection*)	238
Tea House, Glenariff (*Lawrence Collection*)	238
Overall view of The Gobbins Cliff Path	255
Suspension bridge, The Gobbins (*Lawrence Collection*)	255
Milepost (*E. N. Calvert-Harrison*)	256
Trespass board (*E. N. Calvert-Harrison*)	256
B & NCR crest	256

Photographs not acknowledged above are
by the author, or from his collection

IN TEXT

Seals of the constituent companies	22 & 23
Map of the Belfast & Ballymena Railway	44
Map of the Londonderry & Coleraine Railway	65
Map of the Ballymena & Portrush Railway	93
Map of Coleraine	99
Map of the system in 1861	105
Map of railways at Belfast c 1900	113
Map of railways at Londonderry c 1900	115
Map of the County Antrim branches	134
Map of the short sea passage	135
Map of the County Londonderry branches	167

Map of Glenariff Glen	248
Map of Whitehead and Islandmagee and The Gobbins	251
Map of the system in 1903	264

Line drawings by J. D. C. Charlton and E. N. Calvert-Harrison

Foreword

This volume deals with the formation of the Northern Counties Railway and its development up to 1903. The second volume will cover the period from 1903 to 1949 with a brief survey of the years thereafter. Volume III will be entirely devoted to the locomotives and rolling stock, signalling, operating and other more technical aspects of the railway, and will contain the technical appendices with full bibliography and acknowledgements. The historical appendices will be found in Volumes I and II.

For convenience the title *The Northern Counties Railway* is used throughout; it is realised that this is not altogether appropriate for the period 1845–1860, nor correct for the years after 1903, but the title is that by which the railway was generally known to the 'man in the street'.

References to the three County Antrim narrow gauge lines have been kept to a minimum since these railways have already been the subject of an exhaustive study by Dr Edward M. Patterson in his *History of the Narrow Gauge Railways of North-East Ireland* ('The Ballycastle Railway', 1965 and 'The Ballymena Lines', 1968). The same is true of the Portstewart Tramway, which was dealt with by the present author in 1968.

Many photographs of interest will be found in Dr W. A. McCutcheon's *Railway History in Pictures: Ireland* (Volume I 1969, Volume II 1971) and so far as possible duplication of illustrations between these books and the present work has been avoided.

CHAPTER ONE

The Province of Ulster

This is the story of a railway but it is also largely a social history of the two north-eastern counties of Ireland through which that railway primarily ran—Antrim and Londonderry.

THE NORTHERN COUNTIES

North-east Ireland is physically close to Great Britain; in good weather Scotland may be seen from the Antrim coast. In the days before history was written it was this part of Ireland which received the migrant cultures. In the early days of English rule in Ireland the focus shifted to Dublin, but with the coming of the Industrial Revolution the north-east regained its pre-eminence and the linen industry for which the Province of Ulster is famous centred itself in the region around Belfast. The Lagan Valley became an outlying region of industrial Britain and a centre of incipient urban society in what is still otherwise a largely rural society.

In time the importance of linen spread throughout Ulster. Farmers grew the flax crop which provided the basis of the fabric; its sale gave rise to markets in the towns; then it passed to the mills. The final process, of weaving into the fine and strong material known as linen, took place originally in the cottages, but with the Industrial Revolution factories took over. There were few towns in County Antrim which did not have a connection of some sort with linen; County Londonderry was slightly less important in this respect but large quantities of flax were grown there. It was the linen industry which gave rise to the rapid development of Belfast; today's great metropolis developed out of a small town, which, apart from its favourable situation, was closely similar to ten or twelve other Ulster towns. And, since Belfast was the focal point of the Ulster railway network, it may be said that it was linen to which the railways owed their origin; to linen, and to the engineering industries which came into being during the early nineteenth century.

BELFAST

No industrial city in the British Isles has had a more rapid development than Belfast. It received its first Charter from James I in 1613, and this began its rise as a commercial and industrial centre. By 1780 it was the centre of a prosperous cotton industry and though this soon decayed and disappeared, the techniques employed were of value in the linen industry which replaced it. It was a suitable port of export for the finished product; it was easily reached by the then means of communication, and Carrickfergus Bay became Belfast Lough.

Belfast soon adopted the techniques of the Industrial Revolution and it wrought a transformation in the linen industry. Great mills were built and the steam engine took the place of the water wheel; in 1836 fifty of Ireland's 150 steam engines were in Belfast mills. It developed as a conventional industrial centre similar to those of the English Midlands.

It was in early Victorian times that the expansion was most rapid. Belfast was not officially constituted a city until 1888—a step long overdue—a further charter in 1892 acknowledging Belfast as first in Ireland in commercial and manufacturing importance with a Customs revenue second only in the United Kingdom to London and Liverpool. In the early 1850s there began the great shipbuilding industry, established on Queen's Island on land reclaimed from Belfast Lough by William Dargan who will have an important place later in this history. No less striking was the rise in population. In 1841 the total was 70,447, in 1871 174,412, and in 1901 349,180. In 1961 it had risen to 415,856—tenth city of the United Kingdom. The tremendous upsurge of the mid-Victorian era may be attributed to the rise of the shipbuilding and engineering industries.

The development of such industries was surprising in Ireland; devoid of raw materials, virtually everything had to be imported save the flax, raw material of linen. But Ulster produced, like England, a class of sagacious and ruthless entrepreneurs who attracted British capital, and were able to draw upon the abundant sources of labour throughout Ulster. They imported their necessities and exported their finished products, through the great docks which grew up in Belfast.

THE RAILWAY ARRIVES

In such a climate the development of railways was inevitable, and indeed it was necessary for the efficient discharge of commerce and trade. At this time Dublin was the political capital of Ireland—as it remained until partition in 1921—but Belfast had very much the ascendancy of industry. The earliest proposal for railways in Ireland came in 1825 for a system of lines, the principal of which was to link Belfast and Dublin. But the time was not ripe and nothing came of the scheme. The first railway was not authorised until 1826—a line from Waterford to Limerick which did not materialise. The next Act was passed in 1831 and from it grew the Dublin & Kingstown Railway, Ireland's first working railway and primarily a passenger line linking Dublin to the packet port of Kingstown. It was opened in December 1834.

Stimulated by the D & KR, proposals for railways were made in Ulster. The only one which came into being at this time was the Ulster—incorporated on 19 May 1836 to build a line 25 miles south-west from Belfast to Portadown through that Lagan Valley which cradled the linen industry. This line was eventually opened between 1839 and 1842 and in 1848 was extended to Armagh. The gauge adopted was 6ft 2in (the D & K had adopted 4ft 8½in) and this had clearly the makings of confusion.

The Board of Trade sent its chief inspecting officer, Major-General Pasley, to investigate the situation. He took the independent counsel of railway engineers and, sifting the replies he received, it became apparent that the maximum gauge advocated was 5ft 6in and the minimum 5ft 0in. To solve his dilemma it is asserted that Pasley totalled these and halved the sum—thus obtaining 5ft 3in. Whatever the truth of this tradition the Gauges (Ireland) Act of 7 August 1846 enforced this gauge for all future construction and eventually all the existing railways had to regauge in the interests of conformity. In many ways this Irish gauge was a disadvantage for it prevented through running with British rolling stock; but who in 1846 could foresee that railways would become so widespread and important? In other ways the different gauge made the Irish lines totally different to the British and therefore extremely interesting. The Ulster Railway was entirely the product of local enterprise—mainly that of Belfast merchants; the princely sum of £20,000 received from the Treasury built scarcely two miles of track!

NORTH OF BELFAST

The Ulster was planned to serve the area south-west of Belfast where linen had its focus; but to the north and north-west lay an area almost equally prosperous. Ten miles north of Belfast was Carrickfergus, a very ancient settlement and one which had the functions of the county town of County Antrim for centuries until Belfast became a city. North-west was the equally ancient town of Antrim near the shores of Lough Neagh. It was a prosperous market centre. In this area too was the town of Ballymena, a very important centre of the linen trade and by the 1830s containing a population of some three thousand. It was thus the second largest town in County Antrim after Belfast—by 1841 the population had risen to 5,549.

If southern Ulster was a ripe ground for railway promotion, no less so was this region. With the development of Belfast, there was ample traffic potential, not only in linen, but in agricultural produce. There was also the traffic in rock salt from Carrickfergus and raw materials for other small industries. Nor was the other principal constituent lacking—a hard core of astute and prosperous 'merchant princes'. These were to be found in Belfast in plenty; they were the men who had built the Ulster. Their motives were not always above reproach but in the main they were interested in opening up new lines of communication to the hinterland. It was this mixture of commercial pragmatism and altruism which underlay the building of the Belfast & Ballymena line, the first constituent of the Belfast & Northern Counties Railway.

Seals of the constituent companies
(1) Belfast & Ballymena Railway, (2) Londonderry & Coleraine Railway,
(3) Ballymena & Portrush Railway, (4) Belfast & Northern Counties Railway,
(5) Carrickfergus & Larne Railway, (6) B & NCR crest used on publications

Seals of the constituent companies

(7) Ballymena, Cushendall & Red Bay Railway, (8) Ballymena & Larne Railway, (9) Ballycastle Railway, (10) Derry Central Railway, (11) Limavady & Dungiven Railway, (12) Draperstown Railway, (13) Portstewart Tramway

CHAPTER TWO

The Belfast and Ballymena Railway

IN THE STEPS OF THE ULSTER

It was from Ballymena that the first steps came towards a scheme to link that town to Belfast by rail. In Ballymena was a family of Davisons, the present generation being represented by five brothers, Alexander, David, George, John, and Richard. It was Richard, a most able practitioner of his profession of solicitor and Member of Parliament for Belfast with the future Lord Chancellor Cairns from 1852 to 1860, who, early in 1836, suggested that the example of the Ulster might with advantage be emulated. Davison (as he was to recall in 1845) was the subject of not a little ridicule from engineers and others who regarded the scheme he proposed as impossible. Belfast lies in a 'saucer' and the difficulty was to lift any line over the rim. But Davison was not so easily deflected from his purpose. Through his enthusiasm the Belfast merchants became interested and a provisional committee was formed.

This committee took offices in Calendar Street, Belfast. It appointed Samuel Thompson and George Davison as the secretaries *pro tem*; Arbuthnot Emerson (for Belfast) and Alexander and John Davison (for Ballymena) as treasurers; standing counsel were John B. Gilmore KC, Robert Holmes and James Whiteside; Richard and David Davison (who had offices in Castle Place, Belfast) were the solicitors and the parliamentary agent was J. E. Dorrington. Preliminary surveys were undertaken of the proposed route by William Bald FRSE MIRA and Thomas J. Woodhouse, County Surveyor of Antrim, in cooperation with the consulting engineers, Walker & Cubitt of London.

The prospectus was issued on 26 April 1836:

THE NORTH-EASTERN RAILWAY

from Belfast to Ballymena

> By the White-House Shore, Templepatrick and Antrim, with power to make a Branch to Carrickfergus, and extend the main line to Ballymoney, Coleraine and Derry, or either of them, in case the Shareholders shall deem it necessary, with liberty to increase the Capital at any future day for the purposes of such extensions.

The capital of £625,000 was to be made up of £25 shares, the deposit being £1 per share in two instalments. Bankers were appointed in Belfast, Dublin and Ballymena, London, Manchester, Norwich, Liverpool, Scotland and York. The prospectus detailed the objects of the proposed undertaking and it is here reproduced *in extenso*:

> The object of this undertaking is to connect the Port of Belfast with the large market town of Ballymena, from which the line may either now or afterwards be extended to Ballymoney, Coleraine, Newtownlimavady, and Derry, or either of them as the shareholders may deem advisable ...
>
> The distance from Belfast to Ballymena by the proposed line will be about 23 Irish miles [*circa* 29¼ standard miles]; the country through which it passes is rich and fertile and abounding in Agricultural and Manufacturing produce. In the Town of Ballymena (the largest inland Market in Ireland), there are no less than *three* Weekly Markets—one for Pork, Butter and Provisions on Tuesday; a second for grain on Wednesdays; and a large General Market for Linens and all kinds of manufactured and agricultural produce on Saturdays. There are already four Banks established there, and others are being formed, and the *weekly* circulation of money, from an estimate lately made, averages from 25 to £30,000. It is situated in the very centre of the county, surrounded by numerous towns and villages and lying on the direct road to Ballymoney and Coleraine; thus the surplus produce of this rich and extensive County will be conveyed, for consumption or exportation, along the proposed line. At Antrim, the line touches on Lough Neagh; at Ballymena, it is within a few miles of the River Bann ...

It is said that within two days of the publication of the

prospectus the entire share capital had been applied for. On 2 May the *Belfast Newsletter* advertised that the first instalment of the deposit would be received on 3 and 4 May.

RIVALS

Two competing concerns were seeking to build a railway to Carrickfergus at the same time. The first published its prospectus on 2 May 1836; it advocated the building of a line from Belfast to Larne via Carrickfergus. The other rival was concerned only with Carrickfergus, the idea being to build a deep-sea harbour here with the possibility of making the town the packet port for Scotland. The harbour would be connected to Belfast by a seven-mile railway. Neither of these schemes ever got beyond the talking stage; nor did a third, promoted contemporaneously, the Armagh, Tyrone & Londonderry, to run from Armagh to Portrush.

FAILURE

On 12 July the results of the surveys of the North-Eastern Railway, undertaken by County Surveyor Woodhouse, were published:

> The original scheme was to run along the Lough Shore and Strand in such a direction as to make several miles of the Line common to both a Ballymena and a Carrickfergus Railway; however, after carefully investigating the subject, I found that could not be done with the advantage contemplated as it would have the effect of lengthening the Line to Ballymena several miles without effecting the advantage of improving the gradients or rates of inclination in ascending the Hills.
>
> He had then surveyed another route from the shore to the east of the grounds of Parkmount, obtaining an incline of 1 in 90 over the four miles, thence by deep cutting towards Kingsbog.
>
> An incline of the kind I have adverted to could not be worked without an assistant engine, for, although the angle of elevation is the same as those on the Liverpool & Manchester Railway, which in favourable weather, the passenger

trains can ascend very well without assistance, yet for heavy trains and in a bad state of rails, assistant power would be requisite.

He therefore suggested the abandonment of the Carrickfergus branch in its original form; the main line should take the higher route and that to Carrickfergus the shore route. A suggestion had been made, that Ballymena could best be served by running over the Ulster Railway to Lisburn, thence striking off northwards through Glenavy, Crumlin and Antrim (remarkably similar to the route adopted by the Dublin & Antrim Junction Railway, see Chapter 5 below). He rejected this scheme; Ballymena would be 42 miles from Belfast instead of 33 by the route he favoured: the high level line.

A notice from Davison published concomitantly stated that a meeting would be convened 'after the Assizes' to consider Woodhouse's findings. But nothing further was to be done. A sudden slump hit the money market and already by mid-1836 conditions were being compared to the terrible crisis of 1825–6. Clearly in this economic climate the scheme could not be proceeded with.

One of the principal reasons for the slump was the uncertainty centring round the Agricultural & Commercial Bank of Ireland, in which the Davisons were prominent. It appears that a sudden run was made upon the resources of that institution, which was based in Dublin. The state of the money market generally and the unsatisfactory nature of the concern prevented the Bank of Ireland coming to the assistance of the other. In 1838 the Royal Commission appointed to inquire into the most suitable routes for railways in Ireland did not in the Report recommend the building of any lines in the area later to be served by the Belfast & Ballymena. It seemed for a time as though the sceptics had been right when they told Davison that horses and carts would suffice to carry the traffic.

PROPOSED AGAIN

Davison still hankered to see a line between Belfast and Ballymena. In March 1844 in association with his friend

Sinclair K. Mulholland, a prosperous Belfast linen manufacturer, William Coates of the Lagan Foundry, and John McNeile of Parkmount, Belfast, later to be called 'the father of the railway', a new and rather less elaborate scheme was drawn up. The support of influential landowners in the district through which the line was to pass was solicited, and a provisional committee formed, Davison being appointed *pro tem* secretary.

It was decided to employ Charles Lanyon to carry out the preliminary surveys with a view to ascertaining the practicability of the line. Lanyon was in many ways a truly remarkable man. He was born in Eastbourne in 1813 and articled to one of the engineers of the Irish Board of Works in Dublin. He was in 1835 appointed county surveyor of Kildare and a year later transferred to Antrim at his own request to succeed Woodhouse. During his tenure of office he carried out many works of importance in Antrim. Lanyon, being a busy man, delegated much of the work of surveying to his principal assistant, a young man named Robert Young. Davison's proposal involved a main line from Belfast to Ballymena with a branch to Carrickfergus. Lanyon, his preliminaries completed, addressed a meeting held in Antrim Courthouse on 20 May 1844, presided over by Viscount O'Neill and attended by everyone who was anybody in the County Antrim of that day. He pronounced the scheme quite feasible:

> Having been called on to give my opinion as to the practicability of making a line of railway from Belfast to Ballymena, with a branch to Carrickfergus, I have examined the country between those towns, and have no hesitation in stating that the entire line appears quite practicable. My attention has been, at present, more particularly directed to that division of it between the shore and summit level at the King's Moss, it being the only portion on which I expected any difficulty to exist, in consequence of the short distance in which it is necessary to obtain an elevation of 350 feet. I have the satisfaction of stating, however, that, even on this portion of the line, gradients can be had, quite practicable for either system of working which may be adopted, whether locomotive or atmospheric.

The main difficulty was in the exit route from Belfast: the

Cave Hill presented a formidable barrier to an inland route and the coastal route lay along sloblands. Lanyon however was as exceedingly skilled an engineer as he was a talented architect, and surveyed *both* routes, the former to begin at the Antrim Road, the latter at the junction of York Street and Corporation Street, crossing the slobland on an embankment and reclaiming a considerable amount of land. If this latter route were adopted (and Lanyon strongly recommended it) it would be necessary to have a trailing junction between the main and branch lines at a point $6\frac{1}{2}$ miles out from Belfast so as to ease the gradient. The distance thence to Carrickfergus would be $2\frac{3}{4}$ miles and to Ballymena 26 miles, a total of $35\frac{1}{4}$ miles. He estimated the cost at £11,000 per mile, and £385,000 overall for a double line.

And so it was proposed by George J. Clarke JP of Antrim and seconded by John Kane and carried

> That Mr Lanyon be instructed forthwith to complete the survey of the entire Line of Railway, and that for the purpose of defraying the expenses of such a survey, a subscription list be now opened.

It was also carried

> That a Company be now formed for prosecuting the said undertaking; and that Charles Lanyon Esq. be appointed Acting Engineer and William Cubitt Esq. Consulting Engineer, and Richard Davison Esq., Solicitor of the said Company ...

Cubitt's services were unobtainable and those of Sir John Macneill FRS, the leading engineer of the Ireland of his time, were enlisted instead for the purpose of assisting the committee to make final decisions as to the route. On 14 August 1844 'an influential meeting' took place in Belfast

> for the purpose of examining the surveys of the proposed lines, made by Mr Lanyon, the County Surveyor, and of receiving the report of Sir John Macneill, the Consulting Engineer ... Lord Massereene presided ... Sir John Macneill read his report, which was most favourable to the proposed undertaking, and intimated that not only did the line not present any engineering difficulties, but that its

gradients could fairly compete with many of the best English lines on which the largest traffic existed ...

THE PROSPECTUS

Unlike the men of 1836 the committee began at the right end of matters and only now, with the route of its line settled, did it proceed to issue its prospectus. The provisional committee was by now fifty strong, headed by the Rt Hon John Skeffington, 10th Viscount Massereene & 3rd Viscount Ferrard of Antrim Castle. A prospectus, dated 3 September 1844, stated:

> The object of this undertaking is to construct a line of Railway from the great commercial town and port of Belfast, to the large inland town of Ballymena in the County of Antrim, uniting both by a branch line to the seaport and County town of Carrickfergus, thus forming Northward, towards the leading towns of Ballymoney, Coleraine, and Londonderry, an extension of the line of railway communication opened by the Ulster Railway and which is in progress of connexion with the Metropolis of Ireland [Dublin] by a junction line between it and the Drogheda Railway.

The coastal route had been decided upon; it was hoped to reclaim 2,000 acres, concluding favourable terms with the owners of the sloblands.

An exceedingly rosy picture was painted of the financial prospects of the undertaking, based upon traffic surveys undertaken during the months of May and August, it being stressed that these took no account of local passengers, merely those travelling by public conveyance; nor was the traffic in coals and stone included:

TRAFFIC TABLE

	£	s	d
Estimate of passenger traffic at 1¼d per mile per passenger calculated from the ascertained returns for double the existing traffic as usual in railway estimates	40,643	2	0
General merchandise and farming produce	14,659	19	3
Conveyance of mails and parcels	2,000	0	0
	£57,303	1	3

Deduct 45 per cent for working the line
and interest on 1/3 of the capital if borrowed   25,736 0 0

                                                  ─────────────
                                                  £31,567 1 3
                                                  ─────────────

This £31,000, if divided up amongst a paid up capital of £256,666, would bring a dividend of no less than 'nearly 12½ per cent'. There were to be 7,700 shares of £50 each making a total capital of £385,000, the deposit being £2 10s (£2.50). The prospectus concluded that

> A vast increase in general traffic, beyond the ordinary calculations but more especially in passengers on the Carrickfergus branch, must be anticipated from the facilities of sea-bathing and country residences, which are thereby afforded; and experience has proved that, where sealines of railroad communicate with large towns, the passenger traffic arising from mere pleasure excursions is a legitimate subject of calculation.

A good response was made to the advertisements and the capital was accumulated steadily, the Bank of Ireland being the bankers. A considerable proportion of the capital was subscribed by English sources, demonstrating yet again the close links between Ulster and Britain. English investment was a feature common to the early days of many Irish railways; in later years many English shareholders were bought out. Apparently Irish people preferred to let others risk their capital until the venture was proved. In 1848 the B & B had 221 shareholders.

RELATED SCHEMES

The Dublin, Belfast & Coleraine Junction Railway was incorporated on 3 August 1846 for a line with a capital of £642,000 from Armagh through Dungannon, Cookstown, Magherafelt, Ballymoney, Coleraine and Portstewart, with a terminus at Portrush. A branch of this line ran within two miles of the B & B's projected main line at Antrim, and Lanyon was hastily given instructions to prepare plans for a branch line to Randalstown to connect the B & B with the DB & CJ. He was fortunately in time to include the plans for this in the submission to Parliament.

At the northern end of the DB & CJ there was to be a branch from what was later to be Macfin station, to Ballymoney, a prosperous market town. The B & B was largely involved in a new company promoted at this time, the Belfast & Ballymena, Londonderry & Coleraine Railway, which intended to bridge the gap between Ballymena and Ballymoney. The *Irish Railway Gazette* described this line (also known as the Ballymena & Ballymoney) as 'the natural extension of the Belfast & Ballymena Railway, the Directors of which are its chief promoters'. Should the DB & CJ fail to materialise it was intended to extend the $20\frac{3}{4}$ mile Ballymena—Ballymoney section a further $8\frac{3}{4}$ miles to Coleraine and $7\frac{1}{2}$ thence to Portrush, and possibly also form a junction at Coleraine with the projected Londonderry & Coleraine.

Sad to relate the DB & CJ's powers for the acquisition of land expired in 1849, unexercised; and nothing more was heard of this grandiose scheme. The B & B was left with a comparatively useless branch to Randalstown as a memento of what might have been.

TOWARDS THE ACT

It was now necessary to obtain the sanction of Parliament for the B & B's original line, plus the branch to Randalstown. The legal arrangements were all in the hands of Davison; Lanyon and Young dealt with the preparations of the plans and maps. In April 1845 the Bill, having been duly lodged, came up for consideration before a Committee of the House of Commons. The Belfast Harbour Commissioners objected to certain clauses of the Bill. Of late years large sums had been spent in the improvement of the port of Belfast and the Commissioners, apprehensive of possible competition from the harbour at Carrickfergus or from harbours which might spring up along the coast served by the proposed railway, insisted on clauses being inserted for their protection.

The Committee of Parliament in due course reported that

Page 33
(left) The Rt Hon John Young, chairman 1885-1903

OFFICIALS—I

(right) Edward John Cotton, manager 1857-1899

OFFICIALS—II (*above*) Group, 1868: *Left to right* E. J. Cotton *general manager*, Art W. Forde *resident engineer*, Alexander Yorston *locomotive superintendent*, Hugh Ross *go manager*, Charles Stewart *secretary* (*below left*) Bowman Malcolm, locomotive superintend 1876-1903 (*below right*) Walter Bailey, accountant 1887-1903

THE BELFAST AND BALLYMENA RAILWAY

> ... The Company undertaking this project have every appearance of stability; a large proportion of the shares are held in Antrim and Carrickfergus; the statement of traffic which has been submitted to the Board of Trade appears as far as we can judge to be trustworthy, and the district gives a reasonable prospect of success to the scheme from its character as a thriving and well-peopled county.

The Committee had feared, however, that the works would be heavy and costly and were concerned that only a single line was to be laid down though the land to be purchased was sufficient for a double line. The promoters hastened to assure them that large expense was not anticipated and that a second line would be laid when traffic warranted it.

The Bill passed all its stages in both Houses of Parliament to receive the Royal Assent on 21 July 1845 as 'An Act for making a Railway from Belfast to Ballymena in the County of Antrim, with Branches to Carrickfergus and Randalstown'. The capital was fixed at £385,000 in 7,700 shares of £50; when all this was subscribed up to £128,333 might be borrowed. Land was to be taken for a double line and a second line of rails to be laid if and when required by the Board of Trade. Three years were given for the purchase of land and five years for construction.

> ... And be it enacted, That the said Railway shall be laid down and be ever after maintained at a Gauge of Five Feet Three Inches.

The line was to keep close to the existing shoreline of Belfast Lough, not deviating out into the sloblands without the authority of the owners thereof; nor were goods landed at harbours between Carrickfergus and Whitehouse to be carried nearer than one mile to the boundary of Belfast and similarly goods for these harbours must originate more than one mile beyond the city boundary: this was for the protection of Belfast Harbour Commissioners. The exceptions to this clause were coal, coke and other supplies necessary for the railway.

The rates of fares for passengers were laid down at 3d first class, 2d second class and 1d third class per mile. Maximum charges for the several classes of goods were also laid down.

The first directors were named as Nathaniel Alexander MP, Peter Kirk MP, the Hon George Handcock, John McNeile, Thomas Greg, John Harrison, Sinclair Kelbourne Mulholland, John Thomson, William Chaine, George Joy, George Greer, John White, Robert Langtry, Robert Grimshaw, John Kane, William Gray, James McCalmont, Andrew Gihon, George J. Clarke, Thomas McCammon and Edward Walkington.

At the first meeting following the passage of the Act the newly appointed directors chose from their number the Hon George Handcock as first chairman of the company. Handcock was the fifth son of the second Lord Castlemaine, a prominent Irish landowning aristocrat; George, however, chose to enter the business world and had taken a leading part in Irish railway development. At the time his residence was at Randalstown. John McNeile became deputy chairman. Lanyon was appointed engineer. On Davison's being appointed solicitor to the company, Hugh Harrison had taken over the entire secretarial work. On 1 October 1845, however, a permanent secretary was appointed—John Wilson, whose salary was £200 per annum.

WORK BEGINS

Immediately on the passage of the Act, Lanyon began the preparations for the building of the line, dividing it into three working divisions:

Belfast to King's Moss including the Carrickfergus branch	15 miles
King's Moss to Antrim	9 miles
Antrim to Ballymena	11 miles

Things had now advanced sufficiently to permit of advertising for tenders for construction of the railway and this was done in September 1845; tenders were to be delivered to the secretary by 1 October 1845. As a result of the destruction of most of the records of this time we are precluded from noting the details of the tenders received. It is only possible to state that the contract was awarded to William Dargan who promised completion of the works within 21 months of obtaining full possession of the land. About the same time orders were

THE BELFAST AND BALLYMENA RAILWAY

placed for rails and sleepers and engines were ordered from Sharp Bros and Bury, Curtis & Kennedy.

William Dargan, born in County Carlow in 1799, was trained as an engineer and surveyor, his first major work being the construction of the Holyhead Road in Wales under Thomas Telford. He returned to Ireland and set up as a civil engineering contractor. With the coming of railways he added construction of these to his other specialities—canals and roads—and by 1853 he had constructed 600 miles of line and held contracts for 200 more. He was a man of sterling character and one of Ireland's leading capitalists; he employed only the best labour and his men were paid the highest wages of the time.

With the contract signed, the directors resolved to make a considerable ceremony of cutting the first sod; the day chosen was Tuesday 6 November 1845, the ceremony to be performed by Viscount Massereene & Ferrard who had been associated with the railway from the outset. The *Irish Railway Gazette* wrote:

> The field in which the ceremony took place was immediately adjoining the beautiful church and schoolhouse of Whitehouse [about 3 miles out of Belfast], and the arrangements made by the directors for doing due honour to the occasion were executed on an extensive scale, and conceived in excellent taste . . . Round the enclosure were planted poles, bearing conspicuous flags, and facing the road, over the entrance of the barrier, was a broad banner of white canvas, having displayed, in red letters, the words 'Belfast and Ballymena Railway'. Immediately beyond the spot selected for raising the first sod was placed the fine band of the 26th Cameronians . . . whose lively and stirring music added greatly to the pleasant excitement of the scene. . . . His Lordship, throwing off his coat, proceeded to turn up the first sod with a vigour and a good will in the highest degree amusing. The spade was of very handsome manufacture, the shaft of polished mahogany; and the barrow was of equally exquisite workmanship, of the same wood, and beautifully polished and bound with brass . . . His Lordship, having completed the loading of the barrow, wheeled it in right good style along the plank to its extremity, where he emptied it over on one side.

After the ceremony the company adjourned to 'a very elegant collation' in the adjoining Whitehouse schoolhouse. A further feast, this time 'a sumptuous banquet', was held that evening in the Commercial Hotel in Belfast.

LAND DIFFICULTIES

Dargan had promised completion of the works in 21 months from the time of obtaining full possession of the required land. This was now the preoccupying task for Lanyon and his subordinates. The valuation being completed, Davison as solicitor furnished each landowner or tenant with a statement of the land required and the price the railway company was prepared to pay for it. According to Young the majority of the holders declined the offers. Therefore the next step was to summon a competent common jury of County Antrim to hold a 'trial' of the disputed claims. The hearings took place in that courthouse in Antrim which had seen the inception of the scheme. Richard Davison and his partner James Torrens appeared for the B & BR. The claims were eventually settled to the satisfaction (more or less) of both sides.

There were two claims which almost defied settlement. One of these was that of one Patrick McQuillan of Antrim, an innkeeper who ran a lucrative service of stage coaches between that town and Belfast. Naturally he was infuriated when he learned that not only was a railway to be built, taking away his livelihood; but it was proposed to sweep away his fine hostelry, recently erected, on the environs of Antrim. 'He was fairly mad with passion and determined to put the Railway Coy. to every trouble, delay and expense that could be thought of', says Young.

But the directors under Lanyon's advice decided to take the course of least resistance. It was decided to adhere as closely as possible to the intended course but without *touching* McQuillan's house! At the spot a bridge was to be erected to carry the main turnpike road to Belfast over the railway in a deep cutting and this bridge was completed before excavation began. McQuillan put every obstacle he could in the face of the engineers, serving caveats and writs of trespass. Lanyon obtained a report of the position from his close friend George Godwin of the Ulster Railway; eventually the work was completed after considerable expense had been incurred on both sides.

Of rather more importance was the objection lodged by William Chaine of Ballycraigy, Ballymena, one of the largest linen manufacturers in Ulster and obviously a force to be reckoned with. At the time he was more than eighty but retained his full vigour and still rode on horseback. Despite the force with which he prosecuted his suit he treated the railway officials and engineers with great courtesy; the eventual result was not financially very gratifying to the railway and Young suggests that the fact that Chaine took the entire party of jurors in the case into his mansion and regaled them magnificently might not be unconnected with the result.

By May 1846 more of the land had been obtained and the earthworks, 'the key to the operation of the line', were well under way. It is to be presumed that Dargan began work at the beginning of 1846. During the early part of 1846 the contract for the Randalstown branch—not included in the original specification—was awarded to Dargan. The difficulties encountered in obtaining land elsewhere were not encountered here as Lord O'Neill of Shane's Castle, Randalstown, gave most of the required land free.

At this time Lanyon informed the proprietors:

> The earthwork is . . . in a very forward state; more than half, or about 800,000 cubic yards, have already been moved . . . The masonry is also well advanced, as, out of 111 culverts, there are only ten yet to build, and out of 60 bridges, one half have been completed.

The fencing had also been completed; the permanent way materials had been delivered and Dargan hoped to begin track laying within a very few weeks. For the last three months he had had 4,000 men and 600 horses at work.

The superstitious tendencies of the Irish labourers are illustrated by an incident which occurred in the townland of Lenagh, about a mile on the Ballymena side of the junction with the Randalstown branch. Here there was a prehistoric rath, a fortified earthwork, which was supposedly inhabited by the fairies. It had to be removed for the onward march of the railway; but the man sent to begin the work by cutting away the bushes died under mysterious circumstances and the main body refused to have anything to do with the removal. Eventually it was demolished by the use of explosives.

By the spring of 1847 portions of the line were ready for ballasting; Dargan apparently had no locomotives of his own and the company's had not yet been delivered so he was authorised to purchase one second-hand from the Ulster Railway for use in the work. In May 1847 the shareholders authorised the exercising of the powers of borrowing since all the capital had been taken up. It was at this time hoped to be ready for opening on 1 November 1847.

The first of November passed and the directors were now speaking of an opening 'early in the ensuing year'. The delay was principally due to the work of raising the embankment which carried the line along Belfast Lough to a higher level over the waters. Of the permanent way 29 miles had been ballasted and 22 miles laid with rails. The stations, with the exception of Belfast, were progressing favourably—in the interests of economy of finance and time they were temporary structures of wood. Stations were erected on the main line at Greencastle, Whiteabbey, Carrickfergus Junction, Ballynure Road, Ballypallady, Dunadry, Antrim, Drumsough Junction and Ballymena; there were 'flag' stations at Templepatrick (later to be made a full station) and Andraid. The only intermediate halt on the Carrickfergus branch was at Trooperslane; there was none on the Randalstown line.

For Belfast, Lanyon drew upon his architectural talents and produced a grandiose and impressive classical design with central two-storied pillared portico and two pavilions. Behind it was a single passenger platform which contained all the necessary passenger facilities and the B & B's headquarters' offices. The goods facilities were situated behind the passenger platform line under the overall roof.

The shareholders in November 1847 were told by Lanyon that 'the works generally are being executed in a very satisfactory manner by Mr Dargan' and it was intended to be ready for inspection by the Board of Trade on 10 January 1848.

CAPTAIN LAFFAN

It was, however, 28 February before that stage was reached; on that date Captain R. M. Laffan RE carried out his inspection and his report dated 3 March dealt a sharp blow to the *amour propre* of Dargan, Lanyon and the company as a whole:

> The line to Carrickfergus is $9\frac{1}{4}$ miles in length. It crosses the ooze of Belfast Lock [sic] by a high embankment $2\frac{1}{4}$ miles in length. The single line and sidings are laid throughout, but they are laid very roughly, and in many places they are not yet ballasted. One of these unballasted portions, 2 miles in length, is over the embankment above-named. There are no signals yet fixed, a point of extreme importance in the working of any railway, but especially in that of a single line. There are no mile posts or gradient boards along the line . . . The station arrangements are incomplete, the platform at Carrickfergus, a temporary structure, supported by slender upright posts without either diagonal or side-struts, being so slight that a man could shake it with his hands . . .
> Along the remainder of the line to Ballymena and the short branch to Randalstown, the single line is laid, but the sidings are not yet completed. The permanent way is very roughly put down, and in very many places it is not even ballasted. There are no signals . . . mileposts or gradient boards. The cuttings through rock are unfinished, large masses of earth and stones being left in dangerous proximity to the rails. These cuttings, too, are very badly drained; in one instance the water lying in sheets over the ballasting, and the rails being so damp and slippery in consequence, that an engine with 14 tons on the driving wheel, and with only two carriages behind it, could scarcely make any progress . . . On the last 2 or 3 miles near Ballymena the rails had only been laid very recently; they were very roughly put down and the ballasting was incomplete. A bridge over a road on this portion had only been put together in a very hasty manner to meet my inspection. The deflection, owing to the looseness of the framing, was very great, and running the train over it the result was precisely what might have been anticipated from the great deflection and the oscillation produced by

general irregularity of the line; the front wheels of the leading carriage were forced off the line and had the train been moving with any speed the carriage would most probably have been destroyed. In order to determine whether this occurrence might not (as the engineer of the line suggested) have been in some measure attributable to accidental circumstances, the carriage was replaced on the line, and the train run over the bridge a second time at a slow speed; the same result followed; the carriage was again forced off the line.

I am of opinion that it would be unsafe to allow this line to be opened for passenger traffic until the cuttings are completed and properly drained—till the whole of the sidings are laid down—till the permanent way is fairly adjusted and ballasted throughout—and till the signals are erected for the safe working of the line ...

In sending this report to the B & B on 4 March, Captain H. D. Harness RE, secretary of the Railway Department, wrote scathingly:

... And I am to put to you, the great inconvenience to which the public service has been subjected, by notices being sent to this department that the line would be ready for inspection when the works were so imperfect.

A period of furious activity followed during which Lanyon and Dargan sought to retrieve their reputations by ameliorating some of Captain Laffan's strictures. A full month ensued, then on 6 April the directors held their own inspection:

At 11 o'clock a very long train composed of first-class, second-class and third-class carriages, goods waggons, etc., started ... Over several parts of the journey a speed of 48 miles an hour was attained ... It is stated that its completion will bear comparison with any work of equal magnitude in the United Kingdom.

The following day Captain Laffan held a second inspection on behalf of the Board of Trade and his report dated 8 April was rather more encouraging than that issued earlier.

The Company have substituted level crossings for four Bridges ... The Grand Jury gave their consent in each case ... on condition that a station should be established at each crossing, which has accordingly been done.

But he was prepared to overlook this contravention of the Act; he went on:

> The whole of the present single line is in every respect (saving the question of the level crossings . . .) fit to be opened for public traffic and I would beg to recommend that the single line be now opened and that the question of the bridges be reserved . . .

Harness's letter of 14 April was also more cheerful; by the time it was written the railway was already at work since telegraphic authority had been sent to Lanyon:

> I have been directed . . . to inform you, that [the] Inspecting Officer not having reported the opening of the Belfast and Ballymena Railway would be attended with danger to the public using the same, they cannot postpone the opening; but as it appears by his report that the Company have substituted level crossings for four bridges over county roads without any legal authority, it will be the duty of the Commissioners to see that the provisions of the special Act are complied with and the bridges erected in the manner required by law.

OPENING

The directors had meanwhile busied themselves in appointing officers and recruiting staff. Since 1845 they had a secretary; in 1847 Ellis Rowland was appointed locomotive superintendent and in May 1848 Handcock reported that

> In accordance with the wishes of the proprietary . . . your Directors have secured the services of a gentleman of experience and activity, Mr Thomas Housman Higgin, to whom they have confided the entire detail of the management . . .

Little is known of Higgin save that he was an Englishman, and even disregarding Handcock's platitudes, he seems to have been an unusually capable man. The selection of an Englishman—and his successor was of the same nationality—is not remarkable, for railways in Ireland were so new, and so few of the middle classes were disposed to enter their service, that no qualified local men were available.

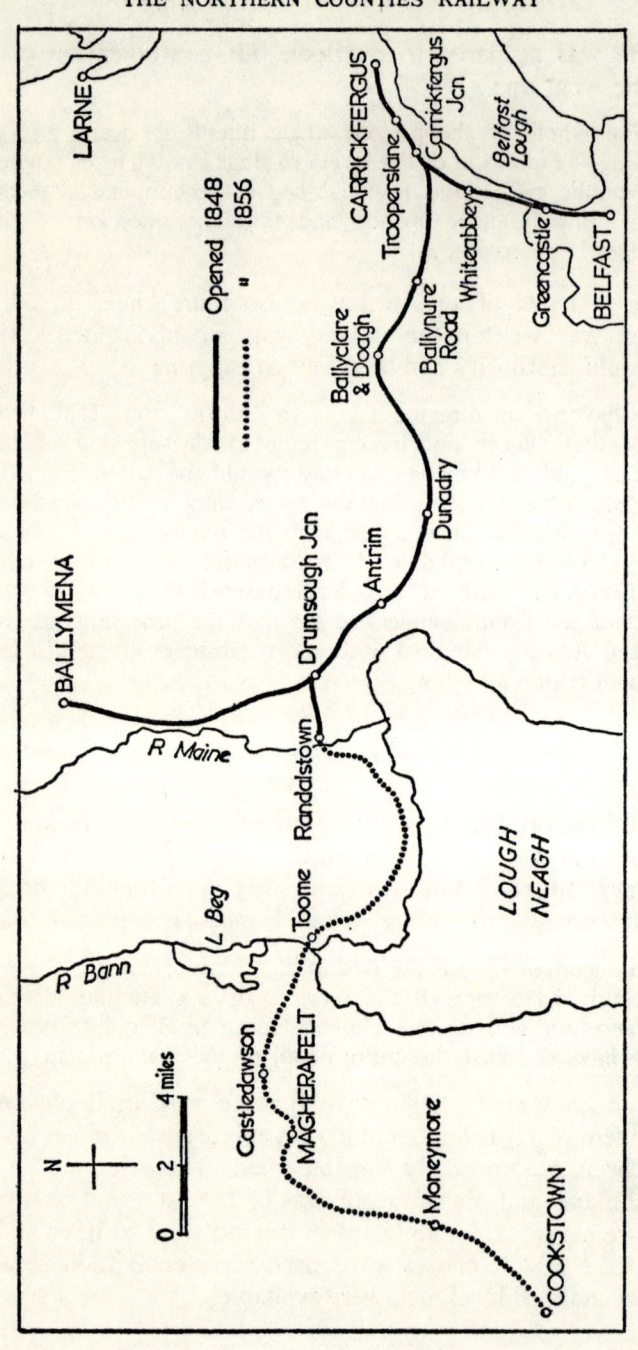

The Belfast & Ballymena Railway

THE BELFAST AND BALLYMENA RAILWAY 45

The telegraphic authority having duly been received from London, advertisements were inserted in the newspapers on 8 April 1848:

> The public is respectfully informed that the Belfast and Ballymena Railway will be opened for Passenger Traffic on Wednesday next, the 12th instant.

On Tuesday 11 April, however, two specials were run; having waited so long to commence operations there was to be no official opening ceremony and instead potential passengers were given a foretaste of railway travel. The *Northern Whig* wrote:

> As was previously announced two trains . . . left the Belfast terminus—one at a quarter past nine, and the other at a quarter past ten o'clock on Tuesday morning. Every carriage was crammed with passengers. The manner in which the duties of the clerks were discharged at the different stations was highly creditable. The trains reached the various places, both going and returning, at the appointed time. Yesterday [Wednesday] four trains were run, all of which were filled. In order to prevent accidents, a pilot engine was sent along the line early on Tuesday morning to see that all was clear; and Mr Lanyon, the Engineer, and Mr Higgin, the Manager, have been indefatigable in their exertions to ensure order, regularity and prevent danger. Praise is also due to Mr Ellis Rowland, the practical superintendent of engines, for the admirable manner in which his department is conducted.

And so the railway was at work. The normal train service was five trains per day each way, the Carrickfergus Junction—Carrickfergus and Drumsough Junction—Randalstown sections being treated as branches. Fares were high: first class returns from Belfast to Ballymena cost 7s (35p), to Carrickfergus 2s (10p), to Antrim 4s (20p). No third class returns were initially issued: the single fare to Ballymena was 1s 6d (7½p), to Carrickfergus 4d (1½p), to Antrim 10d (4p). To encourage traffic return tickets were issued at single fares from all stations on Sundays, and on market days cheap tickets were available.

A system of subscription tickets at substantially reduced rates was introduced between Belfast, Greencastle, Whiteabbey, Carrickfergus Junction and Carrickfergus, for periods of a month, a quarter, half a year and a year. Family tickets were issued, the arrangement being that when two or more persons of the same family purchased subscription tickets at the same time a further 'liberal discount' was allowed.

It should be noted that no goods traffic was carried initially. This was due to the haste in which the line had been completed—the goods sheds were incomplete. The sixth half-yearly meeting in late May 1848 was told by the directors that they

> are fully sensible of the importance of the goods as an adjunct to the passenger traffic; and have instructed your Engineer to expedite as much as possible the erection and completion of the goods stations ...

Since no goods trains were being run certain articles were being conveyed by passenger train 'to a limited extent, and more with a view to accommodating the public than with an idea of profit'. It was stated that it was too early to pronounce upon the results of operation; but, as though preparing the shareholders for a grim report in November, the directors adverted to the depressed state of the country but remarked that 'should the approaching summer and harvest prove favourable to the growth and gathering of the fruits of the earth' matters might yet improve. Lanyon blamed the bad weather for the delay in opening and stated that the total cost of building to date had been £414,386.44

JOSEPH MAUNDER

The company soon faced a barrage of severe criticism of its policies from a section of the shareholders. Toward the end of October 1848 an English shareholder, one Joseph Maunder, called a meeting of fellow-proprietors in the George Hotel, Liverpool. This meeting, as stated in the summons, was

> ... for the purpose of taking measures to induce the Directors so to improve the management of the line that its resources may be fully developed.

Maunder stated that he felt the directors were apathetic and inefficient; further he felt nineteen to be a number too large to conduce to dynamic control. He asserted that almost half the shareholders were Englishmen and the average of the directors' holding only 36, Handcock holding 35. Though the business of the meeting was said by the *Railway Times* to have been 'of a very desultory character' a motion was carried urging that the number of directors be reduced to fifteen, five of whom should be representative of the English shareholders.

There were repercussions of this affair at the next half-yearly meeting on 30 November 1848. Maunder attended and laid a document before it:

> It is . . . expedient that a Committee be appointed, to examine the accounts in order to ascertain the cause of . . . serious discrepancies in the estimate of expenditure and traffic as compared with the prospectus and results; and also, to advise the Directors as to the improvement of the future management of the Railway, with a view to the development of its resources and the prosperity of the Company.

In a long statement Handcock repudiated Maunder's arguments. Maunder declined to withdraw the motion based on his document nor would he apologise for the aspersions he had cast on the directors; and on his motion being put to the vote there were four 'fors' and 55 'againsts'.

THE FIRST ACCOUNTS

The balance sheets of the first six half years are reproduced on p 48, the figures having been converted to decimal currency.

The first balance sheet, of which Maunder had complained, was certainly not commensurate with the figures expected to produce a dividend of $12\frac{1}{2}$ per cent. The chairman, by way of explanation and apology for the fact that *no* dividend could be paid, stated that the directors found the passenger receipts 'disappointing'. They had reduced the second and third class fares in an attempt to obtain additional traffic but it was too soon to estimate the success of this move. The only comfort that could be offered was the statement that work was nearly completed and capital expenditure almost ended. Despite this unpropitious beginning the *Northern Whig* on 8

FIRST SIX HALF-YEARLY REVENUE STATEMENTS—April 1848—March 1851

	April—September 1848	October 1848—March 1849	April—September 1849	October 1849—March 1850	April—September 1850	October 1850—March 1851
Passengers—						
First class	25,044	15,344	23,745	15,908	19,041	15,547
Second clas	60,999	51,202	49,877	54,992	66,820	55,547
Third class	139,010	98,603	133,178	85,367	111,595	98,626
Receipts—						
First class	£2,023.36	£1,385,81½	£2,060.46½	£1,485.89	£1,877.25	£1,552.00
Second class	3.541.24½	2,836.96	2,974.86½	3,128.29	4,193.79½	5,602.99½
Third class	4,226.39	2,973.86½	3,827.40½	2,472.89½	3,147.05	2,867.35
Parcels	983.06½	256.07½	329.12½	280.07	363.79	337.47
Horses	17.01½	28.40	34.72½	28.37½	31.50	33.00
Carriages	44.19	47.05	43.93½	21.85	44.25	18.92½
Dogs	15.75	22.08½	26.16	23.60	18.15	9.76
Goods & Livestock	1,505.02	3,479.09½	4,431.11½	4,609.76½	5,103.21	5.454.56
Mails	—	—	—	—	1,820.21	1,458.42
Miscellaneous	—	—	—	59.77½	104.85	—
	£12,358.29	£11,024.35	£13,727.79½	£12,110.47	£16,974.05½	£15,548.24

May 1849 was writing in its report of the Belfast Share Market, that 'Ballymena rails are enquired for'.

If the first half-year's results were poor those of the second were rather worse. Again no dividend was declared. There was a considerable increase in goods traffic with the running of goods trains consequent upon the completion of the necessary facilities. The decrease of passenger traffic was in part attributable to the winter season and to the potato famine, in regard to which the chairman told the shareholders in May 1849, 'an improvement in the condition of the country is now visible'. Every attempt was being made to encourage traffic by the issue of day excursion and other reduced fare tickets. A point which the directors felt bitter about was that although the mails had been carried since 1 September 1848 and on a small scale since 1 May, the Postmaster-General had not yet agreed the sum to be paid annually for their carriage.

Lanyon's report was more encouraging than the statistics:

> I am glad to state, that the line is generally in fair order, and that we have passed through the winter without experiencing any inconvenience in the working of the line, by subsidence, slips, or otherwise.

Under the terms of the contract Dargan had maintained the permanent way for one year following the opening of the line; and so on 11 April 1849 the company took over this responsibility itself.

By now the receipts had settled down into a regular pattern; that half-year ending in April was rather poorer than that which ended in October, since the former included the winter period and the latter the summer, always more productive of passengers, as well as the harvest season which augmented the goods receipts.

The balance sheet for the April—September period of 1849 was the best to date. A further increase in goods traffic was exhibited; still, the board felt, too much potential railway traffic was being carried on the roads. The goods accommodation had to be improved at Belfast, Ballymena and Randalstown and a 'luggage' engine had to be bought; these items, with additions to the headquarters offices at Belfast, cost £1,600. More importantly to the shareholders a balance of £3,346 was left after the usual subvention to the reserve fund—this permitted the declaration of a first modest dividend of 9s (45p) per £50 share—0.9 per cent. Still there was no settlement with the Post Office. At this time the chairman, Handcock, in complimenting the directors, stated that in his experience 'the working of this line is probably cheaper than any other line in the kingdom'. But another shareholder looked at Lanyon's York Road with disfavour: 'the ornaments at the Belfast station were such as would be fitted to a nobleman's house, or a railway paying twelve per cent'. Handcock told him that a reasonable standard of architecture and appointment was necessary since the building fronted on a main road out of the city.

Another poor half-year was reported in May 1850; the decline in the third class traffic was blamed on the depressed state of the country in the aftermath of the potato famine. The fall in first class passengers prompted Workman to propose the abolition of that class and an improvement of the second class accommodation, which, presently, he said, 'were adapted only to the bringing of prisoners to Carrick gaol'.

An 'umpire' had awarded £4,044.22 for the carriage of mails for the period from 7 May 1848 to 6 April 1850, this not being included in the accounts. A favourable balance permitted a higher dividend of 1 per cent.

At this time the directors were meeting monthly, the traffic sub-commitee weekly. Criticism was levelled at the board and the officers, it being asserted that the accounts were improperly kept. These Handcock indignantly rejected. This particular meeting in May 1850 was unusually protracted—it lasted 'until the candles were lighted'. In November 1850 an exceptionally good report was presented. The inclusion of the item 'Cartage' appeared in 1850 for the first time; this related to the collection and delivery of goods at Belfast and Ballymena, the B & B having laid the foundations of an important aspect of the business. In view of the improved position the dividend was increased to 1½ per cent, still leaving a considerable sum to be put to reserve. Handcock said the increasing receipts were very largely due to Higgin's industry:

> He had seldom met with such an excellent man of business, or one so uniformly unremitting and attentive to his duties.

The final set of statistics for this period to be considered in detail concern the October—March half-year of 1850–1. Despite relatively good returns the dividend was reduced to 1 per cent. Various ideas were being tried to improve passenger traffic; these included the running of an omnibus at Carrickfergus which, leaving for Larne, connected with certain trains. This continued until the opening of the Carrickfergus & Larne line in 1862. Workman proposed the issuing of 'villa tickets' (of which more below); in approving of the proposal (though it was not implemented at this stage), Higgin remarked that a similar scheme had been 'the means of raising a considerable town' on the London & Birmingham Railway.

In June 1851 there were 261 on the payroll: one manager and secretary, one engineer, one locomotive superintendent, one storekeeper, two accountants, nineteen station masters, two clerks, six engine drivers, six firemen, eight guards, forty artificers, eleven pointsmen, twenty-two gatekeepers, six policemen, sixty-seven porters, twenty platelayers and forty-eight labourers. In 1856 the number was 326, in 1858, 723.

TO COOKSTOWN AND COLERAINE

By November 1851 active proposals were afoot for extensions to Coleraine and to Cookstown.

Page 51
BRIDGES

(*above*) Randalstown Viaduct on Cookstown line (*below*) Bann Bridge at Coleraine

Page 52
THE L & C LINE

(*above*) Londonderry (Waterside) station, opened 1875 (*below*) Castlerock station

THE BELFAST AND BALLYMENA RAILWAY

We have already seen the fate of an earlier scheme to join Ballymena and Coleraine; now an extra urgency was lent to the proposal by reason of the fact that the Londonderry & Coleraine Railway was progressing with its main line and with it opened there would be a gap in railway communication between Coleraine and Ballymena. The fortunes of the L & C and the Ballymena—Coleraine line are found in Chapters 3 and 4.

Earlier in this present chapter the abortive scheme to link Randalstown with Cookstown was noticed. The B & B never entirely forgot that its Randalstown branch was something of a white elephant and so in 1851 a new proposal was made within the B & B for an extension to Cookstown via Toomebridge, Castledawson, Magherafelt and Moneymore. The total length of the Cookstown extension was to be 27 miles.

A public meeting was held in Castledawson in January 1852 under the chairmanship of Robert Peel Dawson of that town and the opinions expressed were so favourable that the B & B were disposed to proceed, it being stated that the landowners would give the required land at a 'fair price'. For their part the B & B shareholders at the May 1852 meeting 'favourably received' the proposal, and in September a special general meeting gave authority to Charles Lanyon to make the necessary surveys and prepare the plans. Handcock informed this meeting that

> Since it became known that the directors would apply to Parliament for this Act, they have been officially informed of the intentions of the Londonderry and Coleraine to extend their line from Coleraine along the West bank of the Bann to Castledawson, there to join the Cookstown extension, and thus complete a railway from Londonderry to Belfast. Proceedings were also being taken, and notices given by the landed proprietors, merchants, and others of the northern portion of the County of Antrim, for the formation of an independent company to extend the present line from Ballymena to Ballymoney, Coleraine and Portrush, completing also by this route the most direct communication between Londonderry and Belfast.

A Bill for the Cookstown extension was duly prepared for Parliament by Torrens; when it was approved by a special meeting on 13 May 1853 it had passed the Commons and gone to the Lords. It became law on 28 June 1853 as 'The Belfast & Ballymena Railway Extension Act'.

The new line was to commence at Randalstown, terminus of the existing branch, and 'terminate at or near the Public Road or Street in the Rear of the Market House at Cookstown'. Land was to be taken for a double line though initially the line was to be single. Additional capital of £200,000 was authorised with borrowing powers of £40,000. Much of the land required was in the County Londonderry estates of the Worshipful Companies of Drapers and Salters. The Drapers agreed to give fifty acres free of charge, the Salters fixed a price of £25 per acre on their land. In general much less difficulty than was encountered in obtaining land for the main line was experienced.

The contract was awarded to William Dargan who began work at Moneymore on 24 March 1855—the delay between that time and the passing of the Act may be attributed to the desire to raise capital. Possession of all the necessary land had been obtained by November 1854.

VICISSITUDES

The results over the first few years in the fifties varied; the dividend was mostly over $1\frac{1}{2}$ per cent. From the middle of 1851 Higgin fulfilled also the office of secretary on the retirement of Wilson. It transpired later that for this second charge he was unpaid. He was described in 1853 as 'the life and soul' of the railway, and from 1 November had an increment in salary from £400 to £500.

The first half of 1853 brought a serious fall in receipts; there was an especially disquieting fall in third class passengers of 7,589. The directors stated that the opening of the Londonderry—Coleraine—Ballymena lines was awaited keenly: 'they confidently look forward to the time when the great increase of traffic from these lines must enhance the value of the company's property'.

At this time the Post Office insisted on the mails being carried by the early morning goods trains which was cheaper for the purpose than passenger trains; this Higgin described

THE BELFAST AND BALLYMENA RAILWAY

as 'niggardly and unworthy'. During 1854 the electric telegraph was brought into use throughout the line.

The May 1854 dividend was 1 per cent, there having been an 18½ per cent increase in traffic on the previous half-year's results. It was decided to make certain improvements to York Road terminus preparatory to the opening of the Ballymena & Portrush line; a year later a line connecting the goods yard with the adjacent harbour estate at Albert Quay was opened and it was later stated that this had proved most lucrative, especially for coal traffic.

And the *Railway Times* obviously thought there was very little to complain of; commenting in May 1855 it stated that

> There is little to report of this line, save that it is unostentatiously conducted

and noted approvingly that the capital for the Cookstown extension had been entirely taken up by the existing shareholders 'without preference or priority of any kind'.

The November 1855 dividend rose to a new peak of 5 per cent. Prosperity had arrived. The 1855 working expenses were 41 per cent of receipts; in 1856 expenses had been reduced to 37 per cent. Though the goods traffic at this period exhibited a gratifying upward trend, passenger numbers, especially in the third class, showed rather peculiar fluctuations which one cannot explain by seasonal trends.

During 1855 the founder vice-chairman, John McNeile, died, and was replaced by Robert Grimshaw.

OPEN TO COOKSTOWN

Dargan carried out the work on the Cookstown extension rapidly; it included two massive engineering features which were to be the most outstanding on the B & B. Just outside Randalstown (where a new station had been erected) the River Maine was crossed by a very fine eight-span masonry bridge fifty feet above the water. A few miles further on, the River Bann was crossed by a low-lattice girder bridge which, owing to its position near the outflow of the Bann into Lough Neagh, had a swivel span; 'the Railway [is] carried by a number of wrought-iron girders, covering spans of 79ft 4in, and resting on cast iron cylinders sunk to various depths according to the nature of the foundations and filled with concrete'. The swivel span turned upon a large circular masonry pier. The stations were all designed by Lanyon; Cookstown was especially pleasing, a stone arched canopy covering the platform.

On 13 October 1856 Captain H. W. Tyler RE inspected the new line for the Board of Trade. His report if not altogether satisfactory was in considerable contrast to Laffan's of 1848. He praised the track, which was 76lb per yard flat-bottom rails (then known as contractors' or American section) spiked direct to traverse sleepers 2ft 9in apart grooved by a machine to receive the rail, 'and are thus better fitted for the reception of the rails and the preservation of the gauge'; the ballast was good and sufficient. Nevertheless he did not see his way to authorise the opening. There was an unauthorised level crossing instead of a bridge near Randalstown and the stations lacked 'auxiliary' or distant signals. Level crossing gates were constructed so as to close across the road only. The river bridge at Toome was, save for the opening span, a temporary structure but the plans for the final viaduct were satisfactory. No undertaking as to the method of working had yet reached the Board of Trade.

He left Lanyon with a memorandum of his requirements; on 29 October Lanyon reported that all these had been dealt with but the Board of Trade still refused to countenance the unauthorised level crossing. On 3 and 4 November the B & B wrote to say that the bridge would be built as quickly as possible; the Board responded by seeking Tyler's assurance that apart from the disputed bridge there was nothing to prevent opening and on such being received, permission was given to open on the condition that the bridge was completed within six months.

The line was opened to the public on Monday 10 November 1856, with down trains at 6am, 10.05am, 2pm and 4.35pm and up trains at 6am, 9am, 1.30pm and 6.45pm and two trains each way on Sundays. 'Arrangements are also being made for running a Van and Omnibus to and from Cookstown and Omagh' read the advertisement.

The ceremonial opening had taken place on Thursday 16 October. On that day a special train left York Road at 10.45am driven by Alexander Yorston the new locomotive superintendent. At Antrim a stop was made to pick up Viscount Massereene & Ferrard and his Lordship's guest, His Excellency the Rt Hon George William Frederick KG KP, Earl of Carlisle, Lord Lieutenant of Ireland, and suite. A few miles further and the Vice-Regal train entered upon the metals of the erstwhile Randalstown branch at Cookstown Junction (formerly Drumsough Junction) and so to Toome.

Halting at the Bann bridge the party detrained; Handcock broke 'a good bottle of sherry' over the bridge and requested the Viceroy's permission to name it 'Carlisle Bridge' in His Excellency's honour. His Excellency responded in the affirmative and in a speech expressed the hope that the bridge would continue to carry traffic safely 'to the end of time'. The special then continued on its way to Cookstown, where an address was presented to the Lord Lieutenant and a dejeuner served to a distinguished company in the fine new station. When all were replete resort was had to the train, which left Cookstown at 5.45pm. Belfast was reached at 9.20, the Lord Lieutenant and Lord Massereene having detrained at Antrim to return to Antrim Castle, where a ball was held that evening.

DEVELOPMENTS AT BALLYMENA

Though the Ballymena, Ballymoney, Coleraine & Portrush Junction Railway had been proposed and authorised simultaneously with the Cookstown extension, the former line was at work a year earlier. Since the site planned for the B & P station in Ballymena was more convenient to the centre of the town than that of the B & B, from the opening of the Portrush line in November 1855 the original B & B station was closed and all passenger activities transferred half a mile north to the new station. The goods yard at Harryville, however, remained in use for more than a century.

As will be seen in Chapter 4 the closest links existed from the outset between the B & B and the B & P with several directors common to both, and Higgin managing the Portrush line. The opening of the B & P meant that now there was railway communication between Belfast and Londonderry, the L & C having reached Coleraine in July 1853; but there was not yet *through* communication since no bridge yet existed over the Bann at Coleraine and the L & C's scheme of extension to Castledawson had not materialised. In 1856 the B & B was advertising a ten-hour Londonderry—Dublin journey via Coleraine and Belfast. A tedious one it would have been with at least three changes of train.

THE EXTENSION DISAPPOINTS

The company soon had reason to be dissatisfied with the results of the extension to Cookstown; the Devonshire Commission in 1866 was told that dividends had definitely fallen because of its working. A new timetable was introduced on the line from 1 December 1858. To protests that the trains took ten minutes longer the chairman replied that as the line 'had not given them a sufficient number of passengers' it mattered little how long the trains took! Also 'the greater the velocity, the greater would be the expenses of working'. In May 1859 Workman, a frequent speaker at shareholders' meetings, pointed out that there was an average of only $1\frac{1}{2}$ first class passengers per train on the Cookstown line. He suggested a cut of a quarter in the first and second class fares. To which Grimshaw the vice-chairman retorted that the Cookstown line was 'a great disappointment—perhaps if they were carried free and got their dinners, they would travel. They do not seem to be a travelling people.'

The cost of renewals to the permanent way was a heavy burden. In 1857 Lanyon reported that

> We are still making use of iron for the joint sleepers; in all cases of renewal we introduce fished joints, so that, in the course of a few years, the joint sleepers will be entirely renewed on this principle.

The cost of permanent way maintenance could be up to £4,000 per half year; the original home-grown timber sleepers had been found to be of poor durability and were replaced rapidly with foreign timber.

Nevertheless the dividend remained relatively high between 1857 and 1860, despite the fact that the Cookstown extension and the growing traffic made necessary the purchase of new locomotives and the renewal of older ones; and the construction at York Road of considerable numbers of new wagons.

During 1858 the existing engine shed at York Road, which was wooden, was destroyed by fire; a replacement in timber would have cost £700, but it was decided to renew it in stone at a cost of £1,000. At the same time extensions were carried out at the adjacent workshops and the entire scheme cost some £4,600. The engine shed was a 14-road semi-roundhouse completed in 1861. At this time extensive 'connecting services' were being developed by road; in some cases the car operators were subsidised by the railway.

A NEW MANAGER

In August 1857 Thomas Higgin placed his resignation before the board on the grounds of ill-health. At the meeting of shareholders held on 30 November the chairman, extolling the worth of Higgin and noting that he had for six years acted as secretary unpaid, moved that he be paid a pension of £200 for five years, as he 'had been disabled in the service of the company'. The position of secretary was filled from within the existing staff: Charles Stewart, described as having been 'a valuable auxiliary' to Higgin, was appointed at a salary of £300 per annum. He had been with the B & B since the earliest days. But there was no one at York Road qualified to fill the position of 'Traffic Manager' and advertisements were inserted in the railway periodicals, stating that 'none but a person of experience in railway matters need apply'. The salary was £400.

We know nothing of the other applicants; but there is no doubt that in selecting Edward John Cotton the directors made the most significant contribution to the prosperity of the company that is imaginable. Cotton, a native of Rochester in Kent, where he was born on 1 June 1829, was already in Ireland at the time of the advertisement, having come there in 1853 to Kilkenny as manager of the Waterford

& Kilkenny Railway. At the age of 24 he was then perhaps the youngest railway manager in the British Isles. His railway career had begun in October 1845 when he entered the service of the Great Western Railway in the traffic department at Paddington. Two years later he became a clerk in the embryonic Railway Clearing House at a time when fewer than twenty companies with a mileage of only 700 or 800 were associated with it. There he gained a thorough knowledge of inter-company traffic working arrangements and so was well fitted for a new post with the North Eastern Railway in 1851. Here he was given the task of training the staff in Clearing House business at a time when the NER was rapidly expanding.

The B & B was already aware of the importance of third-class traffic if only from the speeches of Workman. By the time Cotton arrived in October 1857 the work of roofing the third-class coaches, begun in 1856, was complete. In a further attempt to improve the lot of the third class passenger, Cotton gave orders that from 1 April 1859 third class return tickets would be issued from all stations. It is probable that the B & B was the first railway in the British Isles to provide this facility.

Cotton was keenly interested in the development of excursion trains; especially in connection with the Ballymena & Portrush line. Sometimes his enterprise took a bizarre form —in August 1859 an excursionist was drowned at Portrush; because of high seas the body could not be recovered immediately and it was reported that the B & B had issued special cheap tickets to those who went to look for it!

The company came under unfavourable attention from officialdom when a prize fight was held illegally near Cookstown Junction in 1859. A special train was hired, the B & B being told that it was to carry spectators to 'foot races'— scarcely likely since it left York Road at *3.30am!* At Cookstown Junction the passengers struck off across country to the meeting place where, we learn, 'Hussey' McVeigh was bettered by Peter McCann. The running of 'fight' trains became illegal in 1868. The year 1859 also brought the great religious revival and in August Cotton reported: 'The Sunday traffic [over the last month] shows a decrease of £22 16s od, which

THE BELFAST AND BALLYMENA RAILWAY

must, I think, be attributed to the present religious movement in this district. The mill workers are not going to Antrim, etc., in the same number . . . .'

'EAGLE'

On 9 April 1857 engine No 11, *Eagle*, shunting in the goods yard at Belfast, suffered a boiler explosion. This 0–4–2 of 1847 was too light for the main line goods trains and was probably the regular yard shunter. Its boiler pressure was 80lb; there were two safety valves. According to custom one of these was screwed down by the cleaner to 50lb when handing over to the fireman at 8.45am. The driver took charge at 9.30 with pressure at 80lb and the water half an inch from the top of the glass.

Eagle shunted for an hour, then the driver left the footplate to assist the shunter in coupling. By then the engine had been 'blowing off' from both valves for ten minutes. The driver called to the fireman to move the engine and in an attempt to hear better the fireman 'stopped the blowing'. Almost at once there was a violent explosion. The engine was projected over the tops of the wagons some 30 yards. It came to rest on its side and the fireman was found to be 'quite dead' in a sorry condition. Lt-Col Wynne, investigating for the Board of Trade, found that the water had probably been allowed to sink low in the boiler, allowing the firebox crown to get overheated. A sudden generation of high-temperature steam had then probably caused the explosion. The conduct of all concerned was 'most reprehensible'.

Eagle was rebuilt and continued in service until 1883. It was one of the original stud of ten which sufficed until 1851 when a new 'luggage' engine was ordered. In 1856 for the opening of the Cookstown line six passenger locomotives were ordered, and a year later two heavy goods engines.

SHORTAGE OF CAPITAL

Though prosperous at this time the B & B were suffering from a shortage of capital through large expenditure on works. The shareholders' meeting of May 1859 was told the capital of £778,000 had been totally expended and the borrowing powers exceeded by £10,000. It was proposed to make a submission to Parliament as quickly as possible.

It was well known that many of the original wooden stations, intended to be temporary, were in need of renewal; this was especially true of Cookstown Junction. Further, the single line out of Belfast was totally inadequate to deal with the volume of traffic now passing. Workman said that 'the Americans in some places do ten times the traffic on a single line. I know of a company where the receipts are £20,000 a week on a single line.' Handcock replied that perhaps there were more accidents—something the B & B had been almost free of.

As already noticed close links existed between the B & B and B & P, in which William Dargan was the leading figure and virtually the owner. With the connivance of the B & B, the B & P promoted a Bill in the 1858 Parliamentary Session which became law on 28 June 1858. By it the B & B was empowered to purchase the B & P at a future date, the sum required to be paid by the issue of new shares. This power was not exercised immediately; the price had yet to be settled with Dargan.

A complication ensued when on 19 April 1859 the B & P was given Parliamentary approval for the construction of a bridge over the Bann at Coleraine. This, coming after the 1858 Act, could not therefore be included in any sale of the B & P. At the same time the B & B had to consider its own shortage of capital. To take care of all these matters a Bill was authorised at a special meeting on 11 August 1859. Additional points in it were a change of title of the company and authority to regularise the half-yearly meetings hitherto held in May and November—now they were to be held in February and August, permitting of a division of the year into two halves from 1 January. At the last shareholders' meeting held under the old Belfast & Ballymena name in November 1859 Lanyon told the proprietors that 'a considerable number of the rails have been finished with iron clip-joints during the past Summer and I hope that the joints along the whole line will be similarly renewed before the expiration of two

THE BELFAST AND BALLYMENA RAILWAY

years'. The last half-yearly accounts of the B & B for the period October 1859—March 1860 were:

First class passengers	24,031	£2,837.66
Second class passengers	55,540	4,620.64
Third class passengers	173,188	6,300.51
	252,759	£13,758.81
Parcels		617.67
Horses, Carriages, Dogs		91.15½
		£14,467.44
Mails		£732.33¼
		£15,199.97
Goods and Livestock		£14,668.76¼
Rents, etc		231.40
Cartage		971.21¼
TOTAL		£31,071.35½

The declared dividend was 4 per cent.

And so on the passage of the Bill on 15 May 1860 the Belfast & Ballymena Railway ceased to exist and its place taken by the Belfast & Northern Counties Railway. The reason for the change of the old and somewhat parochial title to the more expansionist one will be amply demonstrated in the succeeding chapters.

CHAPTER THREE

The Londonderry and Coleraine Railway

THE TWIN RAILWAYS

The historic City of Londonderry had by 1840 become a thriving settlement of more than 20,000 persons which derived its commercial prosperity from its position, making it suitable to serve as the principal port for the county of Donegal.

The county of Londonderry was perhaps the most important of the Plantation Counties. Inland about twenty miles east of Londonderry was the little town of Newtownlimavady (called Limavady after 1870 and thus referred to here for convenience), a settlement created during the Plantation to replace an earlier town, and north-east of it was the ancient town of Coleraine, which had been the county town in the days before Londonderry sprang into prominence. It lay on another inlet, the River Bann. The inland area between these three places was an extremely fertile agricultural region; Coleraine was an important centre of the linen trade and a small port. There were a few settlements along the coast.

A railway to connect these three centres was an obvious scheme to be proposed at a time when railways were being planned all over Ireland. But when it came it was only part of a much more elaborate scheme.

The County of Londonderry has had for nearly four centuries close connections with the city of London, and it was from that quarter that two railways were promoted in 1844. One was a line from Londonderry south sixty miles through Strabane and Omagh and thence to Enniskillen in County Tyrone. The other was a much more grandiose scheme: as the *Railway Times* wrote, 'this project is . . . one of the boldest yet brought before the public'. An embankment was to be

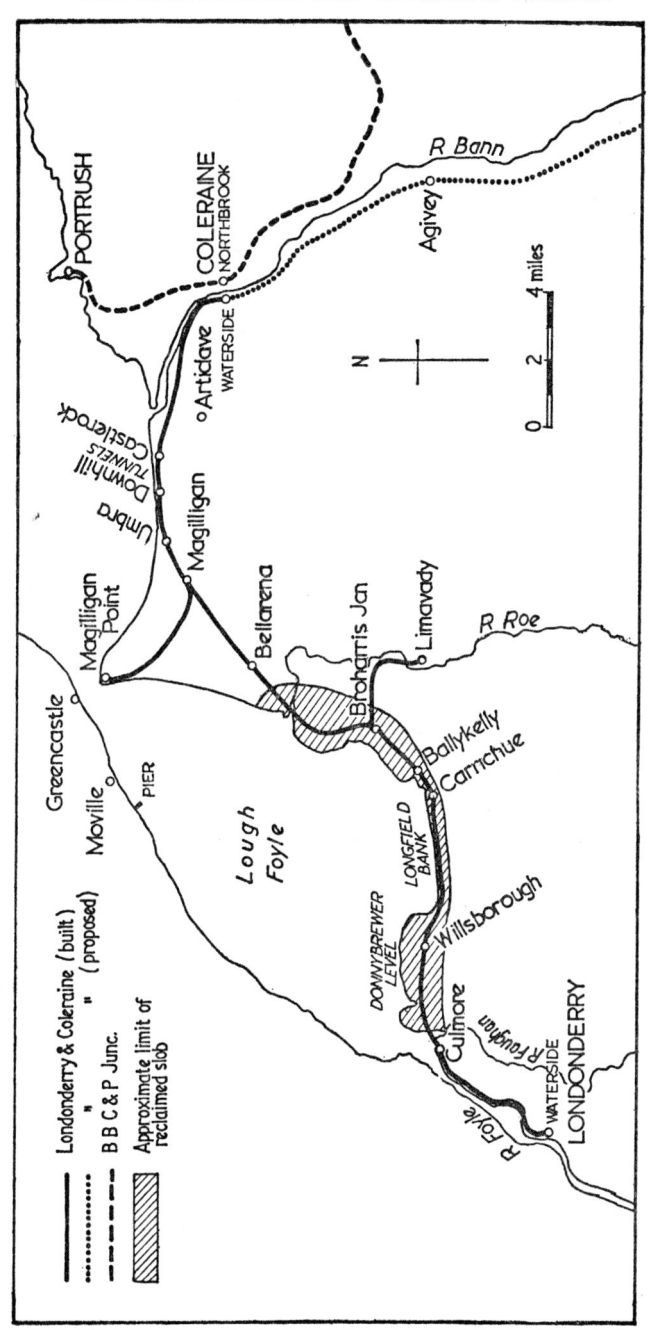

The Londonderry & Coleraine Railway

constructed, starting at a point where Lough Foyle becomes the River Foyle at Coolkeeragh, some five miles north east of Londonderry, and cutting right across the Lough north east to Magilligan Point, a distance of fifteen miles. This would reclaim some 20,000 acres of land, the sale of which would pay the cost of making the embankment and also that of building the intended railway from Londonderry to Coleraine, with a branch to Limavady. Of the provisional committee only two or three were Londonderry men, the rest being Londoners. Robert Stephenson and Charles Lanyon were appointed to make the preliminary surveys. No engineering difficulties over and above the making of the great embankment, and two tunnels where the line bordered the sea near Downhill, were envisaged.

The L & C and L & E shared substantially the same board, the same officers at 5 Church Passage, Guildhall and later at Coleman Street Buildings, London, and the services of the same secretary, Frederick Hemming (which individual constantly became confused and transposed entries in the two minute books). They were to remain closely associated until the L & E became part of the Irish North Western (later the Great Northern Railway of Ireland).

The Board of Trade and the Admiralty had to be approached (since the work would mean the alteration of the shipping channel up Lough Foyle) and then a submission could be made to Parliament, for the authorisation of the land reclamations and 38 miles 8 furlongs 3 chains of railway. A surprise awaited the promoters, however. The Bill was examined by the same Committee which investigated that of the Belfast & Ballymena, and the Board of Trade came out strongly against the scheme, saying that it 'seems to offer no material advantage', and noting that 'the Londonderry & Coleraine scheme appears under an aspect totally different from any other Railway project which has yet come before the Board . . .'. The coastal route was too far distant from pockets of population and it would be some time before people settled on the reclaimed land; there was little through traffic between Londonderry and Coleraine. The Board urged rejection, saying that a good embankment scheme did not require a railway, and vice versa.

THE LONDONDERRY AND COLERAINE RAILWAY 67

Nevertheless Parliament authorised the L & C on 4 August 1854 (and the L & E on the same day). John Lewis Ricardo MP became chairman and John Griffith Frith vice-chairman: a local committee was appointed to deal with day to day affairs; board meetings were held in London. A main line of railway some thirty miles long from Londonderry to Coleraine was authorised, with a four-mile branch to Limavady. The capital of the company was £500,000.

WORK BEGINS

The first half-yearly meeting was held in London in September 1845, the chairman's table being tastefully and appropriately decorated with produce from land 'that twelve months since was covered by the sea at every flow of the tide'. It was stated that work had already begun at Coolkeeragh, Campsie and Longfield; it was claimed that the agricultural value of the land reclaimed would be sufficient to cover the cost of building the railway.

Though work had begun in August it was not until October 1845 that a contract was signed, for the making of the Foyle embankment and the two tunnels necessary to carry the line through the cliffs at Downhill. The successful tenders were from Bromhead & Hemming, who quoted £322,000 for the embankment. Bromhead was a Bristol man; Hemming was from Londonderry, already concerned with reclamation, and conveniently enough was a brother of Frederick Hemming the secretary—though curiously this fact went unnoticed when charges of corruption were bandied about later.

At this stage plant and equipment was being ordered, on the recommendation of Robert Stephenson. Work was concentrated on making the embankment at Longfield, which would reach out to join the main embankment. A pier was built at Coolkeeragh for the unloading of equipment from the steamers. In October work began on the tunnels at Downhill, the sub-contractors being Marshall Bros. 'Several hundred Englishmen were obliged to be brought over, as not an Irishman could be found who knew the use of a drill, or the application of a fuse.' Ordinary tunnelling methods were used in the early stages; a heading or gallery was hewn into the rock from the side of the cliff, fifty feet in length, at the end of which a shaft was sunk 22ft to the level of the railway. Another gallery was made at the bottom running at right angles into the first one, and further into the rock.

There had been considerable ceremony when the first rock was being blasted in November 1845:

> On Monday last the ceremony of blasting the first rock of the series through which the tunnel is to pass at Downhill, was performed by Lady Bruce [wife of the landlord] in presence of an immense body of spectators who had assembled for the occasion. Her Ladyship applied the match in a scientific and truly workwomanlike manner, and the explosion which followed was hailed on all sides with loud blasts of enthusiastic applause. After the blast referred to, Lady Bruce gave a splendid entertainment [at Downhill Castle] to the numerous assemblage which had congregated to witness the interesting ceremonial in question.

The miners from England now created a diversion on their own account; a number of them were arraigned before Coleraine Court for attempting to form a 'combination' but there were no 'Downhill Martyrs' as a result! Work proceeding, the sub-contractors were ready by June 1846 to remove a huge mass of rock—some 30,000 tons—at one blast, hailed as 'The Great Blast', for explosions on this scale were then novel. The L & C took the opportunity of obtaining some revenue and vigorously advertised the event for over a month beforehand. Steamers were chartered in Londonderry and elsewhere to convey spectators to the scene.

A charge of 2,400lb was placed at the end of the gallery already referred to and earth packed in. A small charge of 600lb was then put in position higher up the rock face. When all was ready the 'Electric Fluid' or 'Galvanism', as the detonating agent was variously described, was applied, and 30,000 tons of rock slid gently into the sea. This completed, the contractors held a banquet in one of the partially completed tunnels, which blossomed forth under the light of great chandeliers bearing 350 candles and 1,200 'variegated lamps'. Some 500 persons were regaled in this bizarre setting.

Most of the stone for the embankments was being quarried at Moville in County Donegal, it being then ferried across Lough Foyle. In Londonderry seventy or eighty 'flats' were being built to carry 60 or 70 tons of stone on deck, and five steam tugs for their haulage were awaiting delivery of their 50hp engines. But after this auspicious beginning troubles were at hand.

HARD TIMES

For its difficulties the company had no one but itself to blame; in March 1847 the shareholders were told that 'the works generally have almost kept pace with the funds at the disposal of your Directors'. Work on the tunnels had been restricted early in 1847 to enable work to be concentrated on the main embankment, which progressed little; early in 1846 an Act had to be obtained extending the time limit for the reclamation.

In September 1846 the directors had explained that the delay in commencing the Coleraine end of the main embankment was caused by the heavy demand on constructional plant, which had prevented the delivery of three of the six locomotives previously ordered. Nor were the tugs completed. A hard winter in 1846–7 delayed work further but a start was made at the mouth of the River Roe and 800yd of tunnel was completed. By then work had also at least begun at Magilligan.

In July 1847 the western tunnel at Downhill was completed; work had been delayed by powder smoke hanging in the unventilated atmosphere but in June the headings were successfully obtained under the direction of a talented young engineer, Edward Webb. It was thus the first tunnel in Ireland to be *ready* for use, but as it was 1853 before trains ran through it, two tunnels on the Cork & Bandon line were also competitors for the honour. Some progress was also being made in draining the land at Willsborough, already enclosed by the embankment west of Longfield.

In September 1847 the sensible decision was taken to make the railway follow the Lough shore as it already existed more closely, crossing Hemming's and Robertson's reclamations, instead of carrying it on the main outer embankment. Some of the reclaimed land would however be used for the new course of the railway from Benone to Umbra. As a result the railway would be completed sooner and would run closer to Limavady, and 'the completion of the embankment [would be] hastened by affording the contractors greater facilities for procuring stone, and its carriage over the line as goods will supply revenue'. A new Act was obtained on 14 August 1848. The shareholders' meeting called to authorise the Bill was a lively affair; one Barry said he had visited Ireland two years before and in his view the best plan would be to abandon the entire scheme. Some also believed the crops claimed to be growing on the reclaimed land were non-existent. This Act also made some attempt to put in order the affairs of the L & C; the original company was in effect dissolved and reincorporated, the old shares being cancelled and new ones of similar value issued in their stead.

Since the autumn of 1847 relations had been strained between the company and its contractors; the number of men employed had dropped considerably and according to Hassard, the engineer who had succeeded Lanyon, insufficient progress had been made everywhere. Little work if any was being carried on by the spring of 1848 and in November 1847 a director's report may give the reason:

> I have seen Mr Bromhead, and I perceive that the weight of the liabilities of Mr Hemming in the neighbourhood of the works deters Mr Bromhead from commencing the vigorous prosecution of the works.

The L & C therefore decided to take possession of all plant which it owned, then in the contractors' hands, and register it in its own name; they would then be able to deal with the recalcitrant Hemming from a position of strength. A further report from Hassard in May 1848 was not reassuring; the shareholders constantly asked for details of progress and now when they had them they were anything but cheerful:

> I passed through the Downhill tunnels; they require arching and brick-lining in various portions, and rubbish to be cleared away. Thence to the Benone River the foundation is formed. At Magilligan Strand the embankment constructed has been greatly neglected. At the Roe Mouth a considerable amount of work is done (about three miles) but so imperfectly that serious damage from exposure to the elements has resulted

THE LONDONDERRY AND COLERAINE RAILWAY 71

... At the east end of Robertson's reclamation, some land is cultivated. The system of the embankment at the Roe Mouth is palpably erroneous and imperfect, but can be rendered sufficient ... Longfield embankment is well and substantially built, particularly that portion completed to the tip since the works were then taken out of the hands of Bromhead & Hemming. The Blackbrae embankment, though much out of repair, can be sufficiently secured if the works are discontinued. The contractors have shown an utter disregard of the preservation of plant and materials belonging to the Company, and considerable expenditure must be incurred to collect them together and place them in a place of security.

Little work was still being done. The young engineer named Webb was given leave to make 100yd of embankment using a device of his own invention, a coffer dam which he believed would shut out the water in 18 months instead of $2\frac{1}{4}$ years by conventional methods. But in October 1848 work was suspended altogether for want of money. Hassard was dismissed and Webb retained, keeping a watching brief and acting in such cases as that in January 1849 when the Donnybrewer and Longfield embankments had to be repaired after being breached during a storm. Soon afterwards Edward Preston, who had been one of Hassard's assistants, was appointed engineer, but for two years all that was done was to safeguard the existing embankments. In 1849 Thomas Carlyle, visiting Londonderry and viewing the works, characterised the embankments as 'an attempted futility'. £100,000 had gone and only a quarter of the work was done. The time limit set in the 1845 Act was rapidly approaching and so on 31 May 1850 another Act was obtained, extending the time by a further five years.

The company had long been searching for a contractor to take over the works that Bromhead & Hemming had been relieved of. They had been negotiating especially with William McCormick, a prominent businessman in Londonderry and a railway contractor of some repute. McCormick was a self-made man who had gone to England as a youth and, having achieved some success as a railway contractor, returned to his native city. He was responsible for sections of the Lough Swilly Railway and was involved in the reclamation work.

He met his Waterloo when he began dealings with the L & C; it was no coincidence that on his death in 1878 he was worth only £100. Prior to his death he had been Member of Parliament for Londonderry from 1861 to 1865. The negotiations with him proving successful, a contract between him and the L & C was signed in January 1851; he undertook to complete the line and have it open to Limavady (it having been decided to press towards that point first) by 1 August 1851, and the main embankment completed by the end of that year.

One of the L & C's perennial problems now reared its head —a dispute between the local committee in Londonderry and the board in London, the chairman of the latter since 1849 being Captain Daniel Warren, who had been a stern critic of the previous board. The committee did not agree with the terms of the contract and declined to give McCormick charge of the company's plant. This painful position obtained for a month. Eventually the local members gave way and McCormick began work. The line at this time was completed and usable from Coolkeeragh to Ballykelly but little else had been done save for the rough completion of the tunnels. McCormick began a vigorous prosecution of the works. By the end of 1852 the line between Londonderry and Limavady was virtually completed though the August target date had had to be abandoned.

The L & C was by now in a serious financial position; most of the shareholders were in arrears with calls. The board was anxious to obtain the assistance of the government but had as yet been unable to do so. On 28 May 1852 yet another Act dissolved the company and reincorporated it. The capital was again £500,000. Provision was made for a contribution to the building of a new bridge over the Foyle at Londonderry, which would permit the passage of rail traffic between the L & C and its twin the Londonderry & Enniskillen. This was not accomplished, however, until 1868 (*see* Chapter 5).

TO LIMAVADY AND COLERAINE

A storm in January 1852 caused considerable damage and set things back several months. By September 1852 the line was at last ready for Board of Trade inspection. It was announced that goods traffic would be commenced on 29 September and passenger traffic on 1 October; but Captain George Wynne had other ideas and refused to allow passenger trains to be run. He returned for a second inspection on 16 October:

> I found the sea Embankment of the Railway much advanced since my last inspection but on that part of the line east of 'Tyrrell's Reclamation' the stone pitching on the exposed side of the Railway embankment is not in so forward a state as would in my opinion render the line quite safe, there is a large quantity of stone still required to complete the work and the drawing of this over a *single* line would offer serious obstruction to the passenger traffic and from the numerous sidings leading into the quarries, would not be unattended with danger...

Wynne came back a third time and on this occasion saw fit to authorise the commencement of passenger traffic. So on 29 December 1852 passenger trains began to run over the $18\frac{1}{2}$ miles between Londonderry and Limavady. The line was being pushed onwards from Broharris (later Limavady) Junction to Coleraine; work had to be suspended in late December 1852 while repairs were executed following a storm which caused damage to the embankment at the Roe mouth. But work progressed at the Coleraine end. A brickyard at Articlave employed 150 men in making bricks to line the tunnels: that at the Downhill end was 307yd long, while that nearer Coleraine was 668yd long.

On 14 July 1853 Captain Wynne inspected the $17\frac{1}{2}$ miles from Broharris to Coleraine:

> The permanent way of the Extension as well as the part already opened is single, the only works of importance are the two tunnels . . . they are excavated in the basaltic rock of the district, their sides are lined with masonry and the semicircular arched roof turned in brickwork, their width is only sufficient for one line of rails, the workmanship of them appears to be very good; I found the permanent way properly laid, and well ballasted, and the other works completed and of sufficient strength.

So on 18 July 1853 the Broharris—Coleraine section was opened to all traffic; a celebratory banquet was held in the

Clothworkers' Arms Hotel, Coleraine. The entire line was thus completed, nearly eight years after the original Act of Parliament was obtained.

The Londonderry terminus, appropriately named Waterside, was situated on the eastern bank of the River Foyle, somewhat remote from the city centre and on the fringe of the then boundary. Initially there seem to have been no intermediate stations between Londonderry and Limavady, but Willsborough (renamed Muff in September 1853 and Eglinton in January 1854) at $7\frac{1}{2}$ miles, Carrichue at $12\frac{3}{4}$ miles, Ballykelly at $13\frac{1}{2}$ miles, and Broighter on the Limavady branch at 15 miles were opened during 1853. Culmore, 5 miles, was added during 1854 and from 1855 to 1859 there was a station at Faughanvale, $11\frac{1}{4}$ miles. The junction station at Broharris had no platform and main line trains ran through to Limavady and reversed before proceeding. Between the junction and Coleraine there were stations at Bellarena ($20\frac{1}{4}$ miles), Magilligan ($23\frac{1}{4}$ miles), Downhill ($26\frac{1}{4}$ miles), Castlerock ($27\frac{1}{2}$ miles). Between 1855 and 1856 there was a 'flag' station at Barmouth at $29\frac{1}{2}$ miles and there is some evidence of the existence of one at Umbra, at about 25 miles. The Coleraine terminus, also called Waterside, was on the western bank of the River Bann near the road bridge and was 33 miles from Londonderry. The distance from Broharris Junction to Limavady was $3\frac{1}{2}$ miles.

Leaving Londonderry the line followed the course of the Lough, save for the portion of the embankment across Rosses Bay, as far as the mouth of the River Faughan. It then ran across the Donnybrewer reclamation and followed the line of reclaimed land for $4\frac{1}{4}$ miles to Ballykelly. From there the six miles to Bellarena again traversed reclaimed land. Lough Foyle was left behind and, skirting the foot of the mountains, the line ran across the great raised beach known as the Magilligan peninsula with distant views of the sea and Donegal. At Umbra the line ran inland for a short section; here it still skirted the cliffs. Meeting the sea again, first the shorter tunnel, then the longer, was passed through, and soon the River Bann was seen. This the railway followed to Coleraine and the terminus.

Except for a slight rise into Castlerock there was scarcely

THE LONDONDERRY AND COLERAINE RAILWAY 75

a perceptible gradient on the line, which ran a few feet above sea level throughout. Apart from the embankments and the tunnels and a bridge across the Roe mouth, there was little of engineering significance. The track was of Barlow pattern: cast iron supports similar to heavy chairs in which rested 'T' rails. Sleepers were not used; tie bars at 10ft intervals maintained the gauge.

By early 1851 receipts from sale of shares had been £263,227 and expenditure £262,341, leaving a balance of that time of £886. From 23 December until the end of 1852 the railway carried 724 passengers; during the six months to the end of June 1853 it carried 18,933 (in the same period the Belfast & Ballymena carried 216,969). The chairman jubilantly reported that "'Tis a long lane that has no turning' and adverted to the tourist potential of their line and the proximity of the Giant's Causeway. A monster excursion had been run from Londonderry to Coleraine for Portrush; 1,600 people were conveyed and a profit of £103 was made, the fares having been 2s (10p), 1s 6d (7½p) and 1s (5p) respectively for the three classes.

Ordinarily five trains ran between Londonderry and Coleraine, and four in the other direction, with one each way on Sundays, all trains serving Limavady. Fares were: singles 5s (25p), 4s (20p) and 2s 8d (13½p) for the three classes respectively for the complete journey; and return 7s 6d (37½p), 6s (30p) and 4s (20p) respectively, 'intermediate fares in proportion'.

It is extremely difficult to be specific in dealing with officials of the L & C, for the paucity of documents means that it is impossible to be certain of some dates; the officers did not in general remain long and there was also a rapid turnover of chairmen and vice-chairmen, especially in the later years.

It appears that for a period before opening Robert Dods acted as manager and locomotive superintendent of the L & C, holding similar positions on the L & E. On the opening of the L & C, however, W. R. Boyle became manager and Robert Fairlie (of articulated locomotive fame) assumed the duties of locomotive superintendent. In 1854, Boyle resigned and Fairlie was dismissed, as the new manager, John S. Sinclair, was to be in charge of the engines also. In 1855 he took his departure and Peter Roe became manager with Edward Leigh (later to join the B & NCR) as locomotive superintendent.

There was an equally bewildering series of engineers. Hassard was in charge between 1847 and 1849, when he gave way to Edward Preston. In 1853 Arthur Forde was appointed; it appears that at one time he took a share in management. In 1857 Robert Collins took over and apparently he was retained in a consultative capacity until 1871; Phineas Howell was, at least for a time, his assistant. These three engineers were to become members of the B & NCR staff in due course.

THE MAGILLIGAN BRANCH

The difficulties of completing the main line were enormous. The cost of the railway was some £9,500 per mile and no sooner had Coleraine been reached than a financial depression prevented the sale of £60,000 in debentures to cover costs. A loan of £70,000 had been obtained from the Public Works Loan Commissioners: £14,000 on 6 July 1852, a similar sum on 16 November 1852, a third £14,000 on 3 May 1853, and £28,000 on 19 July 1853. The time for repayment was 13 years; the rate of interest was 5 per cent, later reduced to 4 per cent.

But all this did not deter the directors; one certainly has to admire their staying power. By the beginning of 1853, with their main line not yet completed, they had under consideration the construction of a further branch. It was to be $4\frac{1}{2}$ miles long from Magilligan station to Magilligan Point. Initially there seems to have been some idea of making it to a different gauge to the main line, but this was not pursued.

Sir Hervey Bruce Bt of Downhill (who will be met with further in Chapter 7) gave the land free; therefore neither Parliament nor the Board of Trade was acquainted with the new line. Work began in September 1853. Soon afterwards Bruce began to make difficulties but the L & C's solicitors reported that he could not interfere.

On 27 June 1855 the secretary noted that 'they now had 36 miles of railway actually at work, and many miles more, known as the Magilligan branch, which £300 would complete and fit for traffic'. The branch appeared in Bradshaw for July

1855 and must therefore have been opened about the beginning of that month. Since forty minutes were allowed for the journey of 4½ miles all the signs are that it was worked by horse traction. A service of four trains making connection with main line trains was provided; two evening trains made no connections. There was one Sunday train.

It appears that the branch ceased running during October 1855—though there is no evidence as to the actual date. But in December 1856, at one of the irregularly held shareholders' meetings, the chairman reported that 'finding a small branch they had made to the Coast of Donegal altogether unremunerative, they had altogether abandoned it'. This must mean that the rails were lifted (*but see* Chapter 8), though the course may still be followed.

The reference to the 'Coast of Donegal' alludes to the idea of connecting with a ferry service from Magilligan Point to Donegal; in 1853 the L & C had taken a financial interest in the ferry to Greencastle and 1½ miles of land along the Donegal shore. It was announced that on Saturdays from 18 August 1855 the steamer *Nelson* would connect with the 4pm train from Londonderry to convey excursionists to Moville, returning thence at 6.30am on Monday to connect with the 7.30am train from Coleraine.

Surely the Magilligan branch was the shortest lived branch line on record! Forty years later the B & NCR made attempts to revive it but these came to naught.

THE CASTLEDAWSON EXTENSION

Whatever its financial position the L & C was certainly not bankrupt of ideas. The Coleraine terminus was built as a through station, it being intended only as an intermediate station in an elaborate extension scheme.

The Belfast & Ballymena had under contemplation an extension of its Randalstown branch to Cookstown (authorised 28 June 1853, *see* Chapter 2). The L & C planned to build an extension of their own down the west bank of the Bann south of Coleraine, crossing the river at Agivey 7½ miles south of Coleraine, continuing thence to Castledawson, 38 miles from Belfast on the B & B, thus effecting a through line of railway between Belfast and Londonderry. So on 8 July 1853 the 'Belfast Extension Railway' was incorporated.

At the same time the Ballymena, Ballymoney, Coleraine & Portrush Junction Railway was authorised, and since it was to run to Coleraine from Ballymena, it was clearly in competition with the L & C's extension as far as completing a through route was concerned.

It will be noticed that this extension was authorised within a very short time of the opening to Coleraine. Two months later a contract was signed with McCormick for the building of the first section to Agivey Bridge from Coleraine (some people thought Dargan or Brassey should have been awarded the contract). The ceremony of turning the first sod was performed on 8 September 1853—and nothing further was done. The Belfast Extension Railway was still-born; the L & C found other things to occupy its attention and capital and in due course the powers expired and were not renewed.

The BBC & PJR had been incorporated on the same day, Dargan being its principal figure. On 22 September 1853, cutting the first sod near Portrush, the Earl of Antrim lampooned the L & C's projected extension, putting the position succinctly and with considerable perspicacity:

> There was an Old Lady called the Maiden City [Londonderry] who had been asleep for years, but occasionally woke up and employed Englishmen to do her work—to make a railway where a road was scarcely necessary—but the Old Lady had failed in her object and he believed her projected Railway would never be made one inch beyond Coleraine.

This speech infuriated Londonderry and His Lordship had to apologise; but his words were nonetheless true and the B & P, entirely organised and financed within Ireland, was quickly built and opened to traffic while the Castledawson scheme was quietly forgotten, its second sod remaining unturned.

THE RAILWAY IN OPERATION

The first receipts from the L & C were encouraging enough; the chairman was enthusiastic and reported that hitherto the district had been served by one stage coach and two jaunting cars. Enterprise was not lacking. Day excursion tickets were issued on Fridays—return tickets at single prices valid for 'day of issue only'. Excursion fares were also made available periodically for various special events. Through bookings were operated from the Enniskillen line and excursions run from that line, the passengers having to make the journey between the two stations in Londonderry under their own auspices. Before the opening of the BBC & PJR a four-horse bus with accommodation for 36 passengers ran in summer between Coleraine and the Giant's Causeway via Portrush, while from 1855 a car connected Muff Post Office with the station there, which was some distance away.

On 14 March 1855 the L & C had its first mishap. The mail from Coleraine, consisting of three or four carriages hauled by one of the little Sharp 2–2–0 well tanks, was running round the forty chains' radius curves at Rosses Bay when the engine mounted the outside rail and after running 40–50yd capsized, killing Driver William Dixon and injuring Fireman William Crawley. Lt-Col Wynne could find no cause; he assumed that the long wheelbase of the locomotive was unsuited to the sharp curve. He had of course reacted adversely to this section of the line in 1852.

Another accident occurred at Bellarena on 28 April 1856. The 5pm ex Londonderry arrived and when the passengers had detrained the locomotive backed to get water. The gateman supervised this operation and in his absence the level crossing gates were opened. The train started forward and killed a deaf man of 80, amputating his legs. The gateman was dismissed.

The railway again came under the notice of the Board of Trade for a further accident on 31 December 1858, the details of which reveal the rather slapdash operating procedures which may have contributed to the L & C's poor reputation. The first up train was a goods which picked up three wagons at Castlerock, destined for Bellarena, which were being propelled. In accordance with regulations the driver whistled approaching Magilligan and received a green light signal signifying that the train need not stop. To the consternation of all concerned the train turned into a short siding at the Coleraine end, and, unable to stop, ploughed through the stopblock and the three wagons were smashed. The 'station man' (to use Capt Ross of the Board of Trade's term) was so surpised he fell backwards and was found three weeks later to have a broken thigh. Ross criticised the propelling of wagons on the main line and deprecated the L & C's 'self-acting switches' which on this occasion had failed to act, and recommended that 'indications' be attached. Furthermore there should be separate staff for goods and passengers—the 'station man' at Magilligan was general factotum.

Business at this time was not brisk; it appears that all stations on the main line were 'flag' halts; trains calling only if required.

On 30 June 1856 the staff consisted of 122 men: one manager, one secretary, one engineer, one storekeeper, two accountants, one inspector, thirteen stationmasters, one ticket collector, four clerks, two foremen, four engine drivers, four firemen, four guards, eleven artificers, four pointsmen, eight gatekeepers, three policemen, twelve porters, thirty-four platelayers and eleven labourers.

The last mention made of the land reclamation schemes was in connection with the signing of the contract with McCormick in 1851, whereby he undertook to complete the main embankment by the end of that year. But work had to be concentrated on finishing the railway and by July 1853, with that completed, it was suggested that work on the embankment should be suspended for the time being. The subject cropped up again at the shareholders' meeting in December 1856. The chairman said that 'to the land reclamation they must still look as the great means of retrieving the position of the Company. By March next they hoped to place before the shareholders proposals for giving life again to the reclamation.' In point of fact the great embankment was never completed in its original form. Before anything could be done certain circumstances without the L & C's control militated against a recommencement of work on the reclamation.

THE LINE IS LEASED

By 1855 the financial position of the company was hopeless and the directors decided they had had their fill. The chairman told the shareholders that the position was 'critical' and had caused much 'painful anxiety'. The inability to sell debentures, and to pay interest, still less repay principal, to the PWLC meant that the only alternatives were sale or lease of the line—and since there were no likely purchasers, leasing was the only hope. 'Your directors feel deeply sensible of the failure of expectation and the postponement of hopes.' It was the logical result of the company's financial background; in 1853 the chairman had warned of impending bankruptcy.

At this time Hemming, the secretary since the outset, resigned. In March 1854 he had been described as 'a man of the railway' and compared to Hamlet but a year later he departed and made vigorous allegations against the directors whom he termed 'an unmitigated nuisance' (this he said at a L & E meeting but the boards were virtually identical). He was succeeded by James K. Arthur.

Besides having been contractor during the latter part of the building of the railway, McCormick was a large creditor and he was persuaded to undertake the lease of the line. For this Parliamentary sanction was required and some shareholders were opposed, doubtless feeling that the directors were failing in their duty. But on 23 July 1855 authority was given to lease the undertaking for three periods of seven years, up to a maximum of 21 years.

McCormick took over the working from this date; and shortly afterwards he appointed Peter Roe, former manager of the Midland Great Western Railway, to manage the line. The sanction of the PWLC had been obtained for the lease but no details were finalised and months of discussion proved fruitless. Furthermore, creditors continued to harass the L & C and obtained judgments against the company, succeeding in bringing about a state of utter chaos.

Finally the PWLC stepped in and brought about the termination of McCormick's lease in December 1856, the working reverting to the L & C but under the supervision of the PWLC who apparently retained Roe as their agent. McCormick was permitted to retain the receipts for the period during which he had worked the railway but from these he had had to pay some judgment debts and maintain the stations and works. He had also obtained possession of the rolling stock and on resuming control the unhappy directors had to arrange to repurchase it by weekly instalments!

Improved receipts were noted following the resumption of control by the company and Roe received the credit for this. But still there was insufficient balance to pay in full all the liabilities and interest and finally the L & C urged the PWLC, under their powers as priority mortgagees, to arrange another lease with McCormick in order to prevent total collapse. This the Commissioners agreed to. In May 1858 the chairman told the shareholders that the lease would prevent the line being 'sacrificed' and the rentals would provide a higher net income than direct working. He hoped that they might make something of the line when the lease ended. At the time £552,457 had been received and £561,748 spent, an adverse balance of £9,291.

The lease was operative from 10 April 1858 for seven years. McCormick had to pay £8,500 for the first two years and £10,000 per year thereafter. Roe remained manager: this remarkable man's career had begun as a ticket collector and ended as manager on the Midland Great Western, which he left in a welter of accusations of malpractice. Since he was an enterprising man McCormick evidently hoped that he would make the best of a bad bargain. Roe did his best. He increased cheap travel facilities, introducing free season tickets for builders of houses at Downhill and Castlerock to Londonderry—a variant of the B & NCR's famous villa tickets. He also instituted evening bathing tickets to Downhill; however these were withdrawn because of misuse. Roe always believed in giving the best possible service under the circumstances: he told the Devonshire Commission in 1866 that he had reduced fares by half and countered allegations that he had neglected the rolling stock by saying that on his departure the stock was valued at a higher figure than on his arrival. In December 1855 he had a dispute with the Post Office—represented by Anthony Trollope, who refused to grant a mail contract 'owing to the peculiar circumstances of the railway'. Until a settlement was reached postal services were chaotic—but Roe obtained local support by arranging to carry newspapers free for the time being until the mail train was restored!

THE LONDONDERRY AND COLERAINE RAILWAY 83

NEW DEVELOPMENTS

McCormick's lease of 1858 continued. On 15 May 1860 the Belfast & Ballymena became the Belfast & Northern Counties Railway and on 1 January 1861, as long expected, took over the Ballymena & Portrush line. Between these two events the bridge over the Bann at Coleraine, which had been under consideration since 1853, was put into regular service on 19 November 1860, so that for the first time Belfast and Londonderry were directly connected and the L & C's station at Coleraine was by-passed (see Chapter 4).

Under these circumstances McCormick, who was finding his lease of the line a tiresome and unprofitable business, decided it was high time for him to cut his losses. The position was complicated: the directors were the lessors but theoretically the line was in the ownership of the Public Works Loan Commissioners. Apart from the Commissioners, McCormick was the largest creditor, holding debentures to the value of £63,200.

The L & C went before Parliament in 1859 and on 13 August obtained authority to create debenture stocks of four classes, which were to be used to placate the creditors. During the course of the examination of this Bill, McCormick indicated that he was prepared to cease working at any time on 'equitable terms'. Who was going to relieve him of the L & C, however, was not clear.

But his chance came in 1861. With the B & NC well established and already seen to be a prosperous and well managed concern, he entered into negotiations with the authorities at York Road. McCormick's seven year lease had four years to run; and on 10 April 1861 this remaining portion was transferred to the Northern Counties at a yearly rental of £10,000. The B & NC also purchased outright the L & C's locomotives and rolling stock for the sum of £22,241. This meant that the entire Belfast—Londonderry main line, 95 miles in length, was for the first time under one management. The L & C's Waterside station in Coleraine, on a spur since the opening of the bridge, was very shortly afterwards closed.

Although after 1861 the working of the line was in good hands, the L & C still existed as a leasing company and was still very much in the woods financially. The Act of August 1859 had authorised it to liquidate some of its debts by the issue of debentures of some £250,000. These powers could not be exercised unless approved by the shareholders and creditors and since strong protests were registered nothing could be done.

The directors decided to make a last despairing effort to regain legal ownership of their line from the PWLC. They persuaded some of the creditors to agree to the provisions of the 1859 Bill; the Parliamentary Committee noted 'the peculiar circumstances of the case'. The directors therefore brought forward a Bill similar to that of 1859 in 1861. They sought to rid themselves of the PWLC and keep the other creditors quiet by giving them 'something tangible' which they could at least try to place on the money market. The board claimed that 98 per cent of the creditors supported their proposals, but opposition was lodged by the Fishmongers' Company of London, owners of much land along the Foyle shore. During the Committee stage the L & C was called 'the most unfortunate railway . . .'.

The shareholders noted that the Bill was intended to permit 'of sale or for other purposes'. They disapproved and rejected it. The next year it was again brought forward and by now the position had improved somewhat. The company had succeeded in repaying the entire sum due to the PWLC which had then handed back the line to L & C control. The shareholders proved accommodating and accordingly the Bill was allowed to pass on 17 July 1862. It provided for the issue of debentures similar to the 1859 Act. In the event of anything untoward happening, such as the creditors refusing to accept the new stock, the entire undertaking might be sold. The extreme position was not reached at this time, however, as most of the creditors accepted the debentures.

It is to be doubted whether they received much of a bargain—debentures which were to prove worthless in exchange for debts extending back over twelve or fifteen years. Many decided to cut their losses and sold the newly issued stock for what little it fetched; others waited hopefully, trusting that one day interest would be forthcoming. They must surely have regretted the day they succumbed to the blandishments of the L & C's prospectus.

THE B & NC'S INHERITANCE

The Northern Counties had leased the line for four years at a yearly rental of £10,000. This lease—from McCormick and not directly from the L & C—was due to expire in April 1865. It was extremely unlikely that the B & NC would renew it on existing terms, for it had proved most unprofitable and there had been large expenditure on the permanent way and on renewals of bridges, fencing and other works. There was also a threat of a new direct line from Londonderry to Dungannon and thence to Portadown and Belfast.

Negotiations resulted in the substitution of a 'haulage contract' operative from 10 April 1865 for such time as it was desired to continue it. The terms were more favourable to the B & NC: 2s (10p) per train mile was charged, with mileage in excess of 7,500 per month charged at 1s 8d (8½p) per mile. Any trains which exceeded seven passenger vehicles or 25 goods wagons were to have a pilot engine or be run in duplicate. Track renewals became the responsibility of the L & C: theoretically they had been McCormick's burden during the B & NC's sub-lease. On taking up the lease the Northern Counties had closed Eglinton station and wished to close Ballykelly, but encountered the opposition of the Fishmongers' Company.

The truth of the Northern Counties' contention that the lease had been unprofitable was now clearly seen. Under the haulage contract the L & C's portion of revenue decreased and the debenture interest remained unpaid. The directors proposed to sue McCormick for his handling of the permanent way maintenance and arbitration was sought. The B & NC found the haulage contract much more favourable to itself, the more so when in April 1868 it was renewed on even better terms: 2s 2d (11p) per train mile for the first 7,500 miles per month, 1s 10d (9p) thereafter. Nevertheless B & NC shareholders thought their company had been saddled with 'a bankrupt concern'. The claim on McCormick could not be prosecuted; terms of arbitration could not be agreed and since McCormick was by now bankrupt the L & C was unsure that it could recover the expense of litigation from him.

By 1866 the powers in connection with land reclamation had lapsed and in February the shareholders were told of the sensible decision to dispose of the assets altogether. At long last the company had decided that there was nothing further to be gained from retaining control of a project which had already proved financially disastrous and was never likely to bring any improvement in the future. The purchase was arranged with the Honourable the Irish Society, large landowners in the City and County of Londonderry.

THE END OF THE L & C

The L & C was now purely a holding company, owning its own line and buildings but no longer an owner of rolling stock nor a working company. It was more concerned with trying to liquidate its heritage of debt—debts of all amounts on all sides but now principally arrears of interests due on the host of debentures issued in a headlong attempt to arrest the spiral. The directors could take comfort in the fact that a reasonable service was being given on the line. But they themselves, being responsible for maintenance and upkeep, were faced with the necessity of more and more expenditure as track and bridges required renewal: for example, $2\frac{1}{2}$ miles of track were relaid with 70lb flange rails in 1868-9.

A number of debenture holders approached the B & NCR and succeeded in persuading it to purchase the L & C line. The debenture holders and the B & NC then proceeded to lay a Bill before Parliament which in its preamble pointed out the deficiencies in the track and stations. On 24 July 1871 the Londonderry & Coleraine Railway Company ceased to exist and was vested in the Belfast & Northern Counties Railway. By the Act the B & NC was authorised to raise £135,000 by the issue of new preference shares and to borrow up to £26,666.

So died the L & C—lamented by no one, least of all by its unfortunate shareholders. Had the undertaking been involved only with the railway portion of the original scheme it was well calculated to be a success. But it was coupled with a most ambitious scheme for reclaiming the shores of Lough Foyle, the completion of which was a charge on the railway even after the idea of making the railway follow the embankment over its entire course had been abandoned.

CHAPTER FOUR

The Ballymena and Portrush Railway

EARLY PROPOSALS

In 1848 the Belfast & Ballymena Railway arrived at Ballymena; five years later the Londonderry & Coleraine reached the latter town. There remained a gap of thirty miles between Ballymena and Coleraine; the important trunk route between Belfast and Londonderry was incomplete. In Chapter 2 mention was made of the several attempts, partly under the aegis of the B & B, to close the gap; and of the unhappy history of the Dublin, Belfast & Coleraine Junction Railway. None of these attempts came to anything; the gap was as yet unbridged.

PORTRUSH

Portrush, a little fishing village on a promontory of the Antrim coast north-east of Coleraine, was the site of a harbour made in the 1830s. It formed portion of the estates of the Earl of Antrim, who, being at that time not unduly flush financially, was anxious to develop this promising possession as a seaside resort. And what better means could be adopted than the provision of railway communication? The project would also serve to close the gap between Ballymena and Coleraine.

It was late 1852 when a definite scheme was formulated; it was lent a sense of urgency by the impending opening of the L & C line to Coleraine. The line was to be 35 miles long from Ballymena to Portrush via Ballymoney and Coleraine. A provisional committee was formed under the chairmanship of the Rt Hon Hugh Seymour, 9th Earl of Antrim, and on 8 July

THE BALLYMENA AND PORTRUSH RAILWAY 89

1853 'The Ballymena, Ballymoney, Coleraine & Portrush Junction Railway Company' was incorporated (for convenience it will hereinafter be referred to as the Ballymena & Portrush) with a capital of £200,000 in 20,000 £10 shares with loans of £60,000. Its purpose, as grandiosely set forth in Bradshaw's Railway Manual, was the completion 'of the chain from Dublin to Derry (North-west) and with Coleraine and Portrush (North) and the great trunk from the north to the south of Ireland, and between Portrush Harbour and Glasgow, steamers opening up the beauty of the North &c'.

Land was to be taken for a double line to be laid if and when required by the Board of Trade, though only a single line was envisaged initially. Running powers over the B & B were included, that company to enjoy reciprocal facilities over the B & P. A clause identical with one in the L & C's 1853 Act was included: that both companies would use their 'best endeavours' to promote a Bill for a junction at Coleraine in the 1854 session of Parliament.

The chairman of the new company's board was, understandably, Lord Antrim. Most of the other directors had close associations with the B & B and some sat on both boards. James Thomson of Ballymoney was appointed secretary, the headquarters of the railway being at Church Street, Ballymoney. The estimable Charles Lanyon was appointed engineer and was at work lockspitting the land. It had also been decided that William Dargan be appointed to build the line. Regrettably we have no documentation of the negotiations with Dargan; we know only that he agreed to enter into contract to build the line, and in lieu of direct payment was to take £160,000 in shares. This, being more than three-quarters of the total share capital, made him virtually the owner and the directors—certainly, after the line was opened—mere ornaments. The boardroom was in effect Dargan's residence at Mount Annville. Towards the end of August 1853 the directors approved Dargan's terms and work began almost immediately. On 21 September 1853 the Earl of Antrim performed the ceremony of cutting the first sod in a field near Portrush. It was at this ceremony that he pronounced the valediction on the L & C's Castledawson extension (Chapter 3). Afterwards 'Mr Coleman of the Portrush Hotel' (forerunner of that great hostelry later to become famous as the Northern Counties) provided a luncheon for 150 guests, '@ 4s 3d per head or 4s 6d according to the way in which it will be done'.

Section 34 of the B & P's 1853 Act had stipulated that a junction should be sought at Coleraine with the L & C, though it did not actually authorise it. The two companies could not agree on the siting of the bridge over the river, and proceeded to lay separate schemes before Parliament. The B & P proposal managed to get as far as the House of Lords before it was rejected. The L & C's did not reach that stage, being strongly opposed by the B & P. The rejection came in July 1854; in August Dargan suggested that a further Bill be promoted, this to include a clause permitting sale or leasing of the line. But the directors, noting that the L & C was unco-operative about joint financing, evinced no interest and decided to withdraw from such a course at the present juncture.

WORK PROGRESSES

We know little of the progress of the works for Dargan was much more than contractor; he supplied rails, sleepers and all other essentials. A serious difficulty in the long term arose as early as August 1853. To the west of Portrush was the little village of Portstewart on the coast, which the B & P sought to include in its route. The local landowner, one Cromie, a stern and unyielding man, was a strict guardian of his property. He, rightly or wrongly, believed that the coming of the railway would shatter forever the 'select' character of Portstewart and he early sought to block the line's path. An agreement of some description was made with him on 6 August 1853; what it was we have no means of knowing. But suffice it to say that he declined to honour it and in October 1854 the opinions of 'eminent counsel' were sought, as to how Cromie might be coerced. Far from giving way, he attempted to get his estranged son-in-law, Lord Robert Montagu, to refuse to sign an agreement with the B & P. The B & P never reached Portstewart, the wranglings with Cromie being regarded as a waste of time; a station was erected two miles outside the town.

As early as October 1853 Lanyon was instructed to confer with Dargan 'on the subject of the best mode of getting

Engines and Carriages for this Company'. Dargan replied that it was yet too soon to think about stock but 'the Engines should be ordered soon and the Stock I would recommend the Board to get (which will be ample) is 3 Engines with Tenders, 15 Inch Cylinders'. A month later he wrote:

> There are no better Engines than those latterly made by Messrs. Fairbairn and if their prices are fair I think the Board cannot do better than agree with that Firm.

The Board eventually decided to order seven engines. Carriages were ordered in April 1854 from Wright & Co of London; in September Lanyon was asked to obtain from the B & B, '50 waggons, on best terms, to be made by them' (presumably at York Road) for £78 each, delivered at Ballymena.

Cromie was still making difficulties. In June 1855 he published notice of ejectment from his County Londonderry estates. An acrimonious battle then took place in which both sides spared no punches; Cromie was unsuccessful but the B & P did not get to Portstewart. Land purchase was difficult in general; two committees of directors, the Northern based on Portrush, the Southern at Ballymena, were appointed to decide on points of difference with landowners.

The sites for stations gave trouble also. Dargan was asked in December 1853 whether the station at Ballymena should be on a new site altogether, or whether the B & B station should be used. He replied that 'he was indifferent to where it should be placed'; so with the concurrence of the B & B the B & P erected a new station, nearer the centre of Ballymena, and to this the B & B transferred in due course. Shortly afterwards it was resolved to place Ballymoney station 'at the foot of the Main Street below the School House'. In July 1855 the inhabitants of Ballymoney asked for 'a good covered station'. As a measure of their impotence, or perhaps merely passing the buck, the directors told the Ballymoney people to petition Dargan. There was also trouble regarding the site of Coleraine station; it had been intended to approach the town centre but instead a site at Northbrook was chosen after opposition from Dr Boyd the landowner; the place was cramped and there were level crossings at both ends of the platform.

By November 1853 Dargan had received his entire share

capital, 16,000 £10 shares. There were only 34 other shareholders, all local men, holding some £27,500 in all; the substantial holders were Antrim the chairman and Lanyon the engineer, with £2,500 each—the latter doubtless accepting shares in payment. The *Railway Times* in 1853 described the B & P as a 'contractor's line'.

In September 1854 it had been resolved to have stations erected at Cullybackey, Dunminning, Bellaghy (later renamed Killagan), Glennylough, Ballymoney, Macfin, Coleraine, Portstewart and Portrush. There is no evidence that Glennylough or Dunminning was proceeded with; Dunloy was added between Cullybackey and Ballymoney. Most of the structures were temporary and were replaced in later years.

In April 1855

> Mr Lanyon reported that he had examined the entire Line and regretted that some of the gradients were not so satisfactory to himself as he could wish.

He also complained that the rails were inferior and that larch sleepers were being used instead of Memel. Dargan agreed to amend the gradients, especially that out of Ballymena known as the 'Rock Cutting', and to relay the line with 70lb rails, 'in the event of his not taking the line and paying off the shareholders'. Obviously he was considering the possibility of buying out the remaining share capital.

But work was well advanced. In June Dargan asked for an engine in connection with ballasting. One of the Sharp engines was sold to him on the understanding that when work was completed it would be revalued by Sharp and re-purchased by the B & P.

OPENING

In August 1855 the Earl of Antrim died. He was replaced as chairman by William Wilson Campbell for a short period and then by John McGildowny, the vice-chairman. The director co-opted to fill the vacancy was John Young, later to become famous as chairman of the Belfast & Northern Counties Railway. In August 1855 Dargan expounded an agreement he had made with the shareholders: he was to buy out their holding

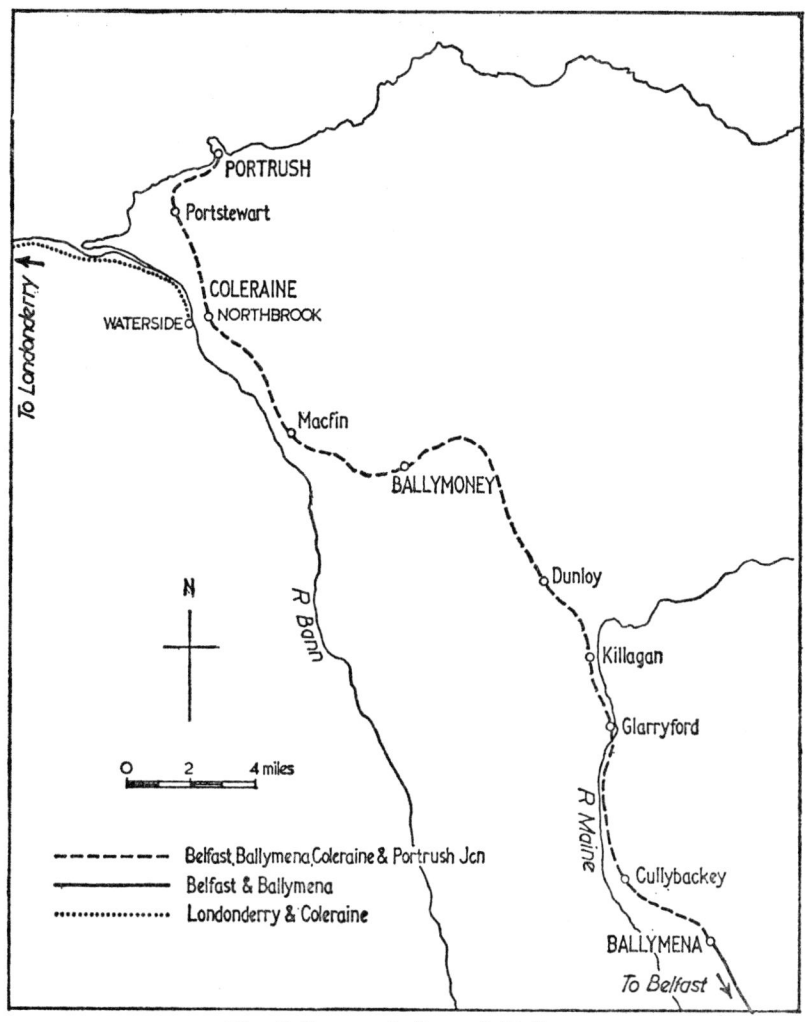

The Ballymena & Portrush Railway

by issuing bonds for three years at 5 per cent, similar to those issued by the Midland Great Western and Dublin & Drogheda Railways. All outstanding accounts were to be borne by the directors.

He begged . . . to express his sense of the exertion and assistance of the Directors and Officers of the Company and as evidence thereof proposed to confer on each member of the Board a free pass on the Railway for life.

These were inscribed on one side: 'Presented by Wm. Dargan to an original promoter of the Line'; on the other, 'B.B.C. & P.J.R. Free Ticket for Life'. The directors were retained, however, to form a local committee of management.

For the Board of Trade inspection on 6 November, the inspecting officer was Lt-Col Wynne, who was attended by Dargan, Edwards (his local superintendent of works later associated with the Carrickfergus & Larne), Lanyon and Thomson, a secretary. Wynne reported:

> I found the permanent way well laid, and the bridges and other works substantially constructed. There are no signals erected on the line, nor have they yet arrived. Neither is there a turntable at the Portrush terminus; but as the Company will undertake to work the line with tank engines, this latter I should not consider a cause for postponement; but the want of signals obliges me to state that, in my opinion, the line without them cannot be opened without danger to the public using the same.

Wynne therefore enforced a postponement in opening for one month and departed leaving Lanyon with a memorandum of his requirements. The permanent way was Greave's patent surface-packed iron sleepers and chairs, being a form of semi-spherodical bowls with the chairs cast on top together with traverse tie-rods. But if the public opening was postponed it was a valuable breathing space, for the line had been built in little more than two years. During this time a memorial from the local clergy was received against the running of Sunday trains (objecting to such trains was then one of the principal tasks of the Ulster clergy). They were told

> That answer be given . . . That this Board of Directors are of the opinion that it would be inconsistent with public convenience to interfere with the running of trains on Sundays.

Clearly economic advantage was to take precedence over religious fervour. But the clergy could take pleasure in the decision of the board to write to Edwards that they believed this Board and the County generally to be quite averse to Men being employed at the Works on Sundays.

They also found time to thank the new Earl of Antrim, who, unable to be present at the junketings on 7 November, had sent a supply of venison to swell the feast.

Rates were also fixed. First class passengers were to pay 2d per mile, second class 1½d, third 1d. A four ton crane was ordered for Portrush and cranes of two tons' capacity for Ballymoney and Coleraine. It was resolved to press ahead with opening Ballymena, Ballymoney, Coleraine and Portrush initially, the others to follow as the buildings were completed and the signals erected.

Higgin, manager of the B & B, was in overall charge of the line. By June 1856 the establishment numbered 112: one manager, one secretary, one engineer, two superintendents, one storekeeper, one accountant, one inspector, eight station masters, five clerks, one foreman, three engine drivers, seven firemen, seven guards, six artificers, fourteen gate keepers, six policemen, twenty-one porters, sixteen platelayers and ten labourers. It was arranged that there be three trains daily each way, the time taken from Ballymena to Portrush 'not to exceed three hours altogether'.

On 12 November Thomson the secretary wrote to the Board of Trade that all signals would be erected by 14 November and Portrush turntable installed by the next week. Tank engines would be used until then with a spare engine at Portrush. Would the Board permit opening on 20 November? But authority was still refused. On 22 November Thomson wrote again, stating that all signals were now in position and the turntable being fitted. On 27 November the Board accordingly permitted the opening with the proviso that until everything was complete only two trains were to be in motion simultaneously and were to pass at Ballymoney. On 4 December 1855 the line was fully opened to traffic; it had already been ceremonially opened when on 7 November a train left York Road at 11.30am and ran non-stop to Coleraine and thence to Portrush. It conveyed, we are told, 'the wealth, intelligence and beauty of the North'. On the return journey it ran non-stop to Ballymena where in the evening a dejeuner, followed by a ball presided over by Dargan, who was much eulogised, was held. The streets of the several towns were gaily decorated with bunting.

So the railway was open to traffic with one of its objectives remaining unfulfilled—the construction of a junction and bridge across the Bann at Coleraine to the L & C. The two stations, that of the B & P at Northbrook, that of the L & C at Waterside, were about one mile apart. Making the best of a bad job the B & P contracted with one Gillespie, and a four-horse bus provided by him was the only means of connection between the two stations. A similar vehicle provided transport between Portstewart station and the town.

DARGAN

It was not at all easy to define the relationship existing at this time between Dargan and the B & P. We have already seen how in August 1855 he 'explained his agreement with the shareholders'. Certainly by the beginning of railway working he had effected a lease or at least a working agreement; he was of course closely involved with the B & B, being engaged in constructing their Cookstown extension and through running took place between Belfast and Portrush under the terms of the 1853 Act with his connivance.

It may seem odd that a railway contractor should own a line. But McCormick had leased the L & C and Dargan was a much more eminent contractor than he, with considerable experience in such matters. Besides being a railway contractor he was one of Ireland's leading capitalists in an age when such men were all important. From the opening of the railway the directors met only infrequently and took no decisions fundamental to railway operation.

THE RAILWAY AT WORK

In February 1856 the directors were complaining that Higgin was keeping them 'in ignorance' of the receipts of the line and that the sites of some of the stations had been changed without their consent. As usual the secretary was told to write to Dargan. On 1 April 1856 Dargan was allotted a further £40,000 in shares and became a director. During the year he was successful in obtaining a mail contract with the Post Office. It was signed in October, a joint agreement with the B & B and L & C and thus obviously concerned the carriage of mails from Belfast to Londonderry. Also during 1856 another religious body—this time the Coleraine Presbytery—with typical bigoted if sincere sabbatarianism, memorialised the board against the running of Sunday trains. As on the last occasion they were unsuccessful. Sunday was a day profitable to both the B & B and B & P. The following year of 1857 must have been a quiet one, for during it the board did not meet at all.

On 25 May 1858 the board met and 'it was proposed by John Patrick Esq. and seconded by Robert Young Esq., and unanimously resolved':

> That the Bill entitled An Act to enable the Ballymena, Ballymoney, Coleraine & Portrush Junction Railway to sell their undertaking to the Belfast and Ballymena Railway be and the same is hereby approved of.

This Bill, passed on 28 June 1858, was promoted by Dargan and the board's approval was merely confirmatory. But nothing towards implementing the provisions was done at this juncture.

The B & P was still determined to have a bridge at Coleraine. A scheme was submitted to Parliament in the Session of 1857–8 as part of the petition for the Act referred to above. This time the company had not only to encounter the intransigence of the L & C but also the opposition of Coleraine. The B & P proposed a bridge of ten spans including one which would open for navigation, to be built 350ft below the road bridge. Commercial and shipping interests immediately asserted that £100,000 had been spent in recent years in improving the navigation of the Bann inland from Coleraine, and a bridge at the site proposed would both impede shipping and preclude further development of the Bann as an inland waterway. The Admiralty, as the body responsible for navigation, was directly interested and appointed James Abernethy CE to hold an enquiry at Coleraine, which took place on 29 March 1858. Eventually he reported in favour of the B & P's scheme, but the time for gratification was short. It must have been extremely disappointing to the promoters when in early May a Committee of Parliament, examining the Bill, deleted the clauses dealing with the bridge, on the grounds that the necessity for it had not been sufficiently proved by the promoters! Consequently the Act of 28 June, as mentioned above, authorised only the future sale of the B & P to the B & BR.

Nothing daunted, Dargan and the Ballymena & Portrush tried again. By November 1858 another scheme was being brought forward. The matter of siting had now to be fought out all over again and W. H. Hemans of the Midland Great Western Railway was appointed by the Board of Works to arbitrate. He recommended in favour of a bridge downstream of the road bridge by about 440yd. Again the Coleraine objectors raised their voices to protest that such a structure would impede shipping; but this time the Bill was successful and on 19 April 1859 a nominally independent company, 'The Belfast & Londonderry Junction Railway', was incorporated. This wholly-owned subsidiary of the B & P was to build the bridge and about 51 chains of connecting line. Shares to the value of £15,000 and loans up to £2,000 were to finance the construction of the single line and the bridge.

> The Bridge or Viaduct across the River Bann shall be constructed on pilework, and so that there be a clear Width of Waterway between the Abutments of not less than Two Hundred and Ninety Feet, and an Opening Span giving a clear Width of Waterway of not less than Forty Feet, and the Soffit of the said Bridge or Viaduct shall be constructed and maintained so as to give a clear Headway of not less than Eleven Feet above High Water Mark at ordinary Spring Tides.

Having waited so long for its Act, the B & P lost no time in taking possession of the land and construction began during the summer. Dargan was the contractor. The deviation line diverged sharply immediately to the north of the B & P's Northbrook station and curved sharply to the left on a downgrade. A straight section brought it in under one road and over another, both bridges being built as part of the works; the latter was a lattice girder structure. An embanked right-hand curve brought the line to the river and the hotly disputed bridge. The new bridge was a structure of quite remarkable ugliness. It was

THE BALLYMENA AND PORTRUSH RAILWAY 99

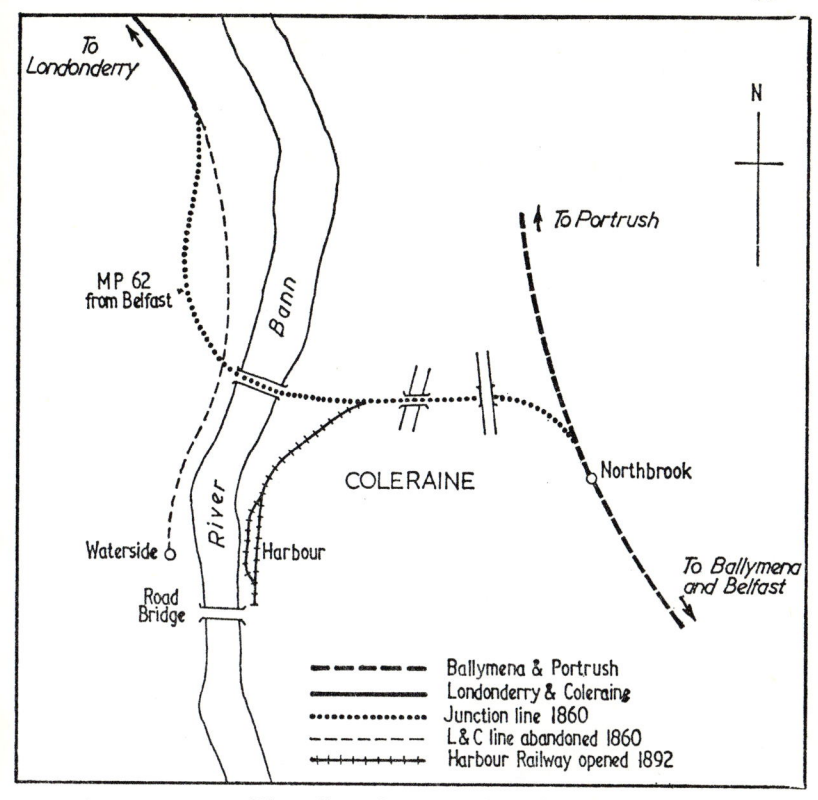

Key:
- Ballymena & Portrush
- Londonderry & Coleraine
- Junction line 1860
- L & C line abandoned 1860
- Harbour Railway opened 1892

The railway layout at Coleraine

built upon wooden piles with a superstructure of iron deck girders on the lattice principle, and slightly on the skew. It was 435ft long with 30ft spans. In the centre was a massive stone pier on which was a revolving span. This, when opened, afforded two spaces for navigational purposes of 41ft 6in—35ft within fenders. Opening was accomplished by means of capstans. On the western bank the new line curved sharply to the right and within a few yards joined the L & C line by a junction facing Londonderry. The L & C's Waterside station was left on a quarter-mile spur.

The local press, noting the progress of the works, began to believe that the bridge was 'too fragile' to carry traffic; it certainly had that appearance but it survived sixty-four years.

It was also pointed out that it did little to enhance the beautiful view from the road bridge downstream.

The Board of Trade inspection was held on 13 November 1860, a few days after the last rails had been laid on the western bank. Captain H. W. Tyler RE was accompanied by Dargan and other officials of the B & P, B & B and L & C. Two hours were given over to the inspection; after investigating the structure from rail level resort was had to a boat on the river, with the purpose of seeing the effect of traffic on the stays. Two engines and a composite carriage were run to and fro at varying speeds. This proved satisfactory. Tyler was concerned at the sharp curves at either end of the bridge—ten chains' radius—and the steep gradient—1 in 75—from Coleraine station to the bridge. He recommended that a speed limit of 10 mph be enforced 'and a notice to this effect . . . conspicuously placed as a warning . . . near each end of the line'. The permanent way, bridge rails with cross sleepers, was generally satisfactory.

As first designed, Tyler noted, the spans of the bridge were to be 40ft wide; but Dargan considered, especially following Tyler's report on the Shannon bridge near Limerick in 1859 and the fact that the structure was partially on a skew, that it would be better to increase the number of spans to sixteen to gain greater strength. Some general strengthening was required: 'the piers of this Viaduct are composed of timber piling only, with cross and diagonal boring and they cannot be expected to last in this position for many years. They will require careful maintenance and should be especially watched' when subjected to the strains of traffic. A further precaution would be the covering of the wooden decking of the bridge with ballast to prevent fire risk. Tyler was in general satisfied (the local press represented him as saying that he had never seen a bridge better constructed!) and he certified the bridge fit for traffic.

The first train to cross the new bridge in regular service was the 10.30am from Londonderry to Coleraine on 15 November, when 'an engine and ten or twelve carriages and trucks' crossed, arriving at the B & P's Northbrook station shortly after one o'clock. It was watched by the chief officials of the B & NCR, the B & P and L & C, and even the Londonderry & Enniskillen;

Page 101
WHITEHEAD

ove) New station, opened 1877, *c* 1900 with train arriving from Belfast (*below*) Promenade built by B & NCR. Note railway lamps

Page 102
LARNE—I

(*above*) Larne Harbour *c* 1876; boat train in old station with PS *Princess Beatr*
(*below*) Larne Harbour new station, *c* 1896. No 49 on train from Belfast. Note clock

for it was the beginning of a new era. The bridge went into regular service on 19 November, and with its opening the L & C abandoned Waterside for passenger traffic. All trains now used the B & P's Northbrook station.

AMALGAMATION

The 1858 Act remained unimplemented. During 1859 Dargan was in active negotiations with the B & B to exercise the powers conferred. The eventual aim was brought a step nearer on 2 January 1860 when a working agreement came into force between the two companies—the B & B was to haul B & P trains on a mileage basis. The B & B took over the management—William Parsons, the B & P's manager, had been appointed after the resignation of Higgin and now became manager of the Portrush Hotel (not then railway property). It was at this time that Dargan was described with perfect accuracy as 'the founder of Portrush prosperity', for already the railway had brought immense benefit to the erstwhile fishing hamlet, now blossoming forth as a select residential area and watering place (though the railway had not reached the harbour).

On 1 February 1860 it was resolved

> That this Company do sell and transfer to the Belfast & Ballymena Railway Company, the Line of Railway from Ballymena to Portrush and the whole undertaking of this Company . . .

Authority to sell the junction railway at Coleraine had not been included in the 1858 Act since that railway had not then been authorised. Meanwhile on 15 May 1860 the Belfast & Ballymena changed its name to the Belfast & Northern Counties, that Act providing for the sale of the junction section. A shareholders' meeting on 18 December 1860 duly authorised the sale and the way was now clear. The sale of the line in its entirety was thus made possible, and arrangements were finalised as quickly as possible.

From 1 January 1861 the erstwhile Belfast & Ballymena, now the Belfast & Northern Counties, took possession of the Portrush line, paying a total of £220,000—£160,000 in new 4 per cent preference shares, also assuming responsibility for the

G

B & P's bonded debt of £60,000. Further, Dargan guaranteed the B & NCR gross receipts of at least £15,000 per annum for five years, while the Northern Counties, for its part, agreed to pay an additional £20,000 in 4 per cent preference shares, should the receipts exceed that figure during the first four years. Of great significance was the fact that the sum to be paid was not stipulated in either the 1858 or 1860 Acts—it had been the subject of negotiation between the B & B and B & NC directors, and Dargan for the B & P. As part of the bargain Dargan became a director of the B & NC, and remained so until his death.

The B & NC had so far only assumed responsibility for the B & P line and the junction line; it had no jurisdiction over the Londonderry & Coleraine's property between the junction and Londonderry. But that close co-operation was taking place between the three companies we cannot doubt; witness the L & C's closure of the Waterside station in Coleraine on the opening of the bridge. McCormick was more disposed to be co-operative than were the L & C directors. We have seen in Chapter 3 how he transferred the L & C to the new Northern Counties company on 10 April 1861. This brought the total mileage under York Road's control to 136.

By a process of acquisition spread over three months the B & NC justified its new title, taking itself beyond its original territory in County Antrim and thrusting far into County Londonderry. Now there was a main line 95 miles long, linking the Northern Metropolis to the Maiden City, with a secondary line to Cookstown and branches to Carrickfergus, Portrush and Limavady. It was with pride that the directors told the B & NC shareholders that they now had Ireland's third most important trunk line under one management, 'uninterrupted and consecutive . . . It is quite impossible for a line under three managements to be worked with the economy of the same length of line under only one management or with the same satisfaction to the public. Every day's experience shows this.'

If the Belfast—Dublin line (opened between 1839 and 1852) was Ireland's principal trunk, and the Dublin—Cork line (opened 1847–9) the second, certainly the Belfast—Londonderry line was third, linking the second city, the commercial capital, to the fifth city of Ireland. Further the Belfast—Dublin

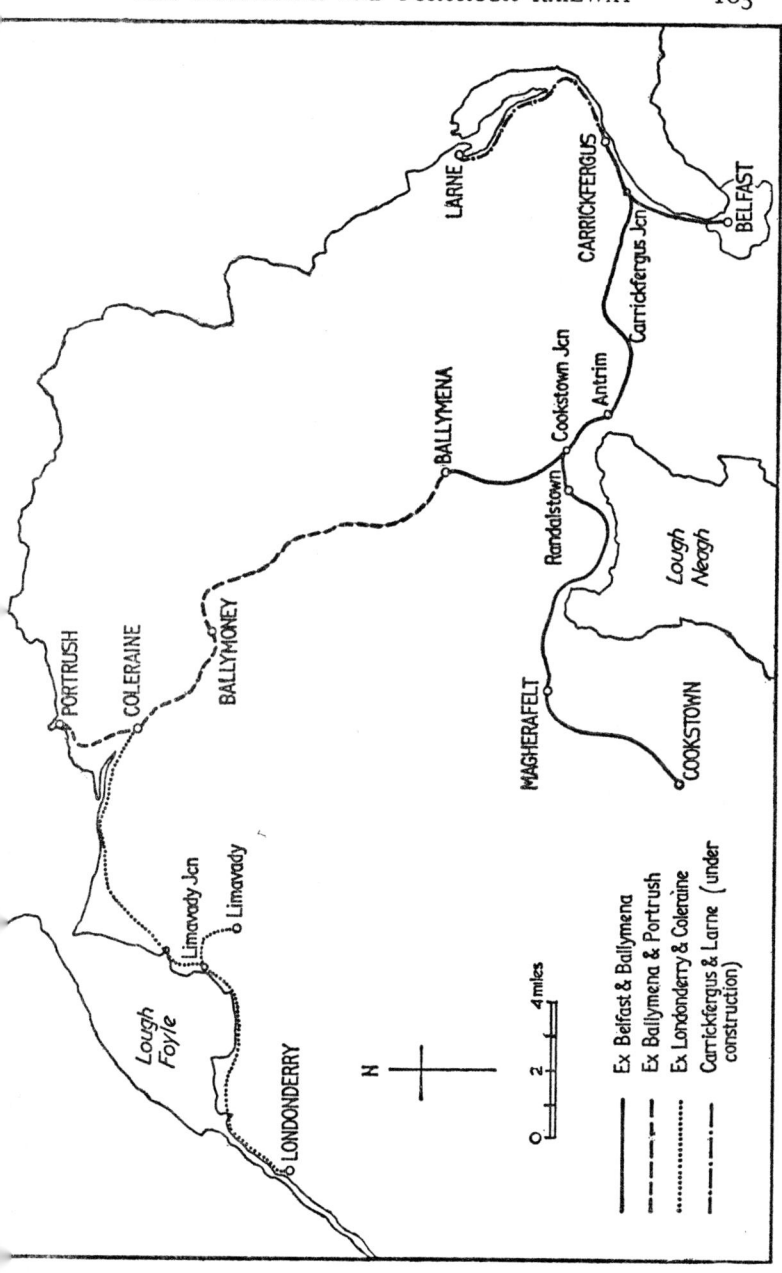

The B & NCR system in 1861

line was under three separate managements until 1875–6, which did not conduce to efficiency and economic working. The Belfast & Northern Counties was now launched on its independent existence of forty-three years; its main network was completed, and it remained to add branches and acquire possible rivals.

The title of the new company soon became abbreviated to 'The Northern Counties'; and with the propensity of the Irish for nicknames, the sobriquet 'Big Nancy Coming Running' became popular. In the early years the term 'Belfast Railway' is sometimes found. Appropriately enough the first armorial device adopted by the company was the coat of arms of Belfast, with the motto *Pro Tanto Quid Retribuamus* (For so much we have received), within a belt bearing the legend 'Belfast and Northern Counties Railway Company'.

CHAPTER FIVE

The Mid-Victorian Years 1860-1880

THE NEW COMPANY

Since the Belfast & Northern Counties Railway was in effect the Belfast & Ballymena Railway metamorphosed into a larger concern, the management remained virtually unchanged. The board of directors was unaltered save for the addition of William Dargan, and the Hon George Handcock remained chairman. Edward John Cotton occupied the managerial chair with Charles Stewart as secretary; Charles Lanyon became consulting engineer and a new post of resident engineer was created, its first incumbent being Arthur Forde. Lanyon, who had engineered practically the entire system of the B & NC, now desired to devote himself to his expanding and lucrative architectural practice and to politics. Alexander Yorston, who had succeeded Rowland as locomotive superintendent in 1849, retained that position.

Some time earlier Lanyon had been instructed to survey the stations on the original line and report on those that required replacement. As soon as the new capital authorised by the 1860 Act was available a programme of expenditure was drawn up:

New station at Jordanstown	£170
Permanent station at Carrickfergus Jct	600
Platforms for Carrickfergus Jct	200
Renewals of permanent way at C'fergus Jct	100
Permanent station at Ballyclare & Doagh	800
Platforms at Ballyclare & Doagh	200
Covered platforms, carriage and engine sheds at Cookstown Junction	1,500

These works, together with new workshops and engine shed accommodation at Belfast, would cost £8,170. To a protest that the works were 'non-essential' Lanyon pointed out that the old wooden stations were expensive to maintain. Jordanstown was a completely new halt built about 1½ miles north of Whiteabbey to serve an expanding and exclusive suburb of Belfast, where was the pleasant villa occupied by the Cotton family. At the same time Lanyon caused to be erected 21 gate lodges at various level crossings, thus making for economies in staff, especially in 'policemen'. The new buildings were completed by the end of 1861 and were described as 'neat and substantial, well suited to their purpose'.

The issue of villa tickets had been considered already, as we have seen in Chapter 2. It was not until May 1860, however, that the scheme for which the B & NC was to be famous for seventy years was instituted. It was announced that a free first class ticket valid for ten years would be granted to anyone building a 'villa' of the annual poor law valuation of £25 or over, within one mile of any of the stations between Belfast and Carrickfergus (such tickets being valid to Belfast) and to Londonderry or Coleraine for houses at Castlerock. Plans had to be submitted to the railway's engineer for approval *before* building commenced. Later the scheme was extended to include the entire Larne line when the extension was opened, and similar arrangements were made for second class free travel for houses with a somewhat lower rateable value. This villa ticket system was the means of developing considerably such suburbs of Belfast as Whiteabbey, Jordanstown, Greenisland, and also Castlerock, but above all it was largely responsible for the rise of Whitehead from very meagre beginnings.

The Cookstown line was still disappointing the company in 1860; it was stated that a reduction in second and third class fares had not had the desired effect and Cotton told the Devonshire Commission that dividends had definitely fallen following the opening. But the amalgamations were expected to bring a great improvement generally and with the bridge at Coleraine open it was hoped to run to Londonderry in four hours instead of six, as formerly.

On 27 November 1860 a special general meeting was called to consider matters of importance for the future. The

Carrickfergus & Larne Railway had been authorised on 15 May and had requested a subscription of £20,000 from the B & NC. This the directors were disposed to grant but the shareholders were less generous and insisted that the subscription be cut to £12,500, to the disappointment of the C & L.

Hardly had the B & NC secured control of a through route to Londonderry than a rival route connecting the Ulster Railway at Portadown to the Londonderry & Enniskillen at Omagh via Dungannon was opened on 2 September 1861. The new company, the Portadown, Dungannon & Omagh, was closely connected with the Ulster and the through route it opened up was some five miles longer than the B & NC's. To prevent a war of rates and fares, negotiations were opened with the rival company which led to an agreement with the PD & OR taking effect from the outset of the new arrangement with the L & C in 1865. Each company was to deduct $12\frac{1}{2}$ per cent for passenger working and 33 per cent for goods from its receipts; the remainder would be pooled and the B & NC would receive 75 per cent of the combined passenger receipts and 66 per cent of the goods.

In October 1862 the Carrickfergus & Larne line opened and was worked under agreement by the B & NC; a new station at Carrickfergus replaced the original B & B structure. The steamer service on the 'short sea passage' from Larne to Stranraer began concomitantly with the railway. Even before the opening of the Larne line serious delays had been experienced as a result of the single track main line out of Belfast. Some shareholders were in favour of delaying doubling until the Larne line had proved itself but Cotton believed widening to be absolutely necessary and Lanyon was given instructions to proceed. In November 1862 the new up line, $2\frac{1}{2}$ miles out to Greencastle, was completed. The $4\frac{1}{4}$ miles thence to Carrickfergus Junction was authorised to be dealt with 'as soon as the season will permit', and this section came into use in September 1863.

The Larne line fulfilled all the apprehensions that had been voiced. In August 1863 the chairman stated that it was being worked 'to some extent at a loss' and the boat was also losing heavily. The service to Stranraer ended at the end of 1863—the B & NC's suggestion of a better boat having been rejected—and this to some extent mitigated losses, though it was a further dozen years before the C & L would be regarded as profitable.

From 1 June 1862 'express' trains began running between Belfast, Londonderry and Portrush, cautiously advertised as taking 'about' $3\frac{1}{2}$ and $2\frac{1}{4}$ hours respectively; not bad for 95 and 67 miles.

ECONOMICS

For two years following the 1860–1 amalgamations the dividend remained at $4\frac{1}{2}$ per cent. Almost immediately after union, however, there was a great upsurge in traffic; the first half year of 1860, for example, brought receipts in excess of £30,000. But still the Cookstown line was considered unsatisfactory and as late as 1870 views were expressed to this effect. Continued lower receipts in the mid-1860s were blamed on the high bank rate and the general depression (though some shareholders thought the latter an invention of the directors and said the Belfast & Ballymena had never been more prosperous). In 1864 the dividend fell to $3\frac{1}{2}$ per cent and goods receipts were considerably down, though the previous year the mineral receipts had been the highest in Ireland. A shareholder asked the chairman for sympathy and it was graciously offered but with the remark that the board needed it too!

By 1866 the position had improved. The C & L and L & C were still unprofitable not to speak of the Cookstown line—but the B & P section was spoken of as 'the best spoke in the company's wheel'. The dividend, it was said, might have been higher but for heavy engineering costs and pay increases. The 1867 dividend of 5 per cent was the highest in Ireland (save for the Dublin & Kingstown whose circumstances were vastly different), and the next year the passenger total of 1,350,000 was the third highest in Ireland.

From the earliest great attention was paid to third class travel. From October 1862 third class carriages were attached to all trains and third class return tickets issued: 'no other company in the United Kingdom does this', it was stated (the first in Britain was the Midland in 1872 when it abolished second class). The policy paid off well and in 1863 third class receipts almost equalled combined first and second class revenue. The shareholders, noting this, urged that nothing be done to detract from the care given to the lower orders, remarking that they were 'the bone and sinew' of the passenger traffic.

Vicissitudes of traffic called for closures of existing stations and the building of new ones from time to time. On the leasing of the L & C in 1861 Willsborough (Eglinton) and Umbra were closed; Jordanstown was opened in 1863 and in 1865 Cullybackey was opened from 1 March while on the same date Dunloy was closed for a time and on 31 January 1867 Macfin also closed. In 1876 another new station was constructed at Kellswater, between Cookstown Junction and Ballymena.

For a considerable time the railway had been operating a cartage service in Belfast and district in connection with goods trains. From 1 February 1869 James Andrews of Belfast undertook this service under lease and into his hands were given the horses and carts.

Strange to relate there was some competition to be encountered from steamer services in the early days. The weekly steamer operated between Londonderry and Portrush by Cameron of the former city caused concern to the B & NC, the Ulster and the Irish North Western, and in 1867 the service ceased when a satisfactory financial understanding was concluded. In 1851 some of the Morecambe—Belfast steamers extended their runs to Londonderry; there had been intermittent Belfast—Londonderry services since 1834. The competition terminated in 1866 when an undertaking was given to the Northern Counties, not to convey local traffic between the two cities. An attempt to revive a Belfast—Londonderry service was made in 1868 but lasted but a few months. Less serious but still significant was the Belfast—Carrickfergus service which creamed off a lot of excursion traffic. In 1868 rail fares were reduced to 9d for a third class return and later to 6d. This had the desired effect; the steamer ceased and the service never revived.

ANTRIM, COOKSTOWN AND BALLYCASTLE

On 11 July 1861 a line which was carefully watched by the Northern Counties was authorised: the grandiosely-titled Dublin & Antrim Junction Railway, an 18 mile line from

Lisburn to Antrim. The line opened on 13 November 1871 and was worked solely by the Ulster; the B & NC station at Antrim was the northern terminus and interchange facilities were provided so that for the first time goods from the south could be routed over the Northern Counties. The facilities for passengers and goods were shared and Antrim became a joint station. The Ulster had been amalgamated with other railways to form the Great Northern Railway of Ireland and this body bought the line outright on 24 January 1878.

In 1864 strenuous opposition was offered by York Road to a Bill promoted by the Newry & Armagh Railway setting out a scheme for a line from Armagh to Cookstown via Dungannon. This was bad enough; but a Committee of Parliament decided that the Dungannon—Cookstown section should be built, not by the N & A, but by the Ulster (lessees of the PD & OR) or the B & NCR or both. 'From the experience we have had of the line to Cookstown it is not such as would justify us in recommending you to make a connection with Dungannon', B & NC shareholders were advised. In 1874 the Ulster promoted the nominally independent Dungannon & Cookstown Railway, a resurrection of the scheme first mooted a decade earlier. The Bill was not opposed by the B & NC and it duly became law with suitable safeguards for York Road. Construction proceeded during the amalgamations which resulted in the formation of the Great Northern and the new GN purchased the incomplete D & C in 1877. The line opened on 28 July 1879, linking the GN's Portadown—Londonderry line at Dungannon to a station at Cookstown which immediately adjoined that of the B & NC. Unfortunately through running was not possible since the stations lay side by side but interchange of goods was possible. Under the terms of the Bill, Belfast—Cookstown receipts were pooled as in the case of the Belfast—Londonderry lines.

In 1863 and 1864 the first proposals for a railway to Ballycastle were made by a nominally separate company, the Belfast, Ballymoney & Ballycastle Junction. In February 1864 the proposal was laid before the shareholders; they did not receive it favourably, being soured towards further ramifications since they blamed the conspicuous lack of success of the C & L for reduced dividends. Not even Cotton's belief that the

THE MID-VICTORIAN YEARS 1860–1880   113

line would pay better—he mentioned 8 or 8½ per cent—mollified them. The board were themselves divided; Dargan and several other directors were of the provisional committee of the BB & BJ and were at pains to point out that Ballycastle was a thriving seaside town of 2,000 inhabitants and had the makings of 'a second Portrush'. Sir Edward Coey pointed out that the shareholders 'had acted rather discreditably on a previous occasion' (in reducing the subscription to the C & L) and Capt Gray believed that 'in point of fact you might as well throw your money into the sea as give it to the Ballycastle Company'.

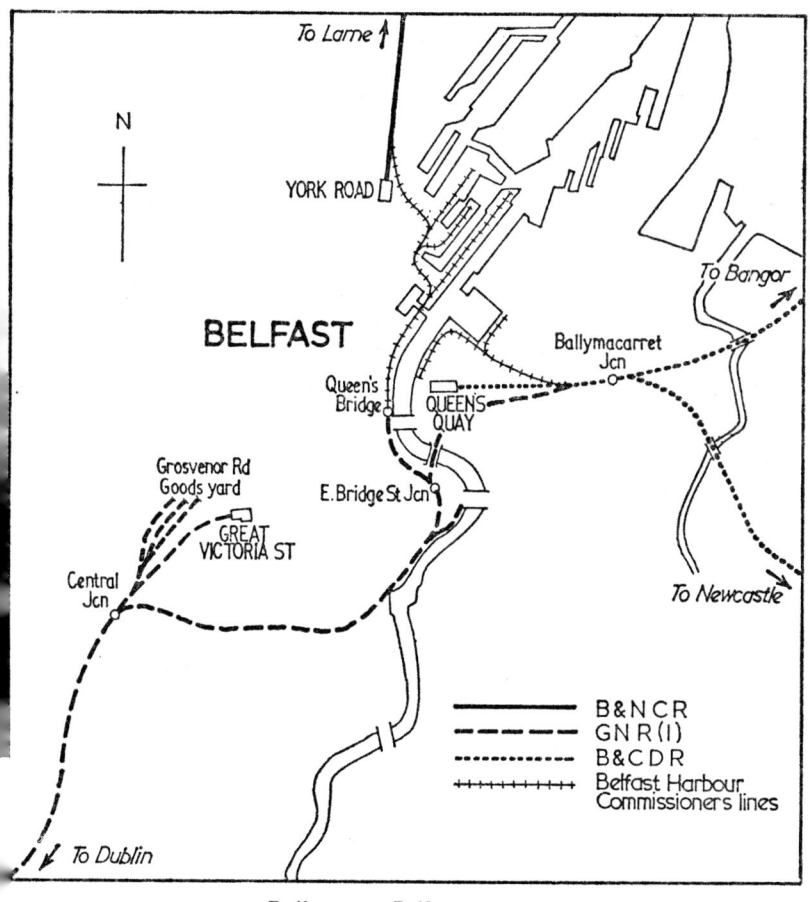

Railways at Belfast *c* 1900

The shareholders thought so too, rejected the motion for a subscription, and the scheme was withdrawn.

THE BELFAST CENTRAL RAILWAY

In the early days of the railway York Road was on the northern edge of Belfast, the line being terminated there to avoid the expense of acquiring large numbers of premises for demolition. But having the terminus $1\frac{1}{2}$ miles from the city centre had its disadvantages, despite the fact that 'Cars and Omnibuses attend'. So considerable interest was evinced in the scheme for a central station mooted by a group of London businessmen in 1863 after similar proposals in Dublin had been rejected.

The Belfast Central Railway was incorporated on 25 July 1865, the scheme providing for a Central station at Victoria Street and connecting lines linking up the three termini (those of the B & NC, Ulster and Belfast & County Down). The scheme was nothing if not elaborate; the B & NC was to be reached by a tunnel under Corporation Street and understandably the capital was fixed at £300,000. York Road was never to be linked up by the Central with the other termini, work but progressed elsewhere in Belfast and in 1875 the line was sufficiently advanced to permit of a passenger service being introduced by means of a bridge across the Lagan by which the Ulster and the County Down lines were linked. In 1867–9 the Harbour Commissioners had laid tramways on the quays and in 1879 a tunnel was opened under Queen's Bridge, which allowed the tramways at the northern end of the quays, already linked to York Road goods yard, to be connected with the Central main line, thus allowing interchange of goods wagons.

The B & NCR had not been altogether inimical to the Central schemes and had delayed improvements at York Road pending developments. Though it did not achieve its aim fully, the Central was very useful as a means of working through goods traffic.

HARBOUR LINES

By the terms of the B & NC Act of 23 June 1864 the company

THE MID-VICTORIAN YEARS 1860–1880   115

was authorised to build a branch line from Portrush station, a distance of three quarters of a mile to the harbour. The cost was £2,951 and the line was opened in June 1866. Under the Act 'no carriage shall be propelled upon the Branch or any part thereof by Steam or by Atmospheric Agency or drawn by Ropes in connexion with a stationary Steam Engine'. Nevertheless steam engines were used; in 1867 an injunction prohibited this and horse traction had to be resorted to from 4 January 1868. By the Act of 30 June 1874 the clause was repealed and steam engines could be employed. At no time were passengers conveyed over this line. Between 1883 and 1893 mixed gauge track was laid, to accommodate goods traffic from the Giant's Causeway Tramway.

From January 1868 connection was established between the Londonderry & Coleraine and Londonderry & Enniskillen lines at Londonderry when the Port & Harbour Commissioners

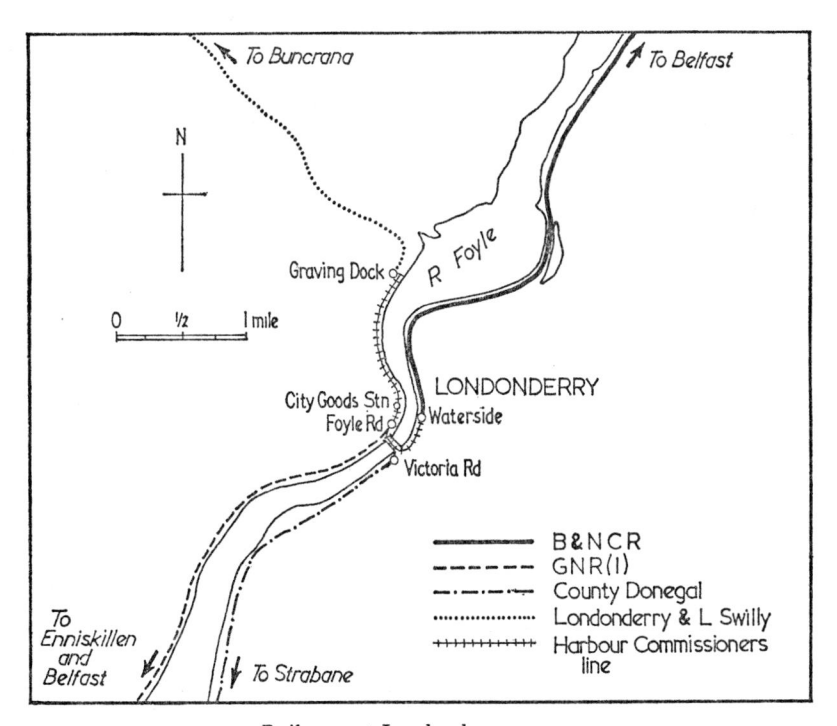

Railways at Londonderry *c* 1900

opened their tramway. This crossed the Foyle on the lower deck of the Carlisle Bridge and linked Waterside with the Graving Dock terminus of the Lough Swilly, then broad gauge, and with the Foyle Road station of the L & E. No interchange of passenger vehicles took place since the entry to the bridge was by turntables and horse or capstan power was used to work wagons across. When the Lough Swilly converted its line to narrow gauge in 1883-5 the tramway became dual gauge and something unique in Ireland could be seen—the Harbour Commissioners' locomotives drawing mixed gauge trains. When the County Donegal Railways opened to Victoria Road, near Waterside, in 1900, connection was also established with that station.

ENGINEERING

The new buildings referred to at the beginning of this chapter did not by any means signal the end of the reconstruction programme. In 1863 £1,500 went to complete the station at Ballyclare & Doagh and a year later £650 was spent at Dunadry for a similar purpose. During 1869 a renewed station at Greencastle was opened and a similar building at Templepatrick in 1871. Goods facilities were not neglected either; in 1866 Belfast goods yard was extended on land purchased from the Harbour Commissioners and in 1868 Ballymena got a new coal yard with associated sidings and goods shed while Cookstown had additional offices built. A new cattle dock was constructed at Belfast in 1869 and new goods sheds at Carrickfergus and Antrim in 1871; at the same time additions were made to the facilities at Killagan. Ballyclare & Doagh station required a new goods shed in 1873 and at this time large sums were spent at Belfast in connection with alterations to the facilities. Carriage sheds were erected at Carrickfergus, Cookstown Junction, Ballymena and Coleraine in 1870; new turntables were fitted at Carrickfergus and Coleraine in 1869 and at Cookstown in 1879. Also in 1879 £1,200 was expended on providing footbridges at several stations.

Throughout these years heavy renewals of the permanent way were taking place and between 1859 and 1862 £62,000 was spent. By 1864 15 miles of the main line had been refitted with fishplated rails and in 1865 204 tons of rails and over 9,000 new sleepers were used. Reballasting was also taking place, especially on the Portrush section, and a ballast pit between Glarryford and Killigan was in use. In 1867 20,000ft of longitudinal sleepers were put into the B & P's Barlow-type track. In 1867 the first order for steel rails was placed; in this the Northern Counties was certainly a pioneer in Ireland though it was several years before such rails were widely used on the system.

The shops at York Road were kept busy during these years with the building of new carriages and wagons and repairs to locomotives and other stock. A total of 91 new wagons was constructed in 18 months in 1864-5 and at this time the company owned the only two boiler trucks in Ireland. It was also unique in permitting the running of privately owned wagons over its line—especially those carrying rock salt from Carrickfergus—and it is likely that these were repaired at York Road. Additions to the works had been made in 1861-2 and constant minor alterations and improvements were made. In 1869 a new sawmill was provided at a cost of £1,500 and in 1872 a new stationary engine and shafting to power the machines. Large numbers of new carriages were turned out to keep pace with the increasing traffic and to replace the obsolescent ex-L & C and B & P stock.

The locomotive stock had remained relatively small but in the late 1860s and into the 1870s a large number of new engines were purchased, especially for goods traffic. In 1870 the shops turned out the first engine to be built there—No 5. In 1871-3 two further engines were constructed and a glance at the costs shows that these were built rather less expensively than others purchased. Their first three products, however, were not entirely new construction but utilised parts of older engines which they replaced; it was not for a further thirty years that York Road was to design and turn out a completely new class of locomotive.

Besides coping with locomotives and rolling stock, permanent way and bridges, the engineering department was also responsible for repairing damage occasioned by 'Acts of God'. In October 1864, for example, heavy flooding washed away much of the line in the Glarryford area and three years later bad weather in January 1867 caused a goods train to be snowed up at Dunadry. Cotton and Yorston went down the line on two engines and succeeded in clearing the main line but the telegraph remained out of operation for a week. The elements also caused continual trouble on the coastal section of the L & C and C & L lines and the latter was also much troubled by landslips in earlier days.

Early in 1866 the reservoir serving York Road station and works burst and inundated the adjacent premises of the Mile Water Spinning Co. This occurred in the period following Forde's death while the position of engineer was being temporarily filled by Yorston, the locomotive superintendent, and claims were made by shareholders that he had not been sufficiently vigilant. The spinning company naturally sought compensation and on the claim being submitted to arbitration the sum of £1,400 was agreed.

THE SHAREHOLDERS

The great interest manifested by the shareholders, not only in their dividend but also in all matters affecting the company, is noteworthy. It was a cardinal rule of the board that all large expenditure must be submitted to the proprietors at a half yearly meeting before being undertaken.

By 1860 all refreshment rooms—Belfast, Ballymena and Carrickfergus—were delicensed for the sale of alcohol. A shareholder requested the directors 'not to continue in their employment or hire, any persons but those of strictly temperate habits'. The chairman told him 'it was better not to press the resolution' and stated that the reason for discontinuing the licences was so as not 'to tempt the servants'.

During the 1862 meetings an allegation was made that a certain first class carriage was totally unsuitable for traffic by a shareholder who often travelled in it. He was told that it was 'a little old' and 'the worst-looking on the line' but at least it *was* clean and comfortable.

The Cookstown line was the subject of an investigation into timekeeping; the railway took 34 miles to reach Toome from Belfast and the road only 22 and the shareholders were afraid that the poor punctuality might enable the competing carmen

Page 119
LARNE—II

) Overall view of Town station, *c* 1885 *(below)* PS *Princess Beatrice* entering Larne Harbour, *c* 1885

Page 120
PORTRUSH

(*above*) New station opened 1893. Note work on clock not complete (*below*) Northern Co
Hotel; gardens in foreground

to steal traffic. The 9.30pm Belfast—Toome was especially bad; one shareholder, getting little satisfaction when he complained in February 1862, undertook to keep punctuality records. Reporting in August he stated that February had been the worst month, when the train was late 81 minutes *in toto* and in four months it had been late on 84 days. But, said Cotton, it was a 'luggage' train and could not be expected to run strictly to time!

The condition of Whiteabbey station caused concern to the Rev Mr Bland. This was one of the original stations, not yet renewed, and the first class ladies' waiting room was off the third class waiting 'shed' so that genteel ladies had to run the gauntlet of the vulgar gaze of the commonalty as they picked their steps through large baskets and bags. It was, he said, his 'third time of asking' and 'he hoped that there would be an immediate performance of the ceremony'. Finally in February 1863 a new station was authorised, at a cost of £300.

Cotton did not suffer fools gladly. It must be presumed that the summer of 1874 was unwontedly tropical in Ulster for a shareholder in August suggested that carriage roofs be painted white. Cotton said that would require a weekly repaint due to the effect of smoke and soot on the light colour. He was asked, would any other light colour do? 'If you paint them any other colour you won't have them white!' he replied. Again a protest was made in 1877 that unnecessary expense was incurred in repainting stock; this brought the retort that 'they need not expect that the ladies would run the risk of getting their dresses spoiled for the sake of the shareholders of the Northern Counties Railway'!

THE LONDONDERRY & COLERAINE

The Londonderry & Coleraine section was a vital link in the main line but it gave constant trouble. When the lease was replaced by the haulage contract in 1865 the Northern Counties put in a considerable amount of work on the track at the expense of the L & C. It was still reported as 'rough' and Cotton and the L & C engineer inspected it; in general, they found, trains 'ran smoothly' though considerable relaying was yet required. Weather was a constant hazard on this section;

in March 1865 sand covered the rails at Downhill, delaying trains—it could easily derail a train; again in November of that year a storm washed away Ballykelly bridge.

Even under the new system of working it cannot be said that the L & C brought much profit to the Northern Counties. A shareholder of the B & NC observed in 1867 that he had never seen 'a more bankrupt looking concern' and personally he intended to take out a life insurance policy before he trusted himself to be carried over it again. He was promptly suppressed by the chairman who drew attention to the fact that there were reporters present!

The story of the takeover of the L & C was detailed in Chapter 3, the date of the Act of amalgamation being 24 July 1871. Since the line was in a serious condition a clause unique in B & NC history was inserted in the Act—for the period taken to complete refurbishment, renewals could be paid for out of capital rather than from revenue. The total cost of the purchase was £256,000. Following the purchase the opinion of 'a qualified engineer' was taken and the directors stated that 'the need for improvements was staring them in the face'. A sum of £30,000 was set aside to rebuild the stations, most of which were in a disgraceful condition, and John Lanyon, son of Charles, was appointed architect.

The new stations were at Londonderry (Waterside), Eglinton, Limavady Junction, Limavady, Bellarena, Downhill and Castlerock. All save the first-named were to the same basic design, varied as required, in ornamented red brick, and these handsome buildings still stand today. Work began in early 1873 and was completed in 1875. Londonderry station was altogether different in style from the others; the old Waterside had long been the subject of much criticism but no one could point a finger at its replacement, a handsome structure in dressed sandstone dignified by a tower with Italianate features to which clock faces were added in 1888. The two-storeyed building provided greatly enhanced accommodation with two platforms covered by an overall roof.

The layout of the goods yard at Londonderry was hampered by the cramped location of the property and it was decided to build a completely new goods terminal on the other bank of the Foyle, which would be more convenient to the city

THE MID-VICTORIAN YEARS 1860–1880

centre. Land was taken near the Carlisle Bridge and the future Great Northern's station in August 1872 and the new station, 'Londonderry City Goods', was opened on 1 May 1877. It was linked with Waterside via the Tramway already mentioned, by agreement with the Port & Harbour Commissioners. In 1897 it was necessary to extend the goods station. The locomotive shed and cattle dock remained at Waterside; the old goods yard became a small marshalling area.

Heavy renewals of the permanent way of the L & C section were also undertaken. When everything was complete the L & C section, hitherto something of which the Northern Counties was ashamed, was brought fully up to the high standards set elsewhere on the system—but not without great cost.

YORK ROAD

From the earliest days Belfast station had had but one platform used for both arrivals and departures. Goods facilities were provided under the span of the all-over roof. The situation had long incurred the disapproval of the Board of Trade and action had been planned but was deferred pending the activities of the Belfast Central. As a result of an accident on 28 August 1873, however, action was taken.

The 3.15pm train from Carrickfergus was running into the platform ten minutes late, having been held outside while the 4pm to Londonderry vacated the platform. As the Carrickfergus train ran inwards the driver saw ahead of him, leaving the siding connecting the passenger road with the engine shed, a light engine, less than 100yd ahead. He braked and reversed; the light engine stopped but the passenger train hit it. It transpired that the light engine usually drew out the carriages of the 3.15 to release the engine and on this day the regular driver was absent; the relief man thought the 3.15 had arrived. Col Rich drew attention, in his Board of Trade report, to the unsatisfactory platform and signalling arrangements and the directors were forced to take action.

In 1873 work began on a new goods shed which would replace the facilities afforded in the passenger area. As soon as it was completed the space occupied by the old goods facilities was utilised to provide an arrival platform and additional siding accommodation and the entire work was completed in August 1875 at a cost of £35,000. Modern signalling was provided as part of the alterations. Meanwhile improved transport between York Road and the city centre was afforded when, in February 1872, the Belfast Street Tramways opened their line which terminated outside the York Road frontage of the station.

MINOR MISHAPS

These years were mercifully free from serious accident, with one exception. There were of course minor occurrences such as that at Coleraine on 3 April 1863 when a pointsman turned a down train into the up loop where it collided with the engine of an up train. Since the accident was 'not wilful' the pointsman escaped with a fine of a guinea.

An accident which might have had serious consequences occurred on 9 February 1863. As the 5pm Ballymena—Belfast train was running about half a mile out of Ballymena the coupling between the third class coach behind the tender, and the first class coach broke. The latter fell on its side but did not drag the other vehicles with it. A few yards further and it might have fallen down an embankment but the driver was quick to stop and only two passengers complained of injury.

An amusing episode took place near Carrickfergus Junction on 11 July 1868. A Cookstown train left Belfast double-headed. At the Junction the pilot engine was detached and prepared to bank the train up Mossley bank. But the banker dropped behind and the driver, observing this, put on steam to come against the train again, doing so with some violence. There was little damage and the train continued to Ballynure Road station where it was discovered that the rear carriage was occupied by members of the Royal Irish Constabulary proceeding to duty in Randalstown on 12 July. They accused the driver of holding 'some damn spite' against them and assured him 'they would make it a dear shunt'! Col Rich found 'pushing' bad practice, only to be resorted to when absolutely necessary.

Coleraine was the scene of an accident on 22 February 1875. The 8.15pm ex Portrush collided with an empty passenger train from Londonderry which was setting back into a siding. The driver of the Portrush train claimed his brakes had failed but the fact remained the distant signal had been against him and Rich accused him of failing to keep a proper lookout. The signalling at Coleraine at this time left much to be desired as did the station generally.

On 2 October 1876 an entire train, a local from Belfast to Ballymena, was derailed at the Belfast end of Cookstown Junction station. It was discovered that an up goods, passing 20 minutes earlier, had so acted upon the switches of a crossover that the indicator gave a false reading. Maj-Gen C. S. Hutchinson blamed the system of wire interlocking in use at the Junction. Three months later occurred the very serious Moylena collision which is the subject of the following section.

Another amusing incident took place near Carrickfergus on 23 December 1878. A mixed train left for Belfast at 7.40am; $1\frac{1}{2}$ miles up the bank it stopped to carry out shunting at Duncrue siding. The train as a whole was too long for the siding and the four carriages, behind the wagons, were left on the main line depending on the guard's van brake, which failed to hold them, and the coaches set off down the single line towards Carrickfergus. They eventually came to a stand $\frac{3}{4}$ mile on the other side of the station, more of their own volition than of any efforts of the staff, Hutchinson discovered. The weather was very severe—there was heavy snow—and this had probably rendered the brake ineffectual. But the staff at Carrickfergus were far from concerned—they knew there was nothing coming from Larne and no one did anything to halt the runaways—save the head porter who threw snow on the rails!

FURTHER WIDENING

The main line was double from Belfast to Carrickfergus Junction; from there on it was single. In February 1871 the decision was taken to double the Ballyclare & Doagh—Dunadry section, $5\frac{1}{2}$ miles, and this was completed a year later. It was then decided to double the $7\frac{3}{4}$ mile intermediate section between the Junction and Ballyclare & Doagh. A delay ensued as a result of the high cost of rails and it was not until the spring of 1874 that the contract was signed. On 1 May 1875 the new up line from Ballyclare & Doagh to Ballynure Road was ready and in November the Ballynure Road—Carrickfergus Junction section was completed.

At this time the price of rails had fallen and the opportunity was taken to double the Dunadry—Cookstown Junction section, 6¾ miles. The new up line was put into use on 5 February 1877 and, again taking advantage of the continuing cheapness in rails, work began on the Cookstown Junction—Ballymena stretch, this being completed in July 1878. This completed a double line from Belfast to Ballymena; there the company rested and there the double line ends to this day. Before the doubling was completed, however, a serious accident took place on 26 December 1876; it brought about the first and only fatality caused by the failure of the company.

The scene was Moylena, about one mile south-east of Antrim, near the pit from which the B & NC drew ballast at this time. At the time the Dunadry—Cookstown Junction section was in process of being doubled; there were passing loops at Dunadry, Antrim and Cookstown Junction. On 19 December a notice was issued by Cotton giving details of a special goods train on weekdays as and from 20 December, leaving Belfast at 8.15am. It was to pass the up mail at Dunadry and the 8.35 ex Coleraine at Antrim. On 21 and 22 December the goods was late and crossed the 8.35 at Dunadry; on 24 and 25 December it did not run. On the 26th it was delayed 8–10 minutes at Dunadry awaiting the up mail to clear the section and left ten minutes late for Antrim.

The 8.35 was timed to leave Antrim at 10.5. On this day it consisted of an engine and tender, two thirds, and a composite brake containing the guard. It left Antrim at 10.6 and when running about 25mph sighted the goods train, made up of a heavy goods engine, brake van, a loaded coal wagon, 17 empties and a second van, 80 or 100 yards ahead. The goods driver had shut off steam descending the 1 in 360 and his train was running about 15mph. The driver and fireman of the 8.35 leaped off the footplate but the crew of the goods stayed at their post and the two engines collided violently. Considerable damage was caused to both trains. The leading coach of the passenger was fortunately empty; it was wrecked and two compartments of the composite behind it shared the same fate. In one of these a Mrs. Lowry was travelling; she was killed outright. Eight other passengers were injured, five seriously.

Col F. H. Rich came to investigate this deplorable occurrence for the Board of Trade. He drew attention to the B & NC's method of working the single line. Since opening it had been worked on the fixed timetable system, that is, trains meeting at prescribed places. If, however, a train was twenty or more minutes late the guard of the train waiting for the single-line section telegraphed to the station in advance and asked permission of the station master there to take his train forward. If authority was given the station master there was to repeat the altered crossing arrangement and both driver and guard gave a receipt to the station master at the station they were leaving in acknowledgement of his authority to start. The delayed train in the opposite direction would then be held at the station in advance.

This had happened on several occasions with the 8.35 and the goods. On the 26th no such interchange of messages took place. The station master at Antrim was reading the gas meter to send the figures to York Road by the 8.35. The telegraph clerk in the office often rang the station bell—the signal to the guard to start the train—and on this occasion he did so at 10.6, thinking everything in order for the train to proceed. The guard, hearing the bell, signalled the train away and jumped into his van. The signalman, seeing all this, lowered the starting signal. The driver claimed to have forgotten the goods and the signalman said he was unaware of the unaltered crossing.

Col Rich dealt sternly with the officials. The accident was the first of its kind; the system of working had worked well since opening and the fact that five separate forms were involved was surely an adequate safeguard, except that there was only the manager's notice of out-of-course specials. He recommended the adoption of the train staff system and improved signalling when the line was doubled. At the Belfast Assizes in March 1877 Andrew McKillop, Antrim station master, John Macrory, driver of the 8.35, and John Turner, the guard, were tried for manslaughter. All three pleaded not guilty and were acquitted. Compensation and repairs cost the company some £7,500.

BLOCK WORKING

In 1869, in reply to a circular from the Board of Trade advocating the adoption of block telegraph working, the B & NC replied that 'the Directors are of opinion that with the comparatively limited traffic, the length of time between the trains, and other considerations affecting the general working, they see no necessity for the adoption of the block telegraph system on this line of railway'.

Following Rich's strictures the company had little alternative but to instal modern equipment. During 1878 the train staff system was made universal throughout the single line; hitherto it was used only between Carrickfergus Junction and Carrickfergus, Coleraine and Portrush, and Limavady Junction and Limavady. The double lines had been worked by time interval; Tyer's two-position block instruments were brought into use between Carrickfergus Junction and Ballymena in June 1878. Ordinary telegraph instruments were used for blocking between Belfast and Carrickfergus Junction (double line) and between the Junction and Carrickfergus (single line), in addition to the staff system. The only other absolute block section at this time was Castlerock—Downhill, for the protection of trains in the tunnels.

A LOOP?

We saw in Chapter 2 why the main line was run to Carrickfergus Junction, necessitating a reversal there for main line trains. As time advanced and traffic increased the position became more difficult and in 1873–4 serious consideration was given to the building of a 'loop' from Whiteabbey to Mossley, $1\frac{3}{4}$ miles long. But such a loop would involve heavy gradients —'such gradients could not be worked with the locomotives then [1848] in use', Lanyon explained. He added that 'it would require a great deal more consideration before they embarked upon it definitely'. It was arranged that Cotton and Collins, the new engineer, should go to England to investigate and report on similar lines there. 'A great deal would depend on the report they would make.' The visit duly took place and as a result 'on more mature consideration' the clauses dealing with the loop were withdrawn from the 1874 Act. It was reported that by reason of the curves and gradients the loop 'would lead to no economy at all', the more so as a pilot engine would constantly be required. But the idea was not dropped, only shelved. On 1 February 1878 the shareholders were asked to approve a Bill which became law on 4 July 1878 providing for

> A Railway, one mile five furlongs and six chains in length or thereabouts, commencing by a junction with the Railway of the Company at the fifth milepost in the townland of Jordanstown in the Parish of Carnmoney, and terminating at a point seven chains eastward of the ninth milepost of the railway in the townland of Ballyhone, in the said Parish of Carnmoney.

Additional finance for the construction was fixed at £190,000; three years were given to acquire land and five for construction.

Hardly had the project been sanctioned than hard times hit the company and the work was deferred. In due course the powers expired and were renewed for a further four years by the Act of 22 August 1881. But by the end of 1882 the scheme had definitely been abandoned; in the straitened circumstances then obtaining the spending of such a large sum, even if it could have been found, could not be justified. The board decided to fit the automatic vacuum brake instead, which 'would save a considerable amount of time between Belfast and Londonderry'.

DIRECTORS AND OFFICIALS

The old men were passing away quickly in the middle 1860s. Lord Massereene who had had such an important part in the early days died in 1863. On 7 February 1867 William Dargan died in Dublin. A subscription of £100 was voted to the fund set up for his widow; his later years had been clouded by declining finances. His work for the Northern Counties had been tremendous though of late years he had not been a frequent attender at board meetings. 'No man had done more for Ireland than the late William Dargan', it was said.

On 20 October 1867 the chairman since 1845, the Hon

George Handcock, died in Dublin. In latter years he had often been the subject of criticism by the shareholders for his non-attendance at directors' and shareholders' meetings and at the August meeting following his death it was demanded 'why should they go to Dublin for a chairman who never attended'. He was replaced by George Jackson Clarke, a prosperous owner of some 2,500 acres whose beautiful Regency house at The Steeple, Antrim, overlooked the main line; he had been associated with the company from the days of 1836.

Charles Lanyon continued to fulfil the position of consulting engineer until 1867 when he joined the board and became vice-chairman. He had been mayor of Belfast in 1862 and from 1866 to 1868 was Conservative MP for the town. In 1868 he was knighted by the Lord Lieutenant. He was by then one of the leading architects in the British Isles with most of the important public buildings in Belfast to his credit.

Cotton's salary at the beginning of his management had been £400; in 1866 it was raised to £1,000, making him the highest paid railway official in Ireland—at the time the Great Southern & Western's traffic manager was in receipt of only £850. Three years later the salary was raised to £1,200, it being explained that he had had a pressing offer to go to India for three years with all expenses paid at a salary of £3,000. 'There are no two opinions as to Mr Cotton's efficiency and ability as a manager'; one had to pay for quality.

The resident engineer since 1860, Arthur Forde, died in office in 1865. He was replaced for a short period by George Orson but in February 1867 Phineas Howell was appointed. His youth was commented upon but it was pointed out that he would make 'a good second' under Lanyon's watchful eye; he had eight years' experience, six with the B & NC and two with Lanyon in his private business. He was to remain until 1873 when on his resignation he was superseded by Robert Collins CE of Londonderry. Collins came from the Lough Swilly Railway whose engineer he had been since 1866: he also had some association with the L & C.

Yorston remained locomotive superintendent until 1868. He was ageing and he did not leave the locomotive stock in any too good order. To replace him Edward Leigh, abandoning the bankrupt Newry & Armagh Railway, came to Belfast. He was to remain there until 1875 when a brief hiatus took place during which Robert Finlay, son of Sir George Finlay of the L & NWR, held the office.

On Finlay's resignation in 1876 due to ill-health, a truly daring appointment of great significance was made. To the responsible position of locomotive superintendent there was appointed Bowman Malcolm, aged only 22. He had entered the locomotive department in 1870 at the age of 16; it was the beginning of 52 years' service. He early marked himself out as an exceptionally capable engineer though he had no formal training. The appointment was to be fully justified. Second only to Cotton, he was the most outstanding personality in the annals of the Northern Counties Railway, and famed throughout the railway world for the success of his compound locomotives.

Malcolm was a stern disciplinarian and expected men to follow the high precepts of his own life. The notices he issued are often full of the virtues of temperance ('You have all known men lose their situations, and bring discomfort, if not absolute ruin, on themselves and their families, in consequence of indulgence in this evil habit—a habit against which, you know, I most strongly set my face, in the interest of the Company', reads one issued in 1889; one of 1886—'Enginemen must not smoke when at or passing Stations; it looks slovenly').

By the 1874 Act the clause of the 1845 Act which required not less than fifteen directors was repealed; now the board must consist of at least six members, this smaller number making for the more expeditious despatch of the increasing volume of business.

THE GOLDEN YEARS

The 1870s were destined to be the most prosperous in the history of the B & NC—a real golden age, during which it established itself for a season as the most prosperous of the Irish companies and 'one of the most prosperous in the United Kingdom', as the chairman said. In 1871 a dividend of $6\frac{1}{2}$ per cent was paid and in 1872 $7\frac{1}{4}$ per cent. From then until 1878 the dividend never dropped below $7\frac{1}{4}$ per cent. In 1873 the Ulster Railway paid $7\frac{1}{2}$ per cent but this was once only; the

Dublin & Kingstown paid more but it was a mere suburban line worked by a larger neighbour. The great upsurge in receipts may be attributed to the general prosperity of Northern Irish industry and agriculture. The year 1872 for example brought an increase of £3,458 in receipts over 1871 so that $7\frac{1}{4}$ per cent could be paid 'without starving the line' as Sir Charles Lanyon put it. A good example of the well-being of the Northern Counties is the fact that in 1873, when it paid $7\frac{1}{2}$ per cent, the mighty London & North Western paid $6\frac{1}{2}$ per cent. As usual much of the credit must go to Cotton; in 1874 it was said that the company 'had the maximum of excellence in management with the minimum of expense' and Cotton was described as being 'omniscient'.

It should be borne in mind that the capital had increased tremendously and the interest charges on preference stocks was considerable. Added to the expense of the improvements all over the system the line was certainly not 'starved' to produce an artificially high dividend. The good times were to be of short duration, however. The dividend in 1877 was $7\frac{1}{2}$ per cent but it was observed that 'an anxious time is approaching'. As it turned out 1878 was the last 'good' year with a dividend of $6\frac{1}{4}$ per cent. The next year it fell to $4\frac{1}{4}$ per cent and until 1889 never rose above $4\frac{1}{2}$ per cent.

CHAPTER SIX

The County Antrim Branches

Four branch lines were constructed in County Antrim by independent companies. Unlike County Londonderry, only one of these was a broad-gauge railway; the others were built to the Irish narrow gauge. The broad gauge line was the oldest of the four and financially it was reasonably successful. The three narrow gauge lines were altogether different; their financial history was exceedingly unhappy.

THE CARRICKFERGUS & LARNE RAILWAY

Unsuccessful proposals for a railway from Carrickfergus to Larne were made in 1836 and 1845. It was more than a decade before any further proposals were made; to understand properly the reasons underlying the construction of the railway we must first look at the 'Short Sea Passage'.

The shortest distance between Great Britain and Ireland is the 22 mile crossing between Portpatrick in Wigtownshire and Donaghadee in County Down. A weekly mail service was established by private enterprise as early as 1662 on this run. The term 'short sea passage' most accurately describes this early route; but for the last century it has been applied to the Larne—Stranraer passage though it is 17 miles longer. This extra distance was compensated for by the easier berthing. In 1846 the government appointed Captain George Evans RN to investigate the best route for the carriage of mails between Scotland and Ireland. He recommended that the theoretical shortest passage be abandoned, and urged the adoption of Cairn Ryan, a small port in Loch Ryan near Stranraer, as the Scottish terminus, and Larne in County Antrim as the Irish. Both provided sheltered anchorages and little expense would be

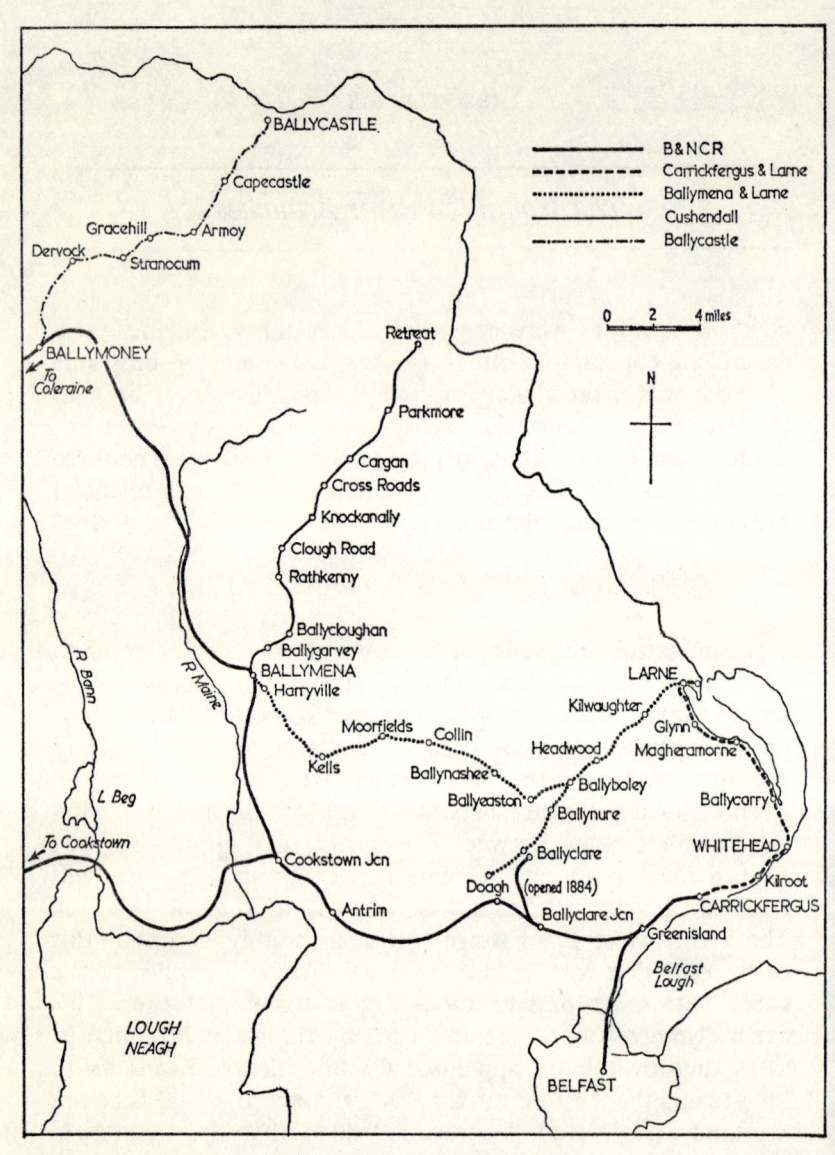

The County Antrim branches

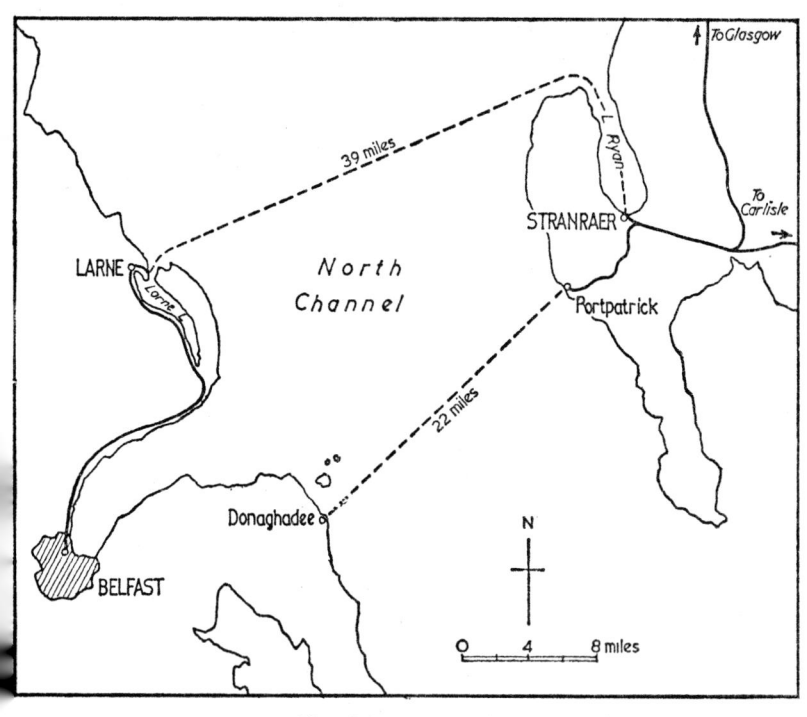

The short sea passage

required to provide the necessary facilities for the steamers.

At that time railway communication in Ulster was in its infancy and it was undoubtedly to advance the claims of Larne that the Carrickfergus & Larne Railway was promoted.

THE 1859 PROPOSAL

Larne lies some 14 miles north of Carrickfergus, terminus of the Belfast & Ballymena's branch opened in 1848. It was with the intention of linking the two towns by rail, and thus opening the way for a steamer service, that a group of businessmen and landowners assembled at 23 Donegall Place, Belfast, on 1 February 1859

> to consider the propriety of promoting a line of Railway in continuance of the Belfast and Ballymena line, to Larne.

The ubiquitous Charles Lanyon was appointed engineer and James Torrens solicitor. These two officials strengthened the link with the Belfast & Ballymena, several of whose directors were on the provisional committee. The meeting decided to approach the B & B 'to ascertain what assistance this meeting may expect'. In due course Lanyon reported that there were two possible routes: inland, requiring heavy works, and a coastal line, also requiring considerable engineering and open to sea damage. Nevertheless the 'shore' route, as it was termed, was chosen. By the end of 1859 the secretary, Samuel Vance, was able to report that £21,500 had been subscribed or promised, and the committee was ready to go to Parliament on the strength of this.

Despite the close links with the B & B that company severely disappointed the embryonic Carrickfergus & Larne in January 1860. The C & L had asked the B & B to subscribe £25,000 and to provide the Parliamentary deposit. Now the B & B proposed to subscribe only £12,500, loaning a further £12,500 at 4 per cent interest. There was nothing the C & L could do but accept and protest, noting that it was largely at the behest of the B & B that the shore route had been adopted.

The Bill was duly laid before Parliament. It provided that the C & L would build a new station in Carrickfergus which would replace the B & B's 1848 erection; this new station was to be half a mile west of the B & B's which would be abandoned, the B & B to pay rental to the C & L for the use of the new facilities. The Bill received Royal Assent on 15 May 1860. Conway R. Dobbs of Castle Dobbs, Kilroot, and James Agnew of Larne became chairman and vice-chairman respectively; several of the other directors were on the board of the Belfast & Northern Counties (as the B & B became on the day the C & L Act was passed). The total length of line authorised was 14½ miles. The capital was fixed at £125,000 in £25 shares; powers were given to borrow up to £41,500 and convert it into debentures. The B & NCR was permitted to subscribe up to £20,000. In August Edward Coey, one of the directors, took charge of the arrangements to hire a steamer and convey a party between Larne and Stranraer to demonstrate the feasibility of running a permanent service and its superiority over the Portpatrick —Donaghadee route. Unfortunately we have no details of this run which appears to have been made by the steamer *Giraffe*.

WORK BEGINS

In July 1860 rails were ordered from the Rhymey Iron Co at £6 7s 6d (£6.37½) per ton, delivery to be begun in March 1861. Lanyon told the board that he was taking sufficient land for a double line and was making overbridges for a double road but underbridges and earthworks were for a single line only. By November eight tenders for the construction of the line had been received. Lanyon went to Leeds to verify the bona fides of Samuel and Frederick Buxton whose tender, at £47,421, was stated to be £12,000 less than the lowest Irish tender. The contract was signed on 12 November but a fortnight later the contractors withdrew from it. The directors thereupon chose John and Robert Edwards, whose tender was £60,720; they agreed to take 20 per cent of the price in shares. The guarantors were William Dargan and Thomas Edwards.

Work began at once and in the first report of the directors the shareholders were told that

> after much consideration [they] have arranged that the station at Larne shall be placed on the slob land at the point of Mr Chaine's property, this being considered the most suitable; and that at Carrickfergus opposite the North Gate ...

Land for eight miles had already been taken; in March sleepers were contracted for with J. P. Corry of Belfast. By May Edwards Bros had 700 men and 89 horses at work; Lanyon thought that more could be employed with advantage and in June he reported there were 1,385 men and 200 horses at work. A month later the totals were 1,472 and 257. Also in June he reported that

> he had laid out the line from the Larne station to the Curran Pier giving facility of approach to either Old or New Pier and given up possession of the land to the Contractor ...

He was instructed to prepare plans for the Larne station building, to include a refreshment room.

In September Dixon of Belfast was given the contract for

the erection of the stations buildings at Larne and Carrickfergus; the latter had to be submitted to the B & NC for approval. In connection with opening the C & L now opened negotiations with the Northern Counties for the working of the line. In time for the opening, a formalised working agreement was prepared and approved by the shareholders. The B & NC was to provide locomotives and rolling stock sufficient to work 'not less than three or more than five' trains daily with one on Sundays, together with the necessary staff; the C & L was to provide materials for maintenance when required. In return the B & NC was to receive 2s (10p) per train mile if three trains ran, 1s 10d (9p) if four, and 1s 8d (8½p) if five. This agreement was binding for one year but could be prolonged if desired. Local traffic accounts were to be audited by the B & NC, 'foreign' by the Irish Railway Clearing House. The B & NC bye-laws were adopted.

TO STRANRAER

While work progressed attention was given to the establishment of a steamer link between Larne and Stranraer, which had replaced Cairn Ryan as the proposed Scottish terminus. The C & L board had 'a very lengthy discussion' on the subject on 6 January 1862. They decided to approach the London & North Western Railway for their views and their assistance, and Cotton, who, representing the B & NC, was taking a leading part, was requested to 'make some private enquiries'. A fortnight later Cotton reported that a steamer 'would likely cost £15,000'. The C & L thought if the B & NC would subscribe £3,000 and themselves £2,000, the Portpatrick and L & NW Companies £5,000, that sum could be found. On 12 February a deputation of the interested railways met the L & NW board in London. Moon regretted his company lacked the powers to subscribe, but might be able to arrange with 'interested parties'. The North Western, Northern Counties and Portpatrick managers were to confer. It was reported that Stranraer Harbour would be ready on 1 July, having 12ft of water at the quayside; the C & L decided to build a new pier and meanwhile James Agnew consented to the use of his, which was to be 'made suitable' at a cost not exceeding £10!

On 28 February Cotton met the managers of the L & NW, Glasgow & South Western, Portpatrick, North British and Newcastle & Carlisle Railways in Carlisle. He submitted a return of cross-Channel passengers from the Northern Counties line. He estimated that in the first years of working a steamer there would be a loss of £2,000 and this might be shared proportionately. He thought it might be best to charter a steamer initially; there were several available. A joint committee was set up with Cotton as chairman. In May fares were fixed and it was decided to proceed with arrangements. Cotton entered into unsuccessful negotiations with the Post Office to secure a mail contract.

A steamer had been bought. It was practically new; named *Briton*, it had been launched early in 1862 by Tod & MacGregor for John Stewart & Co. It was acquired from Stewart in September 1862 at a cost of £12,000 of which the B & NC and C & L paid £3,000, the Portpatrick the remainder. This little paddler had a tonnage of 350, an iron hull, and was 176ft long and 24ft in beam. The C & L appointed Lanyon 'proprietor' of its stake in the boat.

DELAYS

Meanwhile work on the C & L's line was not progressing to the satisfaction of Lanyon. The year 1862 began and it was obvious that no spring opening would take place. In February the delay was ascribed to bad weather, difficulty in consolidating embankments, and a landslip near Glynn. It was with relief that Lanyon noted that the 145yd tunnel near Whitehead was completed. But only one quarter of the permanent way was laid: it was made up of single-headed iron rail in 21ft lengths, fastened to the cross sleepers with fangbolts and spikes and on curves a bracket chair was used as additional security.

In an attempt to speed up construction the C & L had resort to the B & B's expedient and in May Lanyon was instructed to erect no permanent stations between Carrickfergus and Larne —merely temporary platforms 'at the various points where stations are likely to be'. Such platforms were erected at Kilroot, Ballycarry and Ballylig (soon to be called Magheramorne). Lanyon, in explaining the delay, nevertheless believed that the C & L would be completed 'within as short if not a shorter time (considering the nature of the works) than any other similar undertaking'. By September the entire £125,000 in shares had been subscribed; a 36ft turntable had been fixed for locomotive purposes at Larne, with two 12ft tables in the goods yard; signal posts and lamps, similar to those used on the B & NC, had been supplied by that company at £11 10s (£11.50) each; and platform lamps, ticket presses and other requisites had been obtained.

The line was now sufficiently advanced to permit of its being submitted to the inspection of the Board of Trade; 1 September had been tentatively fixed as the date but there were further delays and it was not until 27 September 1862 that Captain F. H. Rich came to inspect the line. He found little to complain of: 'the general state of the line is good'. He noted that 'a covered road to the pier and a new pier are constructing'. Some minor alterations were required to underbridges which had wooden tops and a short length of fencing at the Curran. The general standard of engineering was excellent and his few recommendations had been put in hand. He therefore begged 'to submit that the Larne and Carrickfergus Railway may be opened for passenger traffic without danger to the public using the same'.

OPENED ON TWO FRONTS

The opening to passengers took place on 1 October 1862 with three trains daily each way and two on Sundays. No goods traffic could be undertaken since the facilities were incomplete. On 2 October the *Briton* made her first run in normal service. The weather on this first crossing was so bad that it took four hours instead of the advertised three. The schedule called for the vessel to dock at Larne at 1.35pm and the boat train left for Belfast shortly afterwards. Passengers in the opposite direction left Belfast by the 4pm train and could arrive in London at 9am next morning.

The line had only been opened two months when a serious landslip occurred near Whitehead where the line bordered the sea. There was considerable delay to trains and the steamer. A 'siding' (presumably a loop) was laid to try to prevent a recurrence. The first permanent station, 'of stone and brick', was authorised to be built at Ballycarry in November 1862. It was decided not to build a refreshment room at the Curran terminus of the steamer; that at Larne Town was to be licensed.

In July 1863 Cotton reported that the first nine months of working had lost the Northern Counties £1,087 but this he did not regard unduly seriously since the C & L brought traffic to its neighbour. The receipts from a mail contract would have been welcome but Cotton was unable to obtain one, since the regulations for the operation of mail trains were felt to be too restrictive for the C & L's line.

Lanyon was still far from satisfied with the contractors' performance and in June 1863, following further landslips near Whitehead, he furnished Edwards Bros with a memorandum of his requirements which showed that the line was far from completed. Arthur Forde, engineer of the B & NC, was appointed to assist Lanyon in seeing that these works were carried out. A new ballast pit was to be opened at Kilroot. So far from completing the works Edwards Bros withdrew their men on 2 October and declined to do anything further. Lanyon thereupon set about the completion of the work himself by direct labour; understandably this proved difficult—it was described as 'very tedious' because of the line being in daily use—but by October 1864 all was complete. Sometime during 1863 goods traffic was commenced when the necessary facilities were completed.

A loss had been expected on the steamer service but only of £2,000 per year and it came as a shock when Cotton reported that during the first three months of operation a deficit of £1,536 had been incurred, of which the B & NC and C & L had to bear £331. The Northern Counties directors were of opinion that a bigger boat with greater speed and better accommodation might make the run more attractive; but the C & L had no money to contribute towards such a vessel.

The results continued to be poor in 1863 and on 23 November the Northern Counties intimated that it was withdrawing from its guarantee on 1 January 1864, unless the other partners would agree to join in building a better boat. In view of the losses and the general lack of prosperity of the C & L, they could not contribute and the other railways were uninterested. Accordingly, on 31 December 1863 the *Briton* made its last crossing of the short sea route. It was sold to the Bristol Steam Navigation Co who used it on the Bristol Channel—South of Ireland service until 1890, when it was withdrawn and scrapped the next year.

The mile-long Larne—Larne Harbour section of line became virtually redundant; only a few trains bringing coal from the Harbour used it, though against better days it was kept in repair. The cattle pens at the Harbour were rented to a guard. With the ending of the steamer service the boat trains were withdrawn, and the timetable recast so as to provide three trains daily each way. Another sign of the times was the closing of the refreshment room at Larne for want of patronage. From having been a partner in a cross-Channel steamer service of which much had been expected the Carrickfergus & Larne now found itself a rather minor branch line with a more affluent neighbour.

WHITEHEAD

Five miles from Carrickfergus along the shore was the little settlement of Whitehead, a place with limestone quarries, from which it took its name. When the line was opened there was no halt here; on 8 April 1863, however, it was decided to erect 'a platform and box' and this was opened on 1 May. This first halt was in an isolated and exposed spot on the Carrickfergus side of the tunnel. When an excursion train was run soon afterwards Cotton gave readings from Dickens at York Road to provide funds to hire a band! Though this halt had been open but eight months a memorial, signed by 65 people, was received in January 1864 stating that its site was inconvenient and asking for a new platform nearer the hamlet. This was agreed to and on 1 June the second Whitehead station came into use.

In Chapter 5 reference was made to the institution of villa tickets. In September 1861 the C & L obtained the consent of the B & NC to extend these to their line when opened. Whitehead was an exceptionally agreeable spot reasonably accessible to Belfast; and large numbers of new houses sprang up as a result of the railway and especially of the villa tickets. If Dargan was 'the founder of Portrush prosperity' then the villa ticket is certainly responsible for the development of Whitehead.

In the early part of 1870 a request was received for a new station better appointed and more central to the heart of the developing township. Cotton recommended that a further move be made and the directors agreed to the site 'originally intended'. Howell of the B & NC produced plans for a new building 'similar to Jordanstown or Kilroot' but the C & L found these too expensive. Quarrels with the owner of the land ensued and it was not until September 1875 that John Lanyon submitted a revised plan which, costing between £600 and £700 to execute, was also found too expensive. A month later it was proposed that sleeping accommodation be provided in the new building as local bedrooms for visitors were 'limited'. But this, it was found, would cost £1,500, and, however desirable, was rejected, and Lanyon's plan was adopted.

Early in 1876 the contract was given to J. & R. Thomson at £875, Lanyon being refused a clerk of works on the ground that the contract was too small to necessitate such an official. The B & NC agreed to pay a rental of £20 per annum. This new station, the third to serve Whitehead, was opened for traffic in June 1877. Until 1894 only one platform was provided, but as a result of the provision of the improved facilities Whitehead advanced by leaps and bounds.

DEPRESSED DAYS

In October 1865, £5 was given to a ferryman to provide a boat from Magheramorne (formerly Ballylig) across Larne Lough to Islandmagee and a 'lodge' was to be erected at the station. In May 1864 it was decided to provide a platform at Glynn near Larne and this (which may have come from the original Whitehead station) was opened on 1 October. A siding was also provided here: 'Mr Wilson will agree to send all his goods by railway.' At the same time a carriage dock was built at Larne, and cattle pens at Carrickfergus.

One of the passenger trains had been withdrawn in November 1863; it was restored during the summer of 1864.

A further attempt was made to obtain a mail contract but the Post Office would only offer £100 and Cotton wanted £120. Finally in February 1865 the Post Office offered £30 per year for the carriage of mails by one train per day, and this the C & L accepted. During these times Kilroot station was proving unprofitable and alternated between periods of 'flag' or request stop and complete closure. During 1864, also, a siding was laid across the public road at Larne into the market yard from the goods yard. In September 1864 the original chairman, Conway R. Dobbs, resigned and was replaced by Viscount Templeton of Castle Upton, Templepatrick.

It cannot be said that the cessation of the steamer service brought a marked change in the receipts; a comparison showed that the first half-year of 1863 brought £1,723 from local sources plus £226 from 'through English and Scotch traffic' while the same period of 1864 produced £1,833 locally and £89 from cross-Channel sources—an overall reduction of only £28. There was insufficient balance in either period to permit of the payment of a dividend.

The relationship between the B & NC and the C & L became increasingly close. From the end of August 1865 the Northern Counties became responsible for permanent way upkeep on a temporary basis and shortly afterwards assumed the maintenance of the pitching of the sea walls. In February 1865 a deputation was appointed to wait on the Northern Counties board 'to call their attention to the position of the Carrickfergus & Larne Company and to ask for the alteration of the charges for working the line'. The original working agreement had been renewed in 1863 and 1864 but the company was in dire straits financially. On 23 October the B & NC agreed to work the line under new arrangements:

> ... three trains each way on weekdays and two on Sundays —and to keep up the permanent way, for the sum of £3,000 per annum with fifty per cent added on any increase of gross traffic above £4,500 per annum. Land slips or injury to seawalls to be paid at the expense of the Larne Company.

This the C & L accepted; it was binding from 1 November 1865 for seven years and included insurance, local rates, etc. A joint traffic committee was formed but it met very infrequently.

THE STEAMER AGAIN

The discontinuance of the steamer service at the end of 1863 had not been pleasing to many; notably the Northern Counties, whose proposal for improving the service by the provision of a better boat had been rejected. But at least this initial service had proved the feasibility of the run.

It was not until 1871 that efforts made by the joint committee, especially Cotton, and James Chaine MP, owner of Larne Harbour, came to fruition. During that year the Larne & Stranraer Steamboat Company was formed, capital being subscribed in almost equal proportions on each side of the Irish Sea. Neither the B & NC nor the C & L had Parliamentary authority to subscribe so capital in Ulster came from private hands—mainly those of directors in the two railways. Cotton was appointed general manager.

James Chaine submitted plans in October 1871 for a proposed new wharf at Larne Harbour for the new service. The original 1862 platform was still in existence and the C & L proposed to erect 'a shed' to cover it. A sign of the times was the re-opening of Larne refreshment room; new life breathed at the Harbour. The directors triumphantly reported in February 1872:

> The Railway from Stranraer to Girvan has been commenced and when completed will form, in connection with your Line and the Short Sea Passage between Larne and Stranraer, the most direct route between Belfast and the North of Ireland and the towns of Ayrshire and Glasgow ...

A completely new steamer had been ordered from Tod & MacGregor of Glasgow. The *Princess Louise* was a 497 ton paddle steamer, 211ft long and 24ft in beam, and cost £18,500. An extensive advertising campaign was mounted in April 1872, to which the L & NWR, the Girvan & Portpatrick Railway, the B & NC, the C & L and the Steamboat Co each subscribed £100.

On 1 July 1872 the *Princess Louise* began a daily service between Larne and Stranraer. It must have been a moment of intense gratification to all concerned, and especially to Edward

John Cotton, who had been untiring in his efforts. Unfortunately the *Louise* proved a disappointment. Internally accommodation was of a high standard with a luxurious general saloon and reading and smoking rooms, with special cabins for lady passengers. It soon became apparent, however, that she was incapable of keeping time on the $2\frac{3}{4}$ hour schedule. The cause was lack of engine power—the original engines were of 200hp. Re-engining was several times discussed but finance was tight and the service was not yet firmly established. It was not until 1878 that new boilers were fitted, increasing engine capacity to 347hp, and now the schedule could be maintained with ease.

By the end of 1872 Cotton was telling the C & L that 'the traffic since the commencement has been satisfactory' and showed every sign of improving as the run became better known.

PATTERNS OF CHANGE

We must revert to the second half of the 1860s, a period of mixed fortunes for the C & L. The year 1866 began with the contractors, Edwards Bros, still seeking a final settlement of their account. It was proposed to give them £2,000 in bonds and shares and it appears this offer was accepted. One of the directors returned his free pass: 'I think from the present position of the Railway . . . they should only be used when travelling on *strictly* railway business and I do not require [it] for such . . . .' Indeed the financial position at this time was not bright and in November the directors considered asking the Treasury for a loan of £26,000, but this was not proceeded with.

An attempt was made to increase revenue by offering return tickets at single fares from Larne, Glynn, Magheramorne and Ballycarry to Belfast on Tuesdays. It was also hoped to increase goods traffic, especially in limestone and granite, from the Whitehead area, and a rise of 32 per cent in the goods receipts in the second half of 1867 was ascribed to this. But the cheap tickets proved a failure and were withdrawn. The original secretary, Samuel Vance, resigned on 1 December 1866 and Charles Stewart of the Northern Counties was appointed in his stead, forming another useful contact at York Road. During 1866 a siding was provided at Kilroot at the expense of Conway R. Dobbs, the ex-chairman, for his merchandise and in 1869 that gentleman provided a new station building at Kilroot to the plan of Howell.

A very severe storm at the beginning of 1867 caused much damage to the line near Whitehead tunnel. Extensive and costly repairs were required—at a time when the bank balance was only £39. There was also the curious case of 'ships getting aground at Whitehead harbour and their bowsprits projecting over the railway'. The ballast quarry at Kilroot was sold to the B & NC for £1,000 which sum was very useful but so costly were the repairs at Whitehead that in October the overdraft at the Belfast Bank was £2,960.

Another storm on 31 January 1869 brought tremendous damage to the line in the Glynn area. The line was closed for ten days, being re-opened to goods traffic on 9 February after the dumping of prodigious quantities of stone from Whitehead. The work cost some £400—including £11 for whiskey for the workmen! A director proposed that a recurrence might be prevented if 'a certain weed that grows in the neighbourhood . . . be planted along the embankments of the railway where the tide touches them'. This cost between £4 and £5! Phineas Howell, who, since Lanyon's translation to higher spheres, was engineer, proposed a more scientific solution in the form of 'valves'—cost £150.

The early 1870s were quiet years. The loans were being steadily converted into debentures at 4 per cent; it was gratifying to the directors to report in August 1871 that

> the affairs of the company are progressing so favourably that the liabilities incurred in the first few years of the line are being gradually diminished and will soon be altogether cleared off.

The existing working agreement was due to expire on 1 November 1872. The B & NC pointed out that considerable charges would soon have to be incurred; much resleepering was necessary since the originals had been 'of bad quality from the first', this being 'necessary to make the line fit for running express trains' in connection with the boat. Pending negotiation of a new agreement the existing one was prolonged after 1 November. Finally the matter was resolved in January 1873 when the Northern Counties agreed to renew the old agreement (that of 1865) and to bear half the cost of renewals above £755 10s (£755.50) per annum.

A NEIGHBOUR AT LARNE

In September 1872 the Larne & Antrim Railway, then being proposed, asked for support. It was decided to lodge a petition against the L & A Bill; but then it was thought that, since the L & A proposed to run its rails alongside the C & L between Larne and the Harbour, this might turn out profitable to the C & L. The situation was complicated by the fact that James Chaine MP, owner of Larne Harbour, allowed the C & L to remain there only on sufferance and his name featured prominently in the new company. In June 1873 he completed the new steamer berth at the Harbour and proposed to build a new station and lay the necessary new lines from the C & L's boundary, charging no rent for four years. The C & L therefore decided to give favourable consideration to the request of the Larne & Ballyclare (as the L & A had now become, having altered its proposed gauge from 5ft 3in to 3ft) to gain access to the quays over its property. A temporary platform at least 15ft wide and 200ft long 'as far as possible of old sleepers' was to be constructed and £32 was spent on erecting lamps at the berth, these temporary measures to suffice until the plans of the narrow gauge line were matured.

Towards the end of 1875 a coolness arose with Chaine over Larne Harbour; it came partly from the fact that he had demolished the old C & L pier and replaced it as the steamer berth with his own, for which he now asked £100 per annum rent. As a result it was decided to demand £11,000 from the Ballymena & Larne—still another change of name—for wayleave along the C & L formation and in October 1876 arbitration brought the C & L £5,500 which was used to start a renewal fund. In January 1877 it was agreed to give the B & L use of the platform and cattle docks at Larne Harbour. There were hopes that the B & L would pay half the cost of erecting a more pretentious structure thereat as a joint station. The narrow gauge concern agreed in principle but found the plans too elaborate. Consequently in November 1877 the C & L decided to build 'a new platform with a covered shed 50ft long, Booking and Telegraph Offices to be built of wood'. Chaine was still asking for a permanent arrangement for the use of the quays and during the board meeting on 29 October 1877

> Mr Cotton reported receipt of a telegram from the station master at Larne Station—Mr Chaine was about to allow the rails of the Ballymena and Larne Railway to be laid through the platform of this Company at Larne Harbour. It was suggested that to prevent such repeated situations and the difficulties experienced in getting any satisfactory arrangement carried out at Larne Harbour, that Sir Edward Coey, Sir Charles Lanyon, and Mr Dixon be a committee to consider the feasibility of making a pier at Magheramorne for the steamboat and coal traffic . . .

Nothing came of this latter proposal, however, and the situation improved; in August 1878 the B & L was opened to passenger traffic (having carried goods for almost a year previously) and reasonably harmonious relations obtained for a time.

Towards the end of 1878 Collins, new civil engineer of the Northern Counties, was given instructions to prepare plans for a new terminus at Larne Harbour, 'of as cheap a character as possible consistent with efficiency and arranged for one set of offices only'. In March 1879, however, the B & L agreed to pay half the cost and alterations were made to the plan to accommodate that line. On September Joseph Maguire of Bangor was awarded the contract at £1,260. When work was well commenced the B & L demanded that the cost be reduced. In the meantime Cotton wanted 200ft added to the platform (which was not affected in the rebuilding); the mixed trains, with the wagons in front of the carriages, often had difficulty in unloading the passengers. The contract was cancelled and £160 spent on a 'low-priced temporary station'.

UPS AND DOWNS

The first half of 1873 was memorable: the receipts—no doubt as a result of the steamer service—were so much improved as to permit of the declaration of a first modest dividend on the half year of 1½ per cent. The following half-year brought a dividend of 2 per cent as did the first portion of 1874. From the beginning of 1874 a new working agreement came into force for five years—55 per cent of receipts were to go to the B & NCR which would bear all renewals and maintenance. The second half of 1874 brought 3 per cent; the dividend for the first part of the next year fell to 2 per cent but then rose in the second half to 3 per cent once more.

Storms caused great damage to the sea embankments; in January 1873 1,230 wagonloads of stone were required to fill large breaches in the Whitehead area. Howell thought 'these places will now give no further trouble'. More serious damage occurred in December 1876 between Kilroot and Whitehead. Some passenger trains had to be delayed to allow trains carrying stone filling to pass. There was a serious threat at Glynn where there had been 'movement of the entire side of the hill'.

On 1 December 1883 there was a serious incident at Whitehead when a portion of the tunnel caved in. The line was entirely closed for ten days; goods were sent via Ballymena and the B & L line and passengers walked round the obstruction to another train. The board considered laying a loop line outside the tunnel round the base of the cliffs, but this was found impracticable since Charles Lanyon and James Barton, asked for their opinion, were unable to obtain a curve of more than ten chains' radius. Hardly had this occurred than a very serious storm on 26 and 29 January 1884 washed away the ballast on the sea embankments at several places, damaged the pitching, and eroded much land at Whitehead where the line bordered the sea. Collins was by now engineer; he was given authority to reline the tunnel with 'materials of the best description'. The work inevitably reduced clearances and he later reported that these were only just in accordance with Board of Trade limits. The work here was not completed until August 1886 at a cost of £2,293.

The dividends during the remainder of the 1870s varied between 2 and 3½ per cent. In 1875 a goods shed was erected at Ballycarry and Glynn platform lengthened. There was now money to subsidise local events, for example £9 was paid to provide a band at Whitehead on Saturdays in July and August during 1877, the same figure being advanced by the B & NC. In 1879 four seats were provided at Whitehead (cost £8) and £5 was given to Whitehead Regatta.

The Board of Trade took unfavourable notice of the C & L on two occasions in 1878. Firstly, on 6 March the 5.45pm Larne—Belfast train, consisting of an engine and tender, two thirds, two composites and a van, was derailed in all engine and tender wheels and also one third and compo, at the points of Bank Quay siding outside Larne, which had been opened for coal traffic in 1870. There were no injuries and little damage was caused. Maj-Gen C. S. Hutchinson, investigating, found that the points had not been held properly closed by the pointsman and since the turnout lay on a left-hand curve there was a tendency for the wheels to 'hug' the right-hand rail. Interlocking was required; it cost £120.

Then in August Col Rich, inspecting the B & L, discovered that the level crossing used by both lines at the southern end of Larne Harbour station was unauthorised. Lanyon explained that until recently the road had carried little traffic since a new road had been built north of it; Chaine had a bridge under consideration, though it was not until 1887 that it was completed, the C & L paying one quarter of its cost of £1,400.

In January 1881 Collins drew attention to the present signalling arrangements saying that

> the high rate of speed at which the [boat] express passes through the points, all of which are facing, makes it desirable that a more efficient means be adopted.

At this time he recommended the fitting of facing point locks to all points. His suggestion was underlined on 9 October 1882 when the 12.45pm Carrickfergus—Belfast train was collided with in rear by the 11.40am boat express from Larne Harbour. At this time there was only one platform at Carrickfergus— the up, at which the 12.45 was standing; but there was a through loop. The facing points were not interlocked and were in charge of a pointsman.

The express was late and Driver Samuel Palmer, seeing the distant at clear and the home at danger (sic!), knew that he was to be routed through the loop. As he approached the points he saw they were lying for the platform road. He had already shut off steam in readiness to pick up the train ticket for Carrickfergus Junction and immediately braked; since the vacuum brake was in operation he was able to slow from 35 to about 10mph. The collision was slight but eight passengers complained of injury. The pointsman, George Seymour, debunked and had to be sought by the police. The fireman of the 12.45 with great presence of mind released the brakes of his train and put on steam when he saw the express, thus minimising the impact.

Maj-Gen Hutchinson dealt scathingly with the arrangements at Carrickfergus—on days when the boat express stopped to set down passengers in the loop line they had to dismount on to the ballast! 'It would not have occurred but for the want of modern arrangements.' The Gloucester Wagon Co charged £397 for the new material required to render Carrickfergus safe and the C & L paid £237 of this, the Northern Counties paying the remainder. The latter concern was keen to have a second platform erected but the C & L would not agree.

The old working agreement was prolonged until April 1879; then it was extended to the end of the year but at 52½ per cent of receipts in place of 55 per cent. In October two new proposals were tabled:

1. 22½ per cent of receipts, the Larne Co paying all renewals.
2. 60 per cent of receipts, to include all renewals, the C & L paying the difference in price of rails over £5 5s (£5.25) per ton and receiving credit for price of old rails where such exceeds £2 15s (£2.75) per ton. The C & L, under either proposal to be responsible for landslips, breaches in sea walls, and embankments, same as in all former agreements.

The C & L accepted proposal no 2, and it took effect from 1 January 1880 for an indefinite period. Already the C & L had followed the Northern Counties' lead by ordering in 1876 steel rails at £8 7s 6d (£8.37½) per ton from the West Cumberland Iron Co.

In November 1881 William Valentine, a director, raised yet again a scheme he had been proposing since 1866—'the necessity of doing something to open up Whitehead to excursionists and visitors'. He suggested making a path, a type of promenade, from Whitehead station to the headland known as Black Head.

The cost, estimated at £300, might be shared with the B & NC. Difficulties in obtaining the land prevented completion of the work until 1888; the directors reported that they

> have made arrangements by which excursionists to Whitehead will have a better outlet along the shore towards Blackhead, a walk having been laid out and seats put at several points, together with a large wooden house for picnic parties, or shelter in case of rain. It is hoped these improvements will tend still more to popularise the favourite watering place of Whitehead.

At this time relaying of the main line with steel rails was proceeding and by the end of 1882 half of the $14\frac{1}{2}$ miles was relaid. By 1887 $13\frac{3}{4}$ miles had been thus renewed. The timber bridges were being replaced in iron; that at Larne in 1883 and 1887, those at Magheramorne and Glynn having already been dealt with.

In August 1883 a complaint was received from the British Women's Temperance Association, about 'the exclusive attention given to those who ask for intoxicants' at the Whitehead refreshment room. They wanted tea, coffee and milk to be 'as cheap and easily available as a glass of ale'.

During the summer of 1886 boat trips were operated between Belfast and Larne on Sundays, Mondays and Thursdays by the Bangor steamers. Reduced fares were arranged so that those wishing to return by railway could do so. Alterations in the timetable meant that the up boat train left Larne Harbour at 9.55am instead of 11.5 and the down left Belfast at 4.15pm instead of 4pm; these changes took effect from 1 July. Irregularities having been detected at Whitehead refreshment room, it was ordered to be closed immediately after the passing of the last train of the day; that at Larne had been completely closed in November 1884.

In August 1887 Sir Charles Lanyon resigned from the board because of ill-health; he had been made a director in 1870. The older men were dropping away fast; James Chaine and Sir Edward Coey had gone. In April 1889 the old servant, Charles Stewart, the secretary, died and was succeeded by his son Cecil. An extra train was run during the summer of 1888 in connection with the additional steamer sailing for the Glasgow Exhibition. Whether or not the new paths at Whitehead were

K

responsible, the dividend rose in the second half of that year to an all-time high of 5 per cent—a fact which did not escape Northern Counties shareholders who had once got 7 per cent while C & L proprietors got nothing.

It is time to look again at the Larne—Stranraer steamer service. By January 1873 Cotton was recommending the purchase of a second steamer. At last the service was proving profitable. The B & NC thought the C & L should offer £3,500 but the Larne directors resolved to offer £1,500 'when the service required it'. During 1874 Cotton was making renewed efforts to obtain the mail contract for the route and in 1875 he was partially successful. In October of that year the Northern Counties reported that it had loaned £5,000 free of interest towards the new boat and the C & L offered a similar sum or one quarter of the cost, whichever was less. The new steamer, the *Princess Beatrice*, was launched by Harland & Wolff at Belfast on 7 November 1875; it was 235ft long and displaced 550 tons. The C & L's proportion of the cost, given as an interest-free loan, was £5,953. In 1883 *Beatrice* was given new compound engines and boilers, increasing horse-power to 325.

With her an improved service was made possible; the London departure was the latest of all Irish Sea services and the boat sailed at 9.55am next morning from Stranraer, reaching Belfast via Larne at 1.15pm Irish time. The evening boat train left Larne in the early evening and the travellers reached London early next morning. In 1875 Cotton stated that the other companies concerned were giving a rebate of 20 per cent on traffic originating from the steamer. The C & L agreed to do likewise for ten years. During 1876 through booking from the Midland Railway was instituted. In October 1877 the Stranraer & Girvan line opened, permitting much easier access to Glasgow, and increased traffic resulted. Between 1875 and 1888 the number of passengers using the service increased by 40 per cent while the mail contract increased from £500 to £1,200 per annum. Right at the end of the C & L's existence the *Princess Victoria* came into service; this will be dealt with in Chapter 8.

AMALGAMATION

On 12 February 1889 a committee of the directors met the

Northern Counties board. It was the latter who had raised the question of amalgamation. The C & L authorised their chairman, Macauley, to negotiate with Young of the B & NC. The Larne line's position was strong for now it was prosperous. In April the C & L decided that their terms should be 'stock for stock' and on 24 April Macauley was writing to Gill, new Northern Counties secretary:

> In compliance with the request . . . I now put in writing the verbal offer made by me to your Chairman on the 18th February last regarding the sale of . . . the undertaking of the Carrickfergus & Larne Railway Company. The terms I proposed were as follows: Your Company to get all our assets and on the other hand your Company will take over all our loans on call, and all other liabilities.

The year 1889 continued normally, with a dividend of $4\frac{1}{2}$ per cent. In July the B & NC asked for interlocking frames to be fitted at Whitehead, Magheramorne, Glynn, Ballycarry and Larne Harbour; for Larne platform to be lengthened, and for a second platform to be provided at Carrickfergus. Action was 'postponed' since a merger was imminent.

On 16 December 1889 a petition for amalgamation was signed and duly lodged; on 19 February 1890 a special meeting of shareholders approved of the sale 'stock for stock'. It can be assumed that the Northern Counties took control *de facto* on 1 January 1890; the transfer was legalised on 22 May 1890. The final dividend, for the first half of 1890, was 5 per cent.

So ended the independent existence of the Carrickfergus & Larne Railway. It had been built with one main end in view—the opening up of a short sea passage; when the first attempt failed the company fell on lean times. But no effort was spared to re-establish the service and in time prosperity came—towards the end it rivalled and at times even surpassed the Northern Counties in the percentage of its dividends. But its future clearly lay in the larger concern which had been its neighbour and its working agent.

THE NARROW GAUGE LINES

The three narrow gauge lines in County Antrim which

became part of the Northern Counties Railway are especially interesting. Two of them radiated from Ballymena, the other from Ballymoney. Both of the former owed their development to the exploitation of iron ore in the hills north of Ballymena.

It was in this region that the first narrow gauge railway in Ireland was built to what later became 'the second Irish standard gauge'—it was a small line which ran down Glenariff to the coast at Red Bay, conveying iron ore for shipment from the mines to England. It was unnecessary to seek Parliamentary sanction as the Earl of Antrim was agreeable to the rails being laid over his land. For a time the line, owned by the Glenariff Iron Ore & Harbour Co, worked profitably; it had been opened in 1873, but in 1876 it ceased operation, since the mines it served were no longer economically workable and thereafter it languished, its effects being auctioned in the mid-1880s.

THE CUSHENDALL LINE

Nearer Ballymena, however, iron ore was still plentiful and mining was already in progress. The nearest railway was at Ballymena, some fifteen miles distant. The road to the coast was difficult to negotiate with heavily laden carts; despite the construction of a wire tramway to the coast at Red Bay the most suitable solution was obviously the building of a railway. In 1871 the Ballymena, Cushendall & Red Bay Railway was planned and received its Act of Incorporation on 18 July 1872. By then a junction with the Glenariff line had been decided against nor was there ever any connection with the wire tramway, which was in due course dismantled.

The line was intended to commence at Ballymena and run northwards a distance of $22\frac{1}{4}$ miles to the pier at Red Bay, so that there were two possible outlets for ore. As it was not proposed to carry passengers construction was cheap and facilities of the simplest. This was the first narrow gauge line in Ireland to be *incorporated*. It also had the distinction of reaching the highest point of any Irish line—1,045ft at Essathohan siding. The capital was fixed at £90,000 in shares and £30,000 in loans. Of this the B & NC was permitted to contribute £25,000. But the intake of capital was disappointing and in consequence the first contract dealt only with the building of the $11\frac{1}{4}$ mile

Ballymena—Cargan section. Work proceeded steadily and after fifteen months it was nearly complete. It was partially opened on 26 March 1875 and fully opened on 1 July. By then construction of the other half of the line from Cargan was in hand.

There were numerous lengthy sidings reaching out into the valley from the main line to serve the ore mines. The ore was railed down to Ballymena for transport to Larne Harbour and shipment to England. In the early days before the Ballymena & Larne narrow gauge line was opened the route was via Carrickfergus Junction and the broad gauge. The Cushendall line owned its own broad gauge hopper wagons which ran over the B & NC, there being a trans-shipment gantry at Ballymena.

The line was never completed, either to Red Bay or Cushendall, for the good reason that impossible gradients would have been encountered. Instead it was terminated at Retreat, five miles beyond Cargan, a completely isolated place with no obvious reason for its existence save that it was only four or five miles from Cushendall. To reach Cushendall from Retreat would have involved a frightening descent (as it was there was a gradient of 1 in 37 between Parkmore and Retreat). The opening to Retreat took place on 8 October 1876.

At Ballymena the line ran to the B & NC's passenger station, where were the workshops and trans-shipment gantry. A small engine shed was provided for the company's three small engines. The BC & RB planned several extensions, one of them to serve the market place at Ballymena; but for various reasons none was ever built. In 1880, however, a link line with the Ballymena & Larne was constructed half a mile through Ballymena and crossing the River Maine, paralleling the B & NC.

The early results from the carriage of iron ore were encouraging, despite the cost of transport over a 'foreign' railway, the forty miles from Ballymena to Larne Harbour. In 1878 it paid five per cent and great things were expected of it; but this was the maximum dividend and thereafter things dropped off rapidly, despite management of the line by Cotton. The trouble was that the line had 'all its eggs in one basket'. Its staple was the iron ore; even ordinary goods traffic was insignificant in comparison, and passengers were not catered for. Being thus tied to ore, the Cushendall soon felt the effects of a depression in the hitherto booming ore trade which began early in the 1880s.

In an attempt to earn extra revenue it was decided to seek advice on the possibility of carrying passengers. But the line had not been conceived for such a purpose, and the Northern Counties, investigating, mentioned £9,000 as the sum necessary to put it into a condition fit for passenger working. Such a sum was beyond the means of the Cushendall. During 1882 the Northern Counties strengthened the management by appointing two directors, one of them Sir Charles Lanyon. But the position still declined; ore was simply not being mined, there was little other goods traffic and no passengers.

There was no immediate prospect of an improvement in the iron ore trade; tonnages continued to be insignificant compared with the vast quantities of earlier years. In February 1884 it was reported to the shareholders that 'the results of the working of the line over the past half year have not been satisfactory in consequence of the continued depression prevailing in the iron-ore trade'. The directors had no solution to offer save one; and at an extraordinary general meeting held afterwards the sale of the company to the Belfast & Northern Counties Railway was authorised, receiving Parliamentary approval on 14 July 1884, taking effect three months later. This Act gave the B & NC authority to take over the powers given to the Cushendall to build extensions in earlier days but the larger concern did not see its way to proceed with any of these and instead developed the original line for passenger working.

THE LARNE LINE

We have already seen the reason underlying the building of the Cushendall line and have surveyed the history of the Larne—Stranraer steamer service. Ballymena is only 25 miles from Larne as the crow flies but by railway it was some forty miles, via Carrickfergus Junction. In 1872 a scheme was proposed for a railway to link Larne and Antrim which would have shortened the journey for passengers from Londonderry to Larne considerably. But although the Bill was laid before

Parliament it was withdrawn before passing, for an altered scheme was now put forward. On 5 August 1873 the Larne & Ballyclare Railway was incorporated to be built on the 3ft gauge as against the 5ft 3in proposed for the L & A. Ballyclare was a small County Antrim town a few miles north of the B & NC main line.

Again the promoters changed their objective. While determined to proceed with the Ballyclare line, they decided to strike westwards seventeen miles from a place known as Ballyboley, to Ballymena, thus providing a very considerably shorter through route to Larne. So the company changed its name to the Ballymena & Larne, and as such was authorised on 7 August 1874, this Act repealing the earlier L & B Act. The principal promoter in all these schemes was James Chaine whom we have already met with.

Lack of capital prevented any work being done during 1875 but during 1876 construction had started. Work initially centred on the original Larne—Ballyclare section; this was intended to be completed by 1 March 1877 but the usual difficulties, not least of them the weather, prevented an opening on this date. On 30 July 1877 His Grace the Duke of Marlborough, Lord Lieutenant of Ireland, was conveyed over the line and it was opened for goods traffic on 1 September, though its works were still raw and incomplete.

Work was now proceeding on the Ballyboley—Ballymena section. The station buildings were not begun until almost everything else was complete. Nevertheless the Board of Trade inspector was summoned, and was unimpressed. 'Every station was inadequately furnished in some respect or other, and none of the buildings was finished'. There were unauthorised level crossings, a river bridge was unfinished. The company urged on the contractors and undertook to seek authority for the level crossings, and Col Rich gave his consent to the opening of the line to passengers. On 24 August 1878 the Ballymena —Ballyboley section was completely opened, and the Ballyclare—Larne portion, already in use by goods trains for nearly a year, to passengers. Unfortunately, though the line terminated at Ballymena, it was nearly half a mile from the B & NC station. Early attempts to bridge the gap failed, through the objections of the B & NC, which was perfectly content that the B & L should not be able to cream off boat traffic from the north-west.

In 1877 the B & L went before Parliament with a Bill for eight extension railways. Only three of these were authorised, on 8 August 1878. The most important was an extension of the Ballyclare branch to the little town of Doagh; a second a branch to Kilwaughter, a third a link line at Ballymena. It was this last-mentioned that was first constructed. From the B & L terminus at Harryville the line crossed a main road on a skew bridge and then shared a widened Northern Counties embankment (the broad gauge was then being doubled), going over the River Maine on an additional span on an existing bridge, to join the Cushendall line at a bay platform in the B & NC station. This link, known as the 'High Level Line', was opened on 22 September 1880 and thereafter trains worked through from Harryville—which however remained open a further decade. The opening of the link line meant that ore could now be conveyed direct from the mines without trans-shipment and passengers from Londonderry could transfer across the platform to the B & L train for the boat. Understandably, the new arrangements were not popular at York Road.

The Kilwaughter branch was stillborn but in 1883 work began on the Doagh extension, which was opened for goods on 8 February 1884, and, following strictures from the Board of Trade reminiscent of those of 1878, passenger working began on 1 May 1884. There was considerable potential for the B & L as a whole, an important aspect of the traffic being consignments from Larne to the paper mill at Ballyclare which had a special siding. This meant that the depression in ore which so affected the Cushendall was less felt on the B & L.

The B & L now planned divers other extensions, including one to Portglenone and Londonderry! There was also a scheme for a link with the Belfast Central Railway. These schemes were strenuously opposed by the Northern Counties and others, and while the BC proposal was authorised the Londonderry portion was not, fortunately for all concerned.

B & L results were disappointing. A hard winter in 1880–1 cut receipts from all sources and there were no through bookings to the steamer—as a result of B & NC influence. Ore traffic was poor. Even such as there was did not all go to the boat over the B & L; the B & NC and C & L still carried a fair amount. Indeed it now seemed that Antrim ore would never again enjoy the prosperity it once had, for cheaper and better quality Spanish ores were now freely available in England.

An economy campaign was instituted in an effort to stave off disaster. Staffing, from management downwards, was cut; third class passenger traffic increased a little in 1884-5. But it was still necessary to seek a solution and this the company tried to do by obtaining an Act on 16 July 1885, giving permission to abandon unbuilt branches and to raise a further £30,000 by preference and debenture shares. The economy drive went so far as the withdrawal of the special boat trains from Ballymena to Larne—passengers had to make do with the ordinary trains, rather a case, one feels, of the company defeating its own interests.

In October 1884 the Northern Counties took control of the Cushendall line. Shortly afterwards passenger working began up the valley. The B & L sought to exact a rent for allowing these trains to use the short portion of the link line in Ballymena station. The Northern Counties was incensed—paying rent for using its own property! They threatened to deny the B & L access to the station altogether, but sense prevailed, and no such action was taken.

The powers of the 1885 Act, when invoked, did improve the situation somewhat, but increased interest and the declining standard of the train service brought reduced receipts. In 1886 the Ballyclare Paper Mill requested a reduction in the rates of carriage of esparto grass. From 1886 onwards working expenses spiralled and falling receipts could not keep pace. Receipts in 1887 improved and in 1888 there was even a ¾ per cent dividend. There was, however, only one permanent solution—sale of the line. The Northern Counties was the only possible purchaser and in anticipation of a takeover negotiations had already been opened with the authorities at York Road. On 1 May 1889 the shareholders gave their consent to the amalgamation. The Northern Counties assumed the B & L's debts but the ordinary shareholders got cold comfort—£4 10s (£4.50) per £10 share was all they received. A representative of the B & L was to sit on the B & NC board. The takeover was duly sanctioned by Act of 16 July 1889.

So the Northern Counties extended its network by more than fifty miles between 1884 and 1889, by acquiring two narrow gauge lines. This was the first example in Ireland of a broad gauge company owning narrow gauge lines. Large expenditure was required on both to bring them up to a proper standard—for example, in 1889 B & L stock was fitted with the proscribed Smith non-automatic vacuum brake.

THE BALLYCASTLE RAILWAY

In Chapter 5 notice was taken of the abortive proposal for an extension of the B & NC to Ballycastle. It was ten years before the proposal was brought forward again—this time for a narrow gauge line, which half a century later would become part of the Northern Counties, its eleventh and final constituent.

The line was actively promoted from 1876 onwards; it was planned as a $16\frac{1}{4}$ mile railway running north-east from Ballymoney, to be built on the 3ft gauge already in use at Ballymena. There was no ore at Ballycastle beyond a little coal; this was primarily to be a passenger line, to develop the tourist potential of Ballycastle. Being on the narrow gauge there was no possibility of a normal junction with the B & NC at Ballycastle and there was dissension as to the siting of the terminus there. Finally it was agreed to have a joint station and goods yard. The Act of Incorporation was received on 22 July 1878. The capital was fixed at £90,000 in shares and £45,000 in loans, the B & NC being permitted to subscribe £18,000 and appoint two directors—John Young and Sir Charles Lanyon.

At this time the alternative proposal was again raised—a combination of tramway and light railway, linking Portrush to Bushmills and the Giant's Causeway, with a branch from Bushmills to Dervock on the BR. Later a connecting line to the Cushendall at Rathkenny was planned. Only the Portrush—Giant's Causeway section was built; this was the famous Giant's Causeway, Portrush & Bush Valley Electric Railway & Tramway, the first hydro-electric railway in the world.

Meanwhile the BR began construction in December 1878. The work was at first carried out by Connor who had built the

THE COUNTY ANTRIM BRANCHES 163

BC & RB but as he died after a short time Butler & Fry of Ballymena took over. It had been hoped to have the line in operation for the summer traffic of 1880 but several factors militated against this. Bridges gave trouble, weather hindered progress. The track was extremely light and this early parsimony was something the BR was later to regret bitterly. Sleepers also were poor and in general way and works were constructed as cheaply as possible. By the early summer of 1880 the line was ready for inspection but Col Rich of the Board of Trade overlooked none of its defects and it was 18 October before he would allow it to be opened. A sumptuous banquet was held in Ballycastle in celebration of the auspicious occasion.

A modest service of three trains a day each way sufficed. Public transport in the area was then virtually non-existent and the railway fulfilled a considerable need both in goods and passenger traffic. To facilitate tourists a coach was run between Ballycastle and the Giant's Causeway from 1881 until 1905. The little town of Ballycastle was developing rapidly; good hotels were established and a golf course opened.

But all was not well with the railway. By 1885 little reward had been obtained from the capital invested, and the directors turned on the manager, Silas Evans, who had also connections with the Cushendall line. After some dispute he was forced to resign and, by arrangement with the B & NC, Edward John Cotton took control. He soon made his presence felt in improved mail contracts and savings in the purchase of stores. In 1898 the BR suddenly realised that they had paid him nothing for thirteen years' hard work and voted him £500! Already the permanent way was giving trouble; sleepers were rotting away and the sharp curves at several points 'crept'. Repairs and renewals to the track were a continual and worrying expenditure. The closer links with the Northern Counties forged by Cotton benefited the little railway considerably. As with the larger concern third class traffic was of the utmost importance, and indeed it was not until 1885 that second class carriages were provided (the B & L never had them).

The financial difficulties stemmed from the fact that of the £90,000 of ordinary stock, only £61,000 was ever taken up and recourse was had to loans. Even before opening the Irish Board of Works had loaned £20,000. Even then there was still an overdraft and there were debts to the contractors and engine-builders. The rolling stock had to be bought by a type of hire purchase. In 1884 the BR approached the B & NC for a loan of £12,000 or failing that, to work the line; both proposals were declined. Shortly afterwards Cotton assumed control with benefit to all; creditors were forestalled and matters improved generally. It was not until 1898, however, that a 1 per cent dividend could be paid on the ordinary shares. Improvements at Ballycastle and the purchase of new rolling stock ruled out further dividends until 1906; in that year, 1 per cent was paid and in 1907 2 per cent but then two new engines were obtained and an overdraft became necessary, the dividend disappearing forever.

The death of Cotton in 1899 was a severe blow to the railway; but now Hamilton McAllen, who had been his deputy, took control. Under him the railway functioned reasonably satisfactorily, however unprofitably, until the first world war. This was a severe strain; wages and costs rose while fares were 'frozen' by law. The Northern Counties Committee, as the B & NC had by then become, assisted financially but the BR never recovered. The compensation of some £8,000 paid at the end of the war in 1921 had to go against working losses. The 1922 Railway Commission noted the plight of the BR and recommended its absorption by the NCC. By the end of 1923 the position was untenable with a loss of £3,000 on the year's working and a debit balance in the shares of £4,271. On 21 January 1924 the board resolved to close the line and on 8 February the shareholders consented. On 24 March the line closed.

The new Northern Ireland government were approached, but were not prepared to assist, having more weighty matters to resolve. It remained to the BR to sell the line as scrap or as a going concern. There being no Col Stephens in Ireland the only possible purchaser was the neighbouring concern at Ballymoney, now under the control of the London Midland & Scottish. On 19 March 1924 a deputation of BR directors met Frank Tatlow, a member of the NCC, who gave the NCC's offer of £10,000. This must have been a great disappointment to the men from Ballycastle, for their little line had cost nearly £104,000. They 'asked for more' but Tatlow pointed out the defects in the railway (including the lack of automatic brakes on the rolling stock—by some means or other the BR had always staved off Board of Trade insistence). These would necessitate the NCC spending some £30,000 over three or four years to bring it up to a proper standard.

The debenture holders entered into separate negotiations to try to obtain more from the LMS NCC. There was nearly £30,000 of debenture stock; if only £10,000 were obtained, holders would receive but a third of the value of their holding, ordinary shareholders nothing. Discussions ensued between York Road and Euston (since the NCC officially had no capital of its own) and the LMS authorised the offer to be raised to £12,500. On 4 May 1924 the sale of the BR to the LMS was authorised by the shareholders. No trains ran through the busy summer period of 1924, and the district reverted to the primitive transport of pre-1880 days. On 11 August 1924 the NCC re-opened the line, having re-equipped it, though not until 7 August 1925, by an Act of the new Northern Ireland Parliament, were they officially authorised 'to enter into possession of the line and work it'.

So ended the independent career of the Ballycastle Railway, the last of the three County Antrim narrow gauge lines to come under the control of the Northern Counties. It was another example of the type of railway so often found in Ireland—cheaply built and with a meagre traffic; overcapitalised and never fully subscribed; without any resources to tide it over lean periods. But for the constant support of the neighbour at Ballymoney it would have succumbed far sooner than it did. An earlier acquisition (it had been rumoured as far back as 1886) would have benefited both BR and B & NC considerably, not to speak of the town of Ballycastle.

CHAPTER SEVEN

The County Londonderry Branches

There were four constituent companies of 'the second generation' in County Londonderry, all of which were remarkably contemporaneous, being opened within a three-year period. Each within a period of twelve years became incorporated in the Northern Counties' undertaking. The three broad gauge lines had a common factor—they were all 'sold up' by the Commissioners of Public Works in Ireland, to which body they had turned in desperation when capital failed to materialise. The fourth line was a short narrow gauge tramway and it too was possessed of a most unhappy history.

THE DERRY CENTRAL RAILWAY

PROMOTION

The oldest and most important of the County Londonderry branches is especially interesting in that it was in part a renewal of the Londonderry & Coleraine's abortive scheme for an extension from Coleraine to Castledawson in 1853. The line, proposed in the mid-1870s, was to run through the valley of the River Bann from Coleraine to Magherafelt, entirely in County Londonderry save for a half-mile portion near Macfin which was in County Antrim. The line would link the B & NC at Magherafelt to the main line at Macfin, a distance of $29\frac{1}{4}$ miles. This 'Derry Central Railway' was promoted by prominent County Londonderry landowners, principally the Rt Hon Sir Henry Hervey Bruce Bt of Downhill and his brother Col H. S. B. Bruce of Ballyscullion.

The Act of Incorporation was passed on 11 August 1875. Running powers were granted over the Northern Counties

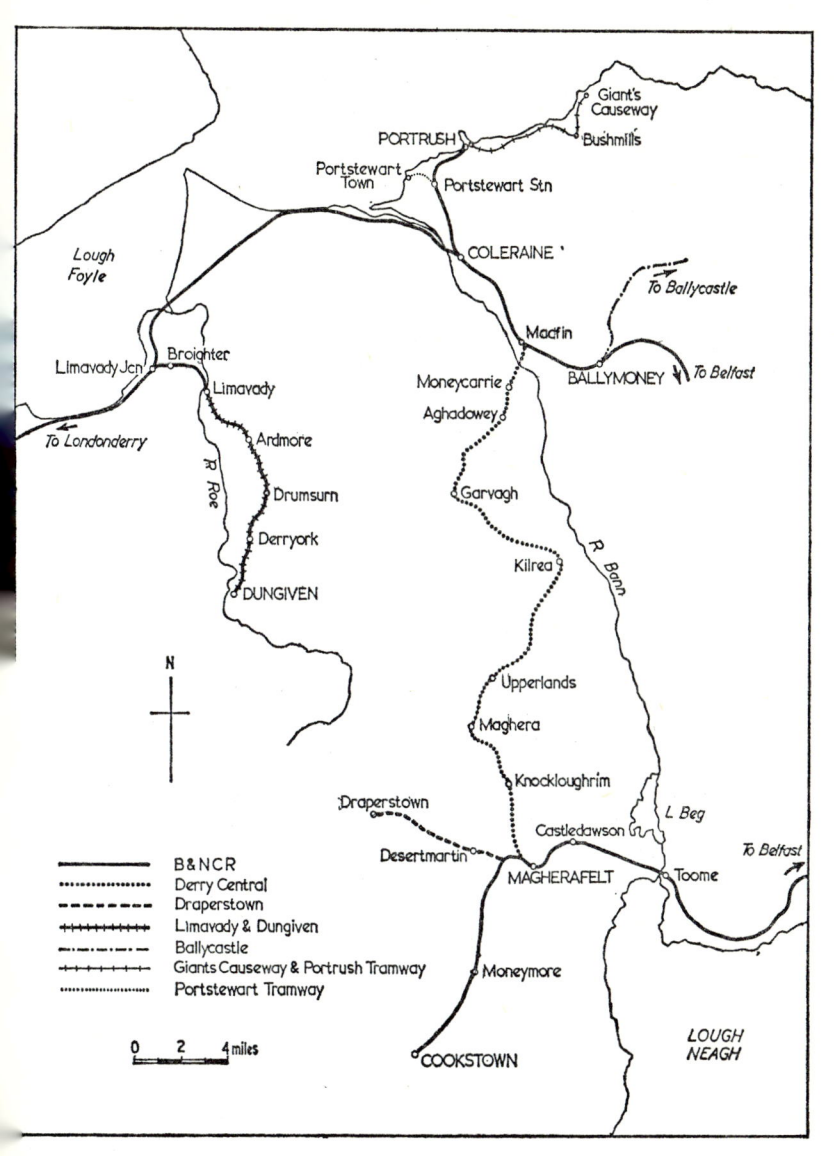

The County Londonderry branches

between the junction near Magherafelt and that station, and between Macfin and Coleraine. Both junctions were to be under the control of the B & NC with whom the DC was given authority to conclude a working agreement. The capital laid down was £220,000 composed of three categories: A—Preference—£85,000; B—County guaranteed—£45,000; C—Ordinary—£90,000. The guarantee on the County shares was to last 23 years and was at 5 per cent. Additional powers for borrowing up to £100,000 were included. Five years were given for the completion of the railway.

Great things were expected of the new line. It tapped a very prosperous district of mid-Londonderry—rich agricultural land with small but thriving market towns and some linen mills. The board met for the first time in Coleraine on 6 September 1875. Sir Hervey Bruce was elected chairman and Glover, a Magherafelt solicitor, was appointed secretary *pro tem*. It was reported that the Marine Insurance Co had advanced £11,155 —5 per cent of the £222,881 estimated to be required for construction. These stocks had been transferred to the names of J. J. Clarke, the deputy chairman, and Daniel Taylor MP. Glover was instructed to approach the B & NC immediately with reference to a working agreement.

By the end of September the DC had appointed James Barton CE of Dundalk as their provisional engineer. Advertisements for a permanent secretary brought 32 replies and after much discussion James Blair Stirling of Ballymoney, described as a 'barony constable', was appointed at a salary of £150 per annum. He was allowed an additional £25 to provide an office in Coleraine and this he did, in the Manor House. His salary was increased to £250 in 1877. Shortly afterwards Barton's appointment was made permanent. He had stipulated his fees at £200 per mile, consenting to take a portion in shares at par.

DIFFICULTIES

The intake of capital was proving disappointingly slow. It was decided to ask local landlords to take shares in payment for their land or to give it free. Local bank managers were to be asked to sell shares and meetings were held in the several

Page 169

YORK ROAD

ve) The station as it appeared after final alterations in 1898. Station hotel to right
(*below*) Layout of station approaches from signal cabin, *c* 1898

Page 170
THE DERRY CENTRAL LINE

(*above*) Coleraine new station, opened 1882 (*below*) Magherafelt—Coleraine train at Magh
c 1900

towns along the route. A request to the Mercers' and Ironmongers' Companies to guarantee £35,000 of stock was disappointing; the Ironmongers offered to underwrite only £5,000!

Attention was now focused on the working agreement. In October Lanyon recommended that the B & NC should exclude the interest on the £25,000 spent on new works, rates and taxes at Magherafelt, if the DC would hand over 75 per cent of its receipts; if these did not amount to £125,000 after ten years' working the arrangement was to continue until that figure was reached.

This the DC rejected, putting forward two alternative proposals of its own; one of which, that set forth by Clarke the vice-chairman, was the basis for the agreement finally jointly signed on 9 October 1876:

> That the working agreement shall continue for 21 years [from the opening of the DC]. The Belfast Company getting 70 per cent according to Mr Clarke's proposal as follows:
> Seventy per cent upon an average of £12,500 to continue at 70 per cent until receipts have reached £13,000.
>
> | | | | |
> |---|---|---|---|
> | 67½ pc up to £14,000 | | 57½ pc up to £18,000 | |
> | 65 | 15,000 | 55 | 19,500 |
> | 62½ | 16,000 | 52½ | 21,000 |
> | 60 | 17,000 | 50 above | 21,000 |
>
> This percentage includes all payments to be made by the Derry Central Company to the Belfast Company for doubling, maintaining and using (single or double) the Line between Macfin and Coleraine and for the use of the Passenger and Goods Stations at Coleraine and Magherafelt and for any alterations in Coleraine station.

This was slightly amended later to include the provision that after ten years the DC was to pay renewal costs of the permanent way, the work to be carried out by the Northern Counties—'the rails should be of iron, and not less than 70lbs per yard'. Signal maintenance was to be included in this charge.

The shareholders gave their approval to the agreement on 10 November 1876 and also to a draft Bill which was to enable the B & NC to subscribe £10,000 in ordinary shares and expend £25,000 on new works required for the accommodation of the

DC. This Bill, passed on 23 July 1877, also ratified the working agreement and provided that all staff, save the secretary and the employees in his office, should be appointed by the Northern Counties. A joint traffic committee, two directors of each company, was to be set up.

The principal engineering feature was a bridge over the Bann about one mile south of Macfin, 165ft long with a swing span to accommodate the sand barges coming downriver to Coleraine. There were 45 other bridges, all save four of which were of masonry and iron. On 5 June 1877 a contract was signed with C. M. Holland of Liverpool whose tender of £84,109 was the lowest of ten received. He was agreeable to take 1,500 shares. But he withdrew his tender in August and shortly afterwards a new contract with him was concluded at £100,000 of which £32,000 was to be in shares. The time limit was two years from 1 September 1877. Work began almost at once.

> It was resolved to cut the first sod of the Railway at Macfin on Thursday the 30th August and the Secretary was directed to issue cards of invitation to the Chairman and Directors of the Northern Counties Railway Company and several others who were named by the Chairman.

Afterwards a banquet was held in the Clothworkers' Arms Hotel, Coleraine.

A joint committee with the Northern Counties was negotiating the purchase of additional lands required at Coleraine and Magherafelt and the alterations needed there. The new station which the B & NC planned for Coleraine did not meet with the approval of the Coleraine Town Commissioners who wanted the site changed but their opposition was unsuccessful. This new station, the need for which had long been recognised, was built on the site of the Ballymena & Portrush's 1855 building and included a special bay platform for DC trains as well as providing greatly increased and improved accommodation. Meanwhile Holland was complaining of difficulty in obtaining possession of the land. In January 1878 the approach to Macfin had to be bought at an exorbitant price as the land was urgently required and there was no time to quibble with the owner. With the additional work the secretary's salary was increased in February 1878 to £300 per annum. Shortly afterwards the rail contract was divided between the Ebbw Vale and Cumberland Steel Cos, delivery to be at Belfast and Portrush. Sleepers were to come from T. G. Seed of Sunderland.

Money was still in short supply. In September 1878 the directors gave their personal security to the Ulster Bank for an overdraft of £15,000. Already it had been decided to approach the Board of Works for a loan—initially £75,000, later raised to £100,000. A petition soliciting this was sent to the Treasury, pointing out that the baronies through which the line passed had guaranteed 5 per cent interest for 23 years on £45,000 payable from the county rates. A finance sub-committee was appointed to keep watch on that aspect.

WORK PROGRESSES

The county surveyor was alarmed at the gradients of the approaches to certain of the overbridges and alterations had to be made. In February 1879 a bridge at Curran collapsed, killing two men; the board regretted that it had not the funds to compensate the relatives. In January 1879 Barton reported that

> The foundations [of the Bann Bridge] have all been got in on the East side of the river and the masonry and swivel pier and the cylinder are above flood level—those of the West side have been begun.

Of the track $20\frac{1}{2}$ miles were levelled for ballasting, and $1\frac{1}{2}$ miles of permanent way had been laid near Kilrea. By July $14\frac{1}{2}$ miles were completed, and Holland had three of his own engines working on the line.

In March 1879 Barton submitted plans of station buildings at Knockloughrim, Maghera, Upperlands, Kilrea, Garvagh, Aghadowey and Macfin. The original intention to build a station at Tirgarvil, between Maghera and Kilrea, had been dropped. These designs, said Barton, 'were as economical as was consistent with durability and convenience'. In July a contract was signed with Dixon & Co for the buildings. In April 1879 the Northern Counties asked when the line was likely to be opened as they wished to plan rolling stock requirements. They were told 1 September was the contract date. In June of that year joint opposition was offered with the B & NC to the Ballymena & Larne's proposed Ballymena—Portglenone narrow gauge line.

Meanwhile the first instalment of the Board of Works' loan —£70,000—was received, and this allowed the contractor and the railmakers to be paid. The Northern Counties estimated the cost of alterations at Magherafelt at £5,000. The DC instructed Barton to prepare a revised plan to cost £1,000. In August the signalling contract was given to McKenzie & Holland for £1,380; advice was sought from the Board of Trade regarding the telegraph instruments and when a reply was received stating that while separate block and speaking instruments were desirable, the Board had no power to insist upon such, the DC decided that speaking instruments could serve both for blocking and communication. Cotton, however, declined to undertake the management unless both types were installed.

The contract date of 1 September 1879 came and the line was not complete. It was now hoped to be ready for 1 January 1880. But Col F. H. Rich, inspecting the line at the end of December, found plenty to complain of; notably the lack of safety precautions at the swing bridge at Macfin where he required a man to be permanently employed until more adequate signalling was erected. Opening had therefore to be deferred until his requirements had been complied with and on 9 February Rich again arrived to inspect. Almost everything he had condemned had been rectified; only a 'lodge' at a level crossing near Magherafelt, improvements to bridge approaches, and some fencing at Maghera and Macfin, were still outstanding. Since these matters were in hand he authorised opening for passenger traffic.

Between his two visits the DC had its first accident ('jointly' with the B & NC). On 20 January the 6.5pm passenger train ex Coleraine for Belfast, on the main line, was partially derailed at the up facing points at Macfin. A special train had reached Macfin from Magherafelt at 5.25pm. The signalling was not complete and the newly laid loop was not yet in use for crossing trains. It was however used to enable the engine of the special to attach two carriages of its train to the 3.30pm ex Belfast. The pointsman forgot to set the points for the main line after this movement and the 6.5 met them in the halfway position, they having been run through by the 3.30. The signals were not yet in operation and so the 6.5 driver had no indication of the position of the points. Maj-Gen C. S. Hutchinson placed the blame on the pointsman's shoulders; fortunately there were no injuries.

THE LINE OPENED

On 18 February 1880 a special train carried the directors and guests over the line and afterwards a banquet was held in Coleraine. The next day, a Thursday, the line was opened to public traffic with three trains each way daily and one on Sundays. Market tickets were issued between Coleraine and Garvagh, Kilrea, Maghera and Magherafelt. One of the first visible results of operation was an application in early March from the mail car operators to the Post Office for an increase in rates, because of the diminution of their traffic caused by the opening of the railway. The DC asked Cotton to request the Post Office to negotiate a mail contract with them and to run its telegraph poles along the railway instead of the county road.

Arguments early arose with the working company that the train service was unsatisfactory. It did little to assuage the critics when Cotton pointed out that the timetable was the work of the joint traffic committee. He undertook to arrange that tickets from DC stations to Belfast would be available for return either via Magherafelt or Coleraine. In March 1880 Cotton suggested an economy—instead of erecting signals and employing a permanent bridgeman the Bann Bridge could be locked by the Macfin—Garvagh train staff. Shortly afterwards it was found that the depth of water underneath the bridge's opening span was insufficient and dredging had to be carried out.

The receipts from the first $4\frac{1}{2}$ months of operation were £1,544 from passengers and £1,260 from goods and cattle. Of this, £2,785 went to the Northern Counties, being the 70 per cent agreed for working. There was a balance of £835 which went towards the Board of Works interest—it had already been decided to seek the balance of £30,000 of the loan. No dividend was declared—nor was the DC ever to pay one. The shareholders were told that 'it is too soon to judge of the traffic of your line, but the Directors are giving careful attention to its development'.

It was at the shareholders' meeting of August 1880 that the vexed question of the 'fourth train'—an additional daily train —was first raised. Another matter raised for the first time was the reduction of the secretary's salary, it being considered by some that with the line opened his duties were 'less onerous'. Taylor, one of the directors, wished to have it reduced to £150. When the board declined his motion he resigned and refused to reconsider his action, despite a pathetic reference by his fellow directors to 'a small difference of opinion'. The shareholders were in favour of the reduction of rates and fares, to which the board would not consent.

The second period of working to the end of 1880 brought receipts totalling £3,881. Of this the DC received £1,052 but from it had to come the secretary's salary and the interest to the Board of Works. By early 1881 a further £25,000 had been received from that Board and was quickly expended; the remaining £5,000 was sought. To try to improve the position Henry Dale was appointed traffic clerk at a salary of £100 in October 1881. At the same time Cotton wrote

> that unless he heard to the contrary he would discontinue [Sunday] trains as they appeared to be doing no business.

The board agreed, if Cotton assumed responsibility for the mails carried on Sundays. At this time Ilbery of the Great Southern & Western Railway was appointed to arbitrate on the costs of running a fourth train daily. The company was much riven on this subject; some thought it absolutely necessary if traffic were to be developed, others believed it superfluous if the existing timetable were recast. The working of the Bann Bridge gave rise to a claim in May for £2.50 from the owners of the Coleraine steam tug *Eagle* which, on one of its pleasure trips upriver, had been delayed awaiting the opening of the bridge. This was to be a recurrent theme in DC history.

UNPROFITABLE YEARS

The year 1881 brought total receipts of £7,743, still insufficient to pay Board of Works interest in full. In January 1882 the Board threatened proceedings unless the arrears were paid within one week but they were staved off for the time being.

Poor Stirling! He had the unenviable position of listening mutely while the question of his salary was hotly discussed yet again at a half-yearly meeting. In April 1882 he told the board

> that in consideration of the unpleasant observations that had been made at the last half yearly meeting (among others) regarding his salary, he was willing, for peace sake, and so far as possible on his part to remove any cause for complaint among the shareholders, and for the sake of economy until the affairs of the Company improved, to submit to a reduction of his salary according to the decision of the Board—from £50 to £100.

Only one director wished the cut to be £100; it was finally made £50.

In April 1882 Holland joined the board. The chairman and deputy-chairman both offered to resign to make way for him but in the event it was Col Bruce who went, giving as his reason his inability to agree with the others on the train service, he being one of the 'three trains daily' school. The DC had by then decided a fourth train was desirable; the Northern Counties stated 4p per mile in addition to the 70 per cent for the existing three trains. Holland guaranteed this for June and July 1882. The Sunday trains, run again in the summer of 1882, were withdrawn from 1 November.

At the end of 1882 the rent to be paid by the B & NC to the DC for use of land at Coleraine was finally settled. In 1882-3 goods sheds were erected at Garvagh, Kilrea and Macfin. The receipts for 1882 were £9,434 and for 1883, £10,118. In July 1883 the Board of Works requested payment of £13,159, arrears of interest and principal. Of course there was no money available to pay this. All the company could do was to assure the Board that 'they are progressing to tide over their difficulties'. The receipts for 1884 showed a decrease, to £9,826.

The only bright spot of that year was Cotton's admission that the B & NC had made an error in measuring the line and the revised measurement was to the DC's advantage. Also in 1884 Clarke the vice-chairman died and Col Bruce was inveigled into rejoining the board in that capacity.

The year 1885 brought a further decrease in the receipts, to £9,432. At the August meeting a shareholder proposed the dismissal of the board but his motion was not seconded. Towards the end of the year allegations were made that the Northern Counties was not properly maintaining the line and it was arranged that Barton should inspect the line before preparation of each half-yearly report. The Board of Works, whose interest in the DC's affairs was naturally very keen, found fault with the manner in which the accounts were presented and this had to be altered. Nor did 1886 bring any improvement—worse, in fact, the receipts dropped to £9,367. It was in this year that the directors lost, by his resignation, the counsel of Sir Charles Lanyon, his place as B & NC representative was taken by John B. Gunning-Moore of Cookstown. The Hopkirk fraud (Chapter 8) occurred at this time; it does not appear, however, that Hopkirk made off with any of the DC's limited finances.

The year 1887 brought constant attempts at economy. In April the insurance on the buildings was reduced from £9,100 to £6,666. When the Garvagh stationmaster requested the redecoration of some of his house he was told 'it was the duty of the Northern Counties Company to keep the stations in proper order'. In July a memorial was received from the residents of Moneycarrie, about 1½ miles south of Macfin, for a halt; a 60ft platform was opened the next year at a cost of £10. In August the appointment of a traffic canvasser was proposed; the expense was felt to be unjustified and the duty devolved upon the secretary, who was told to 'traverse the line' periodically. The 1887 receipts showed a slight improvement, to £9,867.

The fourth train cropped up again in 1888. Cotton agreed to run it on Fridays and Saturdays at no extra cost, provided there were no Sunday trains for eight months of the year. Holland proposed the abolition of second class instead of the fourth train being run. To this Cotton, a firm believer in the three-class system, did not agree; but he did consent to delay the 3.30pm down train to 5pm so as to give better connections from Belfast via Magherafelt. Finally in January 1889 the fourth train was provided, when the B & NC agreed to run it under the existing working agreement. The 1888 receipts were again low, £9,469, the directors bitterly noting that theirs was the only line in Ireland to exhibit a decrease. They managed to persuade Taylor to rejoin the board so they achieved something.

THE SECOND DECADE

It was hardly in a position of strength that the Derry Central entered its second decade. In January 1889 it was decided to reduce first class fares from 2d to $1\frac{3}{4}$d per mile, second class from $1\frac{1}{2}$d to $1\frac{1}{4}$d, and third from 1d to $\frac{3}{4}$d. The new Regulation of Railways Act was a trouble. Cotton reported that since all DC trains were mixed they were contravening the new statute. A special goods train would be required, involving the cancelling of one of the passenger trains. But at least the stock working the line, being Northern Counties owned, had the automatic vacuum brake. At the end of the year requests for stations at Hervey Hill and Milltown were rejected and the overall receipts showed an increase to £10,186.

The new Board of Trade regulations again distressed the directors. They could see no reason why, since they only ran one train faster than 25mph, the others should not be mixed. The receipts of 1890 were £10,503, a slight increase. But in February 1891 the Board of Works pointed out that the arrears of their interest now amounted to £19,546, and Sir Hervey Bruce wrote to Balfour, Chief Secretary for Ireland, for 'aid' in reducing the burden of debt. The DC wished to have the rate of interest reduced from 4 to 3 per cent; the reduction of the sum from £4,000 to £3,000 per annum would have been welcame. But they were unsuccessful.

A further improvement was manifest in 1891 with receipts of £10,730. This was followed by complaints that the Northern Counties was claiming its proportion of excursion tickets to Portrush, Portstewart and Castlerock on tickets *issued* instead of those *collected*. There was also an acrimonious dispute over goods rates during 1892. And as from 1 July 1892 Cotton proposed running a fifth train for goods only. The Northern Counties claimed 5p per mile but then agreed to run it free, after charging that sum during July and August.

On behalf of the DC Cotton went to London and interviewed Maj-Gen C. S. Hutchinson of the Board of Trade to seek a relaxation of the regulations. He was unsuccessful; he reported that Hutchinson was 'very stiff'. On 21 November 1892 Cotton, Wise, Malcolm and Getty, respectively manager, civil engineer, locomotive engineer and traffic superintendent of the B & NC, went over the DC with Stirling, secretary of the DC, surveying improvements required to comply with the new regulations for mixed trains. Wise reported that the present layouts 'were so inconvenient that the working of mixed trains would be attended with great difficulty'. He quoted £1,250 as the sum required to improve matters; this the DC thought 'not justified'. They proposed to revert to the old system of three trains for passengers, the fourth being a goods. Doubtless the fall in receipts in 1892, to £10,222, influenced their decision. They also, in September 1892, rejected a proposal for a station at Killygullib, outside Kilrea.

Towards the end of 1893 a further dispute arose with the B & NC, who had just renewed the timbers of the Bann Bridge with pitch pine, which could not be creosoted and was too expensive for the DC's liking. But 1893 was the best year yet, with receipts of £10,786, though, in the chairman's words, a dividend had to be 'postponed'. This statement was 'greeted with laughter'. An accident at Garvagh on 30 March 1893 shed interesting light on the methods of working. The 8.45am Coleraine—Magherafelt mixed arrived at Garvagh at 9.44 and as the wagons were being backed into the down loop siding they were hit by the 8.55am Magherafelt—Coleraine passenger train, which had failed to stop at the home signal at danger. The driver claimed that he had not seen the home signal owing to its being obscured by steam, but this Maj-Gen Hutchinson declined to accept. On the other hand the driver of the mixed deserved great credit as he had speeded up the reversal of his train when he saw the impending collision. Hutchinson also discovered that the block system was not being properly worked; it was only used to prevent two trains following one another through the section and no advice was sent of departures, only of arrivals. Further the hours of Doyle, driver of the mixed, were overlong—$14\frac{1}{2}$ on four days a week.

The succeeding year of 1894 opened with the DC deciding to petition in favour of the Midland Great Western Railway's proposed line from Kingscourt to Cookstown; 'this project if carried out must be of great advantage to this Line'. The scheme perished on the rock of Great Northern opposition. In April additional sidings were authorised at Upperlands station to serve the great linen mills of Messrs Clark; the Northern Counties paid. There were complaints in 1894 that proper maintenance was not being carried out; Barton, in his report, stated that 'the materials supplied had not in his opinion been used as few old ones were to be seen along the line'. In November, Cotton's scheme to reduce first and second class fares to encourage travel in the high classes was agreed; it was introduced the next year, concomitantly with the B & NC. Good receipts were noted in 1894—£11,150.

In July 1895 the long-suffering secretary James Stirling died. An advertisement for a replacement, quoting a salary of £250, brought an enquiring letter from the Board of Works—what were the duties of the post? They stipulated that no more than £150 be paid. From a list of eighteen applicants Frederick Dawson was appointed. Unlike Stirling he was a trained railwayman, being secretary and manager of the Lough Swilly Railway from 1883 to 1901, which position he retained. He was to go over the line at least twice monthly 'and report to the Directors whether the interests of the Line and the public are properly attended to'—in other words he was to spy on the working company. He was not to have the services of a traffic clerk. In 1895 also the original offices at the Manor House, Coleraine, were vacated in favour of cheaper accommodation at Waterside in Coleraine. The safe was too heavy to be brought upstairs and was exchanged with the Londonderry & Lough Swilly Railway, they paying £5 as the difference in value! The 1895 receipts were up, to £11,673.

The next year brought a decrease to £11,394. At the February meeting Sir Hervey Bruce, vacating the chair as was customary for the certification of accounts, said, with tragic irony,

You are perfectly welcome to move me out of it permanently! I have been fighting these matters for a long time and I feel that I am getting too old for it!

He remained chairman, however. During 1896 the company removed its bank account from the Ulster Bank in Maghera, having been refused an increase in interest on its deposits. The secretary was told to ascertain 'where we can bank most advantageously in Coleraine'. They also withdrew from the Irish Railway Clearing House.

THE END IN SIGHT

In October 1896 Holland proposed that the company should purchase rolling stock and work the line themselves. In November the Derry Central directors decided to offer the line to the Northern Counties for £87,000; £65,000 to pay off the Board of Works, the rest to the shareholders. Gunning Moore, as a member of the B & NC board, said that board might not agree to buy 'but Mr Cotton would recommend it'. The DC board then hedged; they would only agree if the Board of Works *insisted* on selling. It was decided to approach the Great Northern Railway (Ireland) to see if they would take over the working—which would have made for a very interesting situation, for GN trains stopped at Cookstown. In August 1897 Holland was asked if he could find £30,000 for rolling stock in addition to the amount needed to purchase the loan. Meanwhile Cotton agreed to operate a new timetable if one could be agreed.

The receipts for 1897 were the second highest in the DC's history—£11,855. During that year Moneycarrie Halt was closed because of the delays it caused to trains on market days. In October 1898 Holland suggested seeking £60,000 from the Irish banks to buy out the loan; but the 1898 receipts were down to £11,703 and this idea was not pursued.

In January 1899 it was agreed to extend the facilities for Clark's traffic at Upperlands. The secretary was given authority to 'subsidise a car between Magherafelt and Cookstown on market days at Cookstown, if necessary'—this despite the fact that the B & NC ran an excellent train service! The DC's negotiations with the Board of Works infuriated the Northern Counties. The secretary was instructed to modify the wording of the charges made against the working company, which had threatened to stop working DC trains unless this were done. There was a feeling that the government and the Northern Counties were in collusion against the DC: at the shareholders' meeting on 28 February 1899 the following dialogue took place:

> *First shareholder* If we had gone in for the Home Rule Bill we would have got more consideration.
> *Second shareholder* Yes, the government does not do much for its friends!

They noted bitterly that the Ballycastle Railway had been allowed a reduced rate of interest on its Board of Works loan. In July 1899 they gave up the idea of independent working. Col Clark moved

> That in the absence of any assurance that the preference shareholders will consent to a reduction in their interest, this Board is of opinion that no further steps should be taken towards working the Line as an independent concern.

This was passed, the chairman 'strongly protesting'.

Matters were now rapidly moving towards their conclusion. On 7 July 1899 the DC directors met the Board of Works and the B & NC directors in Dublin. Afterwards the DC board recommended their shareholders to approve their offer of £65,000 for the purchase of the loan. A month later the Board of Works appointed R. G. Colhoun, traffic manager of the Great Southern & Western Railway, to hold an inquiry 'on the position and prospects'. This took place at Coleraine on 11 September 1899; seven shareholders gave evidence.

There was an interlude, during which the figures for 1899 became available. The receipts were £11,734, about the average for recent years. The board, defiantly, decided they were in favour of the amended scheme for a line from Kingscourt to Armagh, which was only realised in part long after the DC company was in oblivion!

On 16 March 1900 the secretary went to Dublin to meet the Board of Works. He pressed that the DC be allowed to promote a Bill to obtain running powers from Magherafelt to Cookstown and from Coleraine to Portrush over the B & NCR, and to buy or hire rolling stock. His reason for urgency was that the working agreement expired in February 1901 and unless something was done quickly the line would have to be closed thereafter until the capital could be reorganised. The Board of Works strongly objected to the DC's attitude and threatened to appoint a Receiver. A conciliatory reply was sent, stating that the offending passages had been 'expunged' from the minutes (they are still there!).

On 5 June 1900 the Northern Counties officially notified the DC that they would not work the line after the ending of the agreement. The DC then tried to get the Treasury to receive a deputation. Hopes were raised in August when the GNR (I) asked for the 1899 half-yearly reports, which were reasonably good, but nothing came of this. On 25 September the Board of Works stated £85,000 as their price for the sale of their interest in the DC. The directors offered £70,000 or alternatively asked that the mortgage be reduced to that figure, so that they might purchase rolling stock. By 17 November they were made aware that the Treasury would not accept their offer and 'Sir H. H. Bruce retiring from the room' (he being a diehard) the board passed a resolution appointing a deputation to the B & NC regarding possible sale. They also agreed to seek counsel's advice as to whether 'the Board of Works have the power to sell the line over our heads'. The reply was not reassuring.

But by early December they had changed their minds.

> We the Derry Central Railway Company hereby tender for and agree to purchase from the Commissioners of Public Works in Ireland their interest in the sum of £70,000, £20,000, £5,000 and £5,000 and the arrears of interest now due thereon, charged upon and payable out of the above Railway, for the sum of £75,000.

The results for 1900, the last year of independence, were, ironically, by a small margin the best ever, at £11,894. On 22 January 1901 the directors 'stated that they would not give their personal security for the loan or interest on same'. They resolved

That the Great Northern Railway Company be written to say that the Belfast & Northern Counties Railway decline to work the line after the 28th prox. and to ask if they will be prepared to undertake the working of the Line or to give us any assistance in Rolling Stock.

They also decided to approach Austen Chamberlain, Financial Secretary to the Treasury.

Events passed the unfortunate directors by, however. On 27 February 1901 it was clear that the Board of Works intended to sell to the Northern Counties. On 2 March a letter was read to the shareholders from the Board of Works:

> With reference to the previous correspondence as to the future of the Derry Central Railway: I am directed by the Commissioners of Public Works to inform you that the Board, as the result of a conference between them and the Rt Hon John Young (Chairman) and Mr J. B. Gunning-Moore, a Director of the Belfast & Northern Counties Railway company, are about to enter into an agreement, under the sanction of the Lords Commissioners of His Majesty's Treasury, for the sale to that Company of the Derry Central Railway.

An agreement was signed on 20 March by which the B & NC undertook to purchase the DC and not to raise fares and rates without the consent of the Railway & Canal Commission, and was to develop the line. The board's secretary wrote:

> I am to add that one of the conditions of the proposed sale is that a sum of £20,000 shall be paid by the purchasing company for distribution amongst the shareholders of the Derry Central Company.

Bruce told his shareholders that the whole thing was 'mean'. The B & NC had offered £85,000, he understood; the DC had offered £75,000. The purchase would not help the district; the Northern Counties would run the railway 'without let or hindrance'. He then made a statement which was only too true:

> The majority of the Directors had endeavoured to keep the line out of the hands of the Northern Counties Company as long as they could.

PROTAGONISTS

On 7 March 1901 the Rt Hon John Young appeared before the DC board in Coleraine. After the passage of seventy years one can sense the animosity, which existed between this grand old man of the Northern Counties, aged 75, and Sir Hervey Bruce, doughty champion of the penurious Derry Central, aged 80.

In the course of a long statement Young stated that he was not present as a representative of the Northern Counties,

> I am here by request of the Board of Works to explain the history of this affair . . . Two years ago . . . we offered to renew the working agreement . . . the terms should be submitted to arbitration . . . that offer was neither declined nor accepted . . . Mr Cotton suggested the working agreement should be renewed for another year . . . My Board was content to do that until it transpired that it was the intention of the Derry Central Company to get running powers between Cookstown and Magherafelt. We then thought it was our duty to withdraw that portion of the offer.

Then had come a letter from the Board of Works, stating that they would sell the railway unless a satisfactory agreement were made. Mr Robertson (chairman of the Board of Works) had called the B & NC's proposal 'fair'. Then came a lull, after which he (Young) had met Hanbury of the Treasury in London

> and the result of that interview was that Mr Hanbury practically sold me the line *that day* for £100,000 . . . he was to accept £90,000 and £10,000 was to be distributed amongst the shareholders of Derry Central Line. I said I thought that seemed to me to be a very small consideration . . . but he said he could not increase it . . .

Young still felt that the shareholders were being badly treated and managed to persuade Hanbury to accept £85,000, while the B & NC was to provide £20,000 for the shareholders. Of this sum, Young recommended that £500 be given to the secretary. A special general meeting of the proprietors was held immediately after this, at which the shareholders made the

Page 187
WISE AS ARCHITECT

(*above*) Trooperslane station (*below*) Carrickfergus station

Page 188
TRAINS

(*above*) Cushendall narrow gauge line: train at Ballymena, *c* 1890 (*below*) Royal train Londonderry to Newtownards, 1897

best of a bad job and accepted the Northern Counties' offer. Holland, the largest preference shareholder, accepted 22½p in the pound for his stock. Bruce said 'they had been scandalously treated by the Government' but where were they to get the purchase money?

In June 1901 the directors decided to petition against the amalgamation Bill. They claimed the B & NC had 'broken faith' with the Board of Works by revising rates. The Northern Counties undertook to put this right and guaranteed that it would derive no benefit from the 1,000 ordinary £10 shares it held out of the £20,000 for the shareholders.

On 4 April 1901 the Board of Works took formal possession of the Derry Central Railway and handed it over to the Belfast & Northern Counties. On 17 August 1901 the B & NC obtained full possession when the Act received Royal Assent, after an exceptionally bitter passage through Parliament, of which more in Chapter 10. In the Act it was stated that the DC owed the Board of Works no less than £113,720. The DC board thought so little of it all that they declined to hand over the books and the seal to the York Road authorities!

THE LIMAVADY & DUNGIVEN RAILWAY

The Londonderry & Coleraine had opened its three-mile line to Limavady in 1852. Ten miles to the south was the small town of Dungiven, in the estate of the Skinners' Company, to which an extension had been mooted as early as 1862. In the 1870s the Skinners were improving Dungiven by extensive reconstruction and a group of prominent local men decided to further this by providing railway communication.

THE ACT

So it was on 4 July 1878 that the Limavady & Dungiven Railway Act received Royal Assent. The line it authorised was 10 miles 27 chains in length, from the B & NC station at Limavady (which was to be 'joint') to Dungiven, via Ardmore, Drumsurn and Derryork. The capital was fixed at £75,000 in £10 shares, with borrowing powers up to £25,000. Provision was made for the negotiation of a working agreement with the

Northern Counties who could subscribe up to £18,000 to the L & D.

The offices of the new company were at 'Limavady Terminus' (the B & NC station) and it was there that the board met for the first time in March 1880. S. M. Alexander of Limavady took the chair and David Hamilton, also a local man, was appointed secretary. John Lanyon, son of Sir Charles Lanyon of the Northern Counties, was appointed engineer; on 21 April 1880 a contract was signed with the Londonderry firm of McCrea & McFarland for the construction of the line for the sum of £39,438. The L & D was already in financial straits. On 7 June 1880 the decision was taken to seek a Board of Works loan of £25,000 'at a moderate rate of interest'; meanwhile a bridging loan of £5,000 was obtained from the Ulster Bank. The contractors were complaining that they had not obtained all the land necessary for the line; the company was having difficulty in getting possession in some places. By June 1880 only about half the land required—35 acres—had been acquired, although one-third of the line was ready to receive the track and in August tenders were sought for rails—'especially from Messrs. P. & W. McLellan of Glasgow'.

Since the company's line ran through the land of the Skinners' Company the consent of that Company had been obtained to subscribe a guarantee of 5 per cent on £20,000 of shares for 23 years. In November 1880 the L & D directors learned that in the case of the Draperstown line the Skinners had extended their guarantee to 30 years. They determined to seek the same terms and it was decided to send a deputation to Skinners' Hall, which, however, failed to persuade that Company to extend the period.

When the shares came to be sold it proved rather difficult to dispose of the Skinners' preference stock, and it was again resolved to send a deputation to London. This was received on 30 September 1881. In the course of a long printed statement of the position, the L & D stated that initially it had seemed a 23-year guarantee would suffice but 'times had changed' and the 23 years were not attractive enough to sell the shares. It was only the lack of a 30-year guarantee that was preventing their sale and the completion of the line. The Northern Counties had already subscribed £18,000 and had been induced, if the guarantee were forthcoming, to underwrite the completion and opening of the line. But the majority of the Skinners' Court disagreed with the statement. The deputation came home sorrowing. On 3 November 1881 a further mission arrived at Skinners' Hall; this the Court refused to see personally. A further statement of the position was furnished, in rather blunter terms than the first:

> When your Court in 1877 was pleased to grant the guarantee for 23 years at five per cent on £20,000 it was estimated that such a grant would enable us to raise a sum of £20,000 . . . All our liabilities were incurred in the belief that your guarantee was equal to capital shares to the amount of £20,000 and would have been readily convertible to cash at any time . . . Had the Directors entertained any doubt as to the realisation of this amount . . . they would not have undertaken the Works.

The deputation suggested that 5 per cent be guaranteed for 20 years and 4 per cent for ten years. Not to extend the guarantee would impair the 'good name' of the Skinners' Company and impede the development of Dungiven. Nevertheless the Company decided to take that risk.

An Act was obtained on 19 May 1882. The B & NC was empowered to subscribe a further £30,000 and provide a mortgage of £25,000, raising new capital for the purpose. A year later, on 16 July 1883, in addition to this £30,000 (£10,000 in ordinary shares plus the Skinners' £20,000) they were authorised to subscribe a further £10,000 to complete the line. These shares were taken in the names of George J. Clarke JP DL the chairman, and Sir Charles Lanyon Kt, the vice-chairman. Meanwhile the Board of Works, in reply to the request for a loan of £25,000, stated that the revenue anticipated from the railway was insufficient to warrant such a sum. Disappointed, the L & D could do nothing but accept and opened new negotiations for a sum of £16,000.

CONSTRUCTION

In the second half-yearly report of 1880 Lanyon told the shareholders:

> I regret to say that progress of the works in the last six months has not been all I could have wished, but it must be borne in mind that the contractors had some very serious weather to contend against.

In July 1881 he submitted draft plans of the Dungiven terminus; 'the directors considered the works much too extensive and must have conference before any expenditure is made'. On 26 August 1881 at the instigation of the board the secretary wrote to McCrea & McFarland:

> I hereby give notice that the Directors of the Limavady & Dungiven Railway Company require you forthwith to increase the staff of works, the amount and quality of plant, and otherwise to comply with the terms of your contract in this respect.

The contractors replied '... that on 25 May 1881 we applied to them [the directors] for all the lands necessary to enable us to proceed with the execution of the Works', but they had not obtained full possession until March 1881. And as yet they had received no rails. This bestirred the board's memory and in September 1881 the tender of the Barrow Iron Co was accepted, contingent upon their agreeing to give a discount of $2\frac{1}{2}$ per cent. This they apparently consented to do.

In February 1882 McCrea & McFarland demanded immediately the materials required for the completion of the works. But in July they stopped work altogether since they claimed the earthworks were insufficiently consolidated. In the same month revised plans for Dungiven terminus and the intermediate stations were submitted by Lanyon, approved, and sent to the B & NC for approval. Arbitration of the Board of Trade had to be sought in a dispute with the County Surveyor as to some bridge approaches.

At the August 1882 meeting the directors reported that the track had been completed for $2\frac{1}{2}$ miles out of Limavady and the rest was in hand. But all too soon a setback occurred; in February 1883 the shareholders were told

> ... that owing to a misunderstanding, the Contractors thought fit to stop work on the 13th Day of November ... The Directors hope shortly to be in a position to resume the work ...

THE COUNTY LONDONDERRY BRANCHES

The fact was that McCrea & McFarland were seeking payment. A committee of the B & NC recommended their board to complete the line themselves in view of the large sums they had invested in the L & D. In February 1883 the B & NC sought to arbitrate and McCrea (but apparently *not* McFarland) agreed to accept 200 shares and complete the line. In April 1883 the tender of Silo & Matthews of Belfast was accepted for the stations at Ardmore, Derryork, Drumsurn and Dungiven, and goods stores at Drumsurn and Dungiven, with two gatehouses. W. H. Adair of Belfast was to provide block and telegraph instruments and the Gloucester Wagon Co the signals. In May the Northern Counties provided an additional £10,000 as authorised by the Act of July 1883 to ensure completion and by the middle of that month the track was complete. The flat-bottomed steel rails were 26ft in length and weighed 65lb per yd. The sleepers of Baltic redwood were set in ballast of sand and gravel.

The Board of Trade inspection was fixed for 16 May but had to be postponed as even the temporary station structures were incomplete. It was eventually fixed for 29 June; Maj-Gen C. S. Hutchinson RE was the inspecting officer. He found fault with the fact that a large number of vertical deviations had been made but since no objections had been lodged he passed them over. The steepest gradient was 1 in 69 and the sharpest curve of 15 chains' radius. He was not enamoured of the temporary wooden 'sheds' but in general found the standard of engineering good. Under these circumstances he authorised opening with the proviso that there be a re-inspection when the permanent stations were completed. The line therefore opened to passengers and goods traffic on 4 July 1883. It appears that the stations were not completed until the end of the year.

AT WORK

From the opening of the railway it was worked by the Northern Counties; the provision of a working agreement had been enacted in 1878 and had been the subject of negotiation since 1880. It was finally fixed that the B & NC would work the line for 70 per cent of the receipts for ten years and maintain it at the cost of the L & D. There were three trains each way on weekdays and two on Sundays. Most trains were mixed but goods trains were run for what were termed 'heavy goods'.

The Board of Works approving of the working agreement, it consented to loan capital at 4 per cent interest and thus became mortgagees of the L & D. This loan was received in three instalments:

	£
December 1883	14,000
June 1884	2,421
June 1885	3,180
	£19,601

The receipts for the first half year to the end of 1883 were £740—the shareholders were told that 'the state of trade is not favourable to the development of traffic generally. The number of passengers carried shows that residents appreciate the accommodation offered.' The second half year brought receipts of £902. It was stated that a large traffic in stone was expected from quarries the Skinners' Company intended opening at Dungiven and 'there is also the prospect of a bountiful harvest'. Of these receipts £632 went to the B & NC for working; the remainder virtually all to the Board of Works in interest.

On 9–16 October 1884 a hearing took place in Belfast on the claim of the contractors for payment. The arbitrators awarded McCrea & McFarland £4,293. The L & D asked the Skinners to take shares for this amount and when they refused the Northern Counties paid up! Lanyon in 1885 claimed £1,097 for additional services he had rendered. The board offered him 150 guineas 'made solely from their desire to avoid the publicity of any dispute with their Engineer'. He issued a writ but did not proceed with it, and finally accepted, at the end of 1886, £105 in cash and £800 in shares.

The second half of 1884 brought an increase in receipts of £194. The Skinners appointed G. L. Young, their local agent, as a director. The year 1885 brought a decrease in receipts— 'the general depression in trade and commerce affects your Railway in common with nearly all other railways in this country'. This was despite the issue on Tuesdays and Fridays of cheap excursion tickets to Castlerock, Portrush and Portstewart.

The board from 1886 met very infrequently, generally only to approve the half-yearly accounts. The interest to the Board of Works on the loan was falling into arrears and the surplus revenue, after payments to the B & NC for working, simply could not meet the debts: 'to the Board of Works towards interest' was the phrase usually employed. The accounts settled down to a regular pattern with revenue of between £800 and £1,100 per half year. From time to time shareholders asserted that the Northern Counties was obtaining too large a proportion of excursion and third class fares and charging too much for materials used in permanent way maintenance. A mails contract with the Post Office for £25 per annum was negotiated in 1889. A proposal in 1890 to provide a cattle dock at Drumsurn was not implemented, doubtless for lack of cash.

The 1889 Regulation of Railways Act hit the company, as it did so many small Irish lines, hard. It was decided to protest to the Board of Trade; but despite Cotton's pleas the Board would not sanction more than one mixed train daily each way. Fortunately the L & D was worked on the block system and the stock the B & NC used had the automatic brake.

The existing working agreement with the Northern Counties expired on 5 July 1893. The B & NC proposed altering it to a minimum of £3.50 per mile per week; later they altered it to £36 per week. Eventually the B & NC decided to charge 85 per cent of receipts, and this was approved of by all concerned. An immediate result of this revised agreement was that the surplus available 'towards Board of Works interest' decreased from about £200 per half year to under £100 on average. The new agreement was binding for seven years.

The receipts continued their accustomed pattern, increasing one year, falling another. Market tickets were introduced in 1897 between Dungiven, Limavady and Londonderry. The working agreement made in 1893 expired on 1 July 1900 and it was only in August that the L & D board met to consider its renewal; this was effective for six years with the concurrence of the B & NC. With the takeover of the B & NC complete the L & D was worked by the Northern Counties Committee and in August 1903 a meeting took place with Joseph Martin, the NCC's assistant manager, suggesting a better service in connection with main line trains so as to facilitate travel to Castlerock and Portrush. It was also suggested that the NCC make a siding at Drumsurn. Later it was put to the committee that they should erect a goods shed at Derryork. The connection with the NCC was strengthened in 1905 when, on the death of Hamilton, Henry Cowie, brother of the NCC's manager, became secretary.

THE BOARD OF WORKS

During the first half of 1906 the receipts allowed the payment of £124 to the Board of Works in interest. But in July the Board, noting that the working agreement had again expired, proposed to sell the line to the NCC. A special general meeting was held in Limavady on 26 November 1906. Henry Cowie submitted details of the negotiations between the Board of Works and the NCC. The loan debt was now £19,061 and there were arrears of interest of no less than £11,306. The Midland Railway's Act authorising purchase of the B & NC had had a clause inserted for settlement of the situation as it then existed by arbitration. 'Investigations . . . showed this would leave nothing for interest.' The Board of Works therefore had to consider *its* position.

> The Board had to consider whether the best course for all parties would not be that they should sever the connection and realise something to go in diminution of the heavy loss of the Government with the Limavady & Dungiven Railway, to the Exchequer under an arrangement which should secure the future working and maintenance of the line.

This proposal had the consent of the Lords Commissioners of His Majesty's Treasury and the Board, as mortgagees, had therefore opened negotiations with the NCC for the sale of the line for £2,000. The Board of Works stood to lose £28,907 after the NCC had paid the £2,000.

The shareholders accepted that nothing could be done to retrieve the situation but appointed a deputation of the chairman, the solicitor, and a shareholder, which met the NCC in Belfast on 24 January 1907, to seek something for the shareholders. S. M. Macrory the chairman had previously furnished each member of the NCC with a statement pointing out that the Dungiven Line was constructed mainly with a view to prevent the opposing railway promoted by the late James Chaine Esq., M.P., being run between Ballymena and Londonderry . . . directly opposed [to] the Northern Counties system.

The Rt Hon John Young, chairman of the NCC, replied

that his recollections of the circumstances was that the formation of the Limavady & Dungiven line was pressed upon the Board of the Belfast & Northern Counties Railway by numerous deputations apart from any opposing scheme of railway construction and that in response to representations they made a subscription of . . . £18,000 and the Northern Counties Company agreed to take up £20,000 of shares guaranteed by the Skinners' Company . . . This money having been spent and the line still unfinished, the Company were obliged to advance the necessary funds [£20,000] to complete the undertaking, with the result that in all they had subscribed £58,000.

When they had paid £2,000 to the Board of Works they would have expended £60,000 which was 'a very high price' and therefore the NCC could not accede to the request of the deputation.

From February 1907 the L & D was in the possession of the NCC but it was not until 9 August 1907 that the purchase was legalised by Act of Parliament.

THE DRAPERSTOWN RAILWAY

The third of the broad gauge branches in County Londonderry was the shortest of the three, and like the others it had an exceedingly unhappy financial history, never paying a dividend to its ordinary shareholders in the twelve years of its independent existence.

INCORPORATION

To the west of Magherafelt, southern terminus of the Derry Central Railway, lay the small town of Draperstown, one of the plantation towns erected by the Drapers' Company. Certain local gentry decided to form a company to build a railway to connect the town with Magherafelt, thus providing an outlet for both passengers and the agricultural produce of the district.

This Draperstown Railway was incorporated on 22 July 1878 with a capital of £40,000 made up of £10,000 of 'A' Preference Stock and £30,000 of 'B' or Ordinary Stock with borrowing powers up to £20,000. The B & NC was authorised to subscribe up to £8,000 in 'B' stock and to work the railway when opened. The date of incorporation was less than three weeks later than the Limavady & Dungiven, and the same as the Ballycastle. The line authorised was just over eight miles long, stretching from a point one mile west of Magherafelt to Draperstown; for running powers between Draperstown Junction and Magherafelt the DR was to pay £60 per annum.

During the entire period of the DR's existence the chairman was the Hon Robert Torrens O'Neill MP of Shane's Castle; the other directors were also local men. The Northern Counties, by virtue of its large holding, nominated one director: until 1888 Samuel Black, thereafter John B. Gunning-Moore.

Since the London Companies had a substantial holding in local land it was early decided to apply to the Drapers', Salters' and Skinners' Companies to guarantee large blocks of shares. Under the terms of the Act the working agreement with the B & NC, when concluded, had to be submitted to them for approval before guarantees could be given. During 1880 negotiations with London progressed. The Salters' Company agreed to guarantee 5 per cent on £2,000 in preference shares for 30 years, following a visit to London by the chairman and the DR's solicitor, Glover. A later deputation succeeded in obtaining the consent of the Skinners' and Drapers' Companies to purchase preference stock at 5 per cent interest of, respectively, £5,000 and £10,000. Despite this the inflow of local capital was far from satisfactory; nevertheless the directors decided to proceed with the works. They appointed Charles Stewart of the B & NC as secretary and F. J. Hopkirk, the accountant, as their auditor. Board meetings were held in Magherafelt or Belfast as required; shareholders' meetings generally in Draperstown.

The DR first chose James Barton CE of Dundalk as their engineer, but there was a dispute over payment. Eventually in September 1880 the services of John Lanyon, at work on the

THE COUNTY LONDONDERRY BRANCHES 199

Limavady & Dungiven, were obtained, at £1,400; he agreed to take £250 in ordinary and £250 in preference shares, and was to begin preliminary work forthwith. The following working agreement was sealed at York Road on 29 November 1880:

> RESOLVED that this Company will work the Draperstown Railway for Ten Years from the opening of the line, giving three trains on weekdays and one train on Sundays each way, supplying all rolling stock necessary for that purpose, for the sum of £2,000 per annum, which would include the maintenance of the line (but not renewals or rails, sleepers, or fencing) and the use of Magherafelt station as it now stands, also the running over of this Company's line between the point of junction and the said Magherafelt station.
>
> Should the receipts of the line not amount in any year to a sum sufficient to pay the said £2,000 the deficit to be made good in subsequent years.

CONSTRUCTION

Lanyon, now at work laying out the line, proceeded to advertise for tenders, and by 18 February 1881 eleven had been received. The contract was awarded to J. & W. Grainger after their bona-fides had been checked, theirs being the lowest at £14,596. It was finalised at £15,000, with £10,000 of this being paid in preference shares. The construction work commenced in late 1881 and was expected to be completed by the end of 1882. Originally it had not been intended to have any intermediate stations but by early 1882 the board was thinking in terms of a station at Desertmartin, with perhaps a 'flag' station at Kilcranaghan. Late in 1882 Grainger was entrusted with constructing the station buildings and goods stores at Desertmartin and Draperstown, but Kilcranaghan did not become a halt, despite the requests of the local people; a later proposal in 1886 failed since a landowner would not grant right of access over his land. The signalling contract was given to the Gloucester Wagon Co whose tender was the lowest; Draperstown Junction and Draperstown were to be block posts and the line worked on the train staff system with block instruments obtained from W. H. Adair of Belfast. It was only in February 1883 that the final position of Drapers-town station was decided. A few chains of the authorised route were abandoned and the site fixed at Maghera Road.

THE LINE OPENED

In May 1883 Maj-Gen C. S. Hutchinson held what was termed an 'unofficial' inspection—he was in the area inspecting the Dungiven line. He stated that a turntable was required at Draperstown and this was put in hand. On 18 July he held his 'official' inspection, and passed the line as fit for traffic, his only complaint being a level crossing at 5 miles 65 chains which should be replaced by a bridge within two years. Fencing in some places required completion. Trees at the junction required cutting back and clocks and 'a name' were lacking at Desertmartin and Draperstown, while Magherafelt needed an additional crossover. The permanent way was satisfactory; it was of flat-bottomed steel rails varying in length from 18 to 26¾ft secured to sleepers by bolts and dog spikes. The ballast was of gravel. The steepest gradient was 1 in 61, the sharpest curve of 14 chains' radius.

On Friday 20 July 1883 passenger traffic began, worked by the Northern Counties. That night a great public entertainment was held in Draperstown which, it was hoped, would lay the foundations of a healthy relationship between the railway and the public. The goods stores, however, were incomplete so goods could not be carried; Lanyon stated he could get no satisfaction from the contractors. The engine and carriage sheds at Draperstown were also incomplete. But on 8 October 1883 the line was finally fully opened to all types of traffic. In July the total expenditure had amounted to £35,960.

The financial position was poor. Many shares were in arrears and by no means all the authorised capital had been taken up. During 1883 it was decided to apply to the Irish Board of Works for a loan of £15,000, authorised by the 1878 Act. The Board demanded a deed for £3,000. This the company acceded to and in November the loan was received, repayable in 25 years at 4 per cent interest. A bridging loan of £1,000 had been obtained from the Ulster Bank. Difficulties also arose with the County Londonderry Grand Jury, whose surveyor required improvements at various bridges. The arbitration of the Board of Trade had to be sought, involving the DR in further expense.

The Northern Counties did not officially accept responsibility for the line until the end of 1884. Up to the end of 1883 receipts were £290 for passengers and parcels and £99 from cattle. This was stated to be 'not altogether unusual, under the circumstances, for it is at all times difficult to break up the established mode of transit and introduce a new system into a district'. The total receipts for the first half of 1884 were £514, leaving a balance of £63 when the B & NC was paid, which was considered satisfactory in view of the prevailing depression. But the second half of the year, with receipts of £496, brought a loss of £71—with Board of Works' interest standing at £159. By 1885 the directors were seeking an additional £2,000 from the Board of Works which was not forthcoming. Lanyon and the solicitor Glover were seeking payment. In June 1886 the Board of Works agreed to a mortgage of £2,000, but in August were making pressing demands for arrears of interest, and the chairman paid £181 from his own pocket. The Derry Central asked the DR to join in a deputation to the Board to seek a reduction in rates of interest; but there is no evidence that this was ever appointed. The year 1886 was unsatisfactory; 1887 brought a slight improvement, but in 1888 there was a bank overdraft of nearly £150. And 1888 brought no financial improvement.

In May 1889 the secretary Charles Stewart died, his son Cecil B. Stewart being appointed. Soon a demand from the old man's executors for the arrears of his salary came to hand; there was no money to pay this or Lanyon and the directors continued to stall right to the end, claiming Lanyon was charging for $6\frac{3}{4}$ miles instead of the 6 miles 3 furlongs 100 yards actually built! Cecil B. Stewart died in 1892 and further claims from *his* executors arose. W. R. Gill, who had succeeded Charles Stewart as B & NC secretary in 1887, was appointed.

The Regulation of Railways Act of 1889 was causing the DR trouble; at least its trains had the automatic brake and it, like the Derry Central and Dungiven, was fully signalled and interlocked. But hitherto all trains had been mixed; under the new

Act such trains were strictly limited. Cotton tried to obtain a relaxation from the Board of Trade but could get nothing more than permission to run one mixed train daily each way. The Board of Works, ever watchful, declined to allow a small surplus in revenue to be paid to C. B. Stewart's executors—it had to go to pay their interest.

By early 1893 the Northern Counties was drawing attention to the fact that the working agreement expired in July of that year. In February it was decided to seek a renewal of the working agreement on the same terms, though the DR knew full well the B & NC lost by it. The working receipts for 1892 showed a large decrease over 1891. The Northern Counties submitted a draft of the new working agreement—they would now work the line for 70 per cent of receipts or a minimum of £3.50 per mile per week. Since this would leave nothing to pay interest the Board of Works wrote, denouncing the proposal as 'impracticable':

> Unless [the terms] are modified, there will be no option but for the Board to recommend to the Lords Commissioners of Her Majesty's Treasury the sale or closure of the line.

The B & NC therefore made a new offer—to work the line for three years at 85 per cent of the receipts plus £60 per annum rent for Magherafelt station. The Board of Works proposed 80 per cent for five years. Finally it was agreed that the B & NC would take 85 per cent of receipts or £3.50 per mile per week, for seven years, but would not charge rent for the use of Magherafelt station. This revised agreement took effect from 1 August 1893.

THE END OF THE LINE

On 30 October 1894 a salutary letter was received from the Board of Works pointing out that arrears of interest now stood at £3,248. They had received an offer of £2,000 from the Northern Counties for the purchase of the line. This they were disposed to accept, and

> to enter into and take possession of the line, stations, station buildings, and all property of the Company as soon as terms have been arranged with the Northern Counties Company.

The Solicitor will then proceed to the line on a day to be fixed and take actual possession, and put back the station masters etc., as caretakers and servants for the Working Company.

The Draperstown board could do nothing. The company's property was to be disposed of over their heads. It was explained to them that under Section 45 of the Act incorporating the Irish Board of Works it had authority to enter into possession of mortgaged property. On 25 February 1895 the Board of Works took formal possession of the line and the B & NC took over ownership of the DR, possession being confirmed in the Act of July 1895. The final meeting of the Draperstown board took place in December 1895, when they decided to seek free passes over the Northern Counties line. A final surplus of £33 was handed over to Stewart's executors and Lanyon was left to take issue with the Board of Works.

THE PORTSTEWART TRAMWAY

The fourth and last of the County Londonderry branches was destined to be the smallest constituent of the Northern Counties Railway. Perhaps it is incorrect to term it a branch, as it was an isolated line of narrow gauge, less than two miles long. In Chapter 4 we noted that the Ballymena, Ballymoney, Coleraine & Portrush Railway did not reach Portstewart because of the opposition of the local landowners. The local people were enraged, the more so when they observed the beneficial effect rail communication had on the neighbouring Portrush. Portstewart remained a minor seaside watering place, with its railway station $1\frac{3}{4}$ miles from the town centre.

As early as 1861 the Portstewart Tramway Company sought authorisation to connect town and station; for a roadside tramway only an Order-in-Council was necessary. This scheme appears to have had the backing of George Francis Train, pioneer of street tramways. Again the opposition of the landlords proscribed the project and for a time it lapsed. Another nine years passed and then it began to dawn on Cromie, the dominant landowner, that a railway to Portstewart might not altogether be a bad thing. He it was who took the chair at a public meeting in Portstewart in October 1871 to consider a resurrection of the 1861 scheme which he had killed.

It appears that Cromie now offered the land free of charge to the B & NC for the construction of the line, something akin to a light railway, to link town and station. At this time the 5ft 3in gauge was envisaged, doubtless to facilitate through running with the B & NC. But that company declined to undertake the construction of the line, though it agreed to support an independent company, as well it might, since it stood to benefit.

The 1871 scheme lapsed; it was revived in 1878-9, this time the line to be a tramway and not a light railway, on the 3ft gauge. It was to follow the county road from the station to the town, a distance of 1 mile 62 chains. The application for an Order-in-Council was duly lodged at Dublin Castle; and meanwhile the promoters sought to extend the line to Coleraine. Nothing further was heard of this scheme which would undoubtedly have encountered the opposition of the B & NC. The Order-in-Council was granted on 26 April 1880. Capital was fixed at £5,000 in £10 shares, with borrowing powers for a further £1,666. The Northern Counties, true to its promise, took £2,000 in shares. E. J. Cotton was appointed manager, thus strengthening the connection between the tramway and the B & NC.

Butler & Fry built the line; a portion was in tramway formation, the remainder in normal railway track. It was single throughout, save for two passing loops. A depot building was erected on the Parade (later the Promenade) at Portstewart to house the rolling stock. Track laying was commenced on 21 April 1882. Following delay over the Board of Trade inspection the public opening took place on 28 June 1882 with the usual ceremonies; only passengers and light goods were carried. The locomotive was a conventional four-wheeled tramway steam engine with small tramcar trailers. This was in fact the first roadside tramway in Ireland. The new line was of tremendous benefit to Portstewart and through bookings were available over the Northern Counties whose Portrush branch trains connected at Portstewart station. It was stated that the tramway had cost £2,500 per mile to build, and the working expenses were estimated at 7d per mile. Interest of 5 per cent was forecast. Certain B & NC officials, including Malcolm as locomotive engineer, were appointed to the company's service at purely nominal salaries. The Northern Counties' local permanent way men carried out such maintenance to the track as was necessary.

The first traffic returns were encouraging; rolling stock proved insufficient to give connection to all trains and a second locomotive was purchased. But no dividend was declared. This was a portent of what was to come. By 1885, when in dispute with the Grand Jury over fencing erected on Portstewart Parade, it was disclosed that the tramway was overdrawn by £348, notwithstanding a bridging loan from the B & NC of £966. For some time the finances improved somewhat. The directors became incensed with the B & NC, feeling that they should receive a greater proportion of through booking receipts. When Cotton declined to alter the existing arrangement they considered taking the management into their own hands, but wisely desisted.

The year 1892 brought a claim from a local man, O'Neill, for the liquidation of a mortgage he held. The directors, seeking a scapegoat, turned on the Northern Counties and resolved that henceforth they would appoint their own officials without reference to the B & NC. But only a week after this, the company, on 15 October 1892, was declared bankrupt. Some shareholders suggested Cotton as a suitable person to be appointed receiver, but the directors would have none of this and a Portstewart man, S. R. Henry, was appointed. His offer to lease the tramway for ten years at £100 per year was deferred and nothing developed.

As if this were not bad enough difficulties arose with the rolling stock and track, which the impoverished condition of the company had not allowed to be properly maintained. Then the B & NC shareholders complained that no dividend had ever been received on the £2,000 invested in the tramway; but the chairman said the traffic accruing to the B & NC was ample remuneration. The next year, 1894, the B & NC wrote off its loan of £600. The end came in early 1897 when Robert O'Neill, a Coleraine solicitor and a large creditor, instituted proceedings to wind up the concern. The directors decided not to oppose him and took the only course open to them—sale of the line as a going concern.

On 22 March 1897 the case opened before the Master of the Rolls in Dublin. Debts were revealed on all sides. On 22 July the court decreed that £1,043 be paid to the B & NC (which had joined with O'Neill in the action) and £782 to O'Neill. Meanwhile the Northern Counties had made the only offer for the line, a comparatively small one of £2,100. Henry, now acting as liquidator, confirmed that this would clear all debts, and on 1 June 1897 the tramway was merged in the B & NC, Parliamentary sanction being obtained in 1899.

There is no doubt that this was the most sensible course. The traffic offering was totally insufficient to support such a small independent line. Had the B & NC decided to build and work the line at the outset, matters might have taken a different course. As it was the tramway came to that concern cheaply, though large expenditure was necessary over the next few years until the line developed as a valuable ancillary to the broad-gauge system.

CHAPTER EIGHT

The Late Victorian Company 1880-1899

The year 1880 is as good as any other to close one chapter and open another in the history of the Northern Counties Railway. The years from 1860 to 1879 had been years of amalgamation and consolidation and they had been in the main outstandingly prosperous. Now a period of depression beset the country as a whole and was reflected in the fortunes of the railway. But the company pursued a policy of expansion and after a while the bad days were replaced by better ones, though the old prosperity never again fully returned. The company broke new ground, branching into the field of hotels; and did everything possible to encourage tourism—to which may be ascribed some degree of the improvement in the finances.

Perhaps the modest prosperity of the 1890s is more remarkable than the spectacular success of the 1870s if we remember that in the five years prior to 1893 no less than £450,000 was added to capital; the servicing of this huge sum in addition to the existing stock was no mean task, yet it was accomplished.

HARD TIMES

In the 1880s the whole of Ireland was in a depressed condition. These were the terrible days of the Land War and general agrarian unrest which was reflected in the industrial areas of the north-east, and the B & NC suffered severely. From $6\frac{1}{4}$ per cent in 1878 the dividend fell to $4\frac{1}{4}$ per cent the next year and to $4\frac{1}{8}$ per cent in 1880. In 1881 it was 3 per cent, in 1882 4 per cent, $3\frac{3}{4}$ per cent in 1883 and in 1884 only 3 per cent. The next year was even worse with a fall to $2\frac{3}{4}$ per cent.

Under the circumstances it was not to be wondered at that the shareholders, so long accustomed to receiving 5 per cent or more, should object to the large sums which were subscribed to the branch lines being independently promoted in Counties Antrim and Londonderry, to the extent of £170,000, and the expenditure on the automatic brake and block system. Particularly irksome to them was the purchase in 1884 of the Cushendall line—especially at a time when ore traffic had greatly diminished—at a cost of some £130,000; and the apparently unending expenditure on the Northern Counties Hotel, not to speak of the new branch to Ballyclare.

The shareholders' meeting in February 1885 brought matters to a head. In reference to the rural character of most of the board it was suggested that new blood would be welcome—'instead of having country gentlemen not conversant with business' some of the hard-headed commercial acumen of Belfast should be brought to bear. The shareholders set up a committee to investigate matters in general and in particular the polemical purchase of the Cushendall line. In May 1885 the chairman for eighteen years, George J. Clarke, one of the 'country gentlemen', vacated his office and was replaced by John Young of Galgorm Castle, near Ballymena, owner of some 1,600 acres. Young was a most remarkable man; he had been born in 1826 and became a Master of Arts at Trinity College, Dublin. He had been a director of the Northern Counties since 1859 and was prominent in linen circles in Belfast, being at one time chairman of the Linen Merchants' Association and also president of the Belfast Chamber of Commerce, and chairman of the shareholders' committee of the Northern Bank. He was deeply interested in the Irish university question—a thorny one in the nineteenth century—and was a member of the Senate of the Royal University of Ireland and a member of Convocation of Queen's College, Belfast (now Queen's University). He was often invited to stand for Parliament but never consented, preferring to devote himself to his business interests; he was sworn of the Irish Privy Council in 1886 and later granted the honorary degree of Doctor of Laws for his work in education. Bringing his commercial ability to bear he now set about a reinvigoration of the Belfast & Northern Counties.

The August 1885 meeting was unusually bitter, lasting for five hours. A calumniation of the board was delivered in such terms that Reade, a director, was moved to retort that 'he did not expect to find that the prejudice incited by the Nationalist Press against the landlord class prevailed here'. This was greeted with shouts of 'Order', 'Sit down', 'Withdraw'. In the end it was decided that three new directors, R. W. Kelly, W. J. Pirrie and Wilson, be appointed, the first-mentioned being chairman of the Belfast & County Down Railway in which capacity he had proved an able administrator and had retrieved that concern from its financial plight. Under the newly strengthened board prosperity slowly returned as the economic situation in the country eased—though never quite to the level of the 1870s; from 2 per cent (caused by extraordinary circumstances) in 1886 the dividend rose to $3\frac{1}{2}$ per cent in 1887, $4\frac{1}{2}$ per cent in 1888 and $5\frac{1}{4}$ per cent in 1889. Thereafter until 1903 the dividend never fell below 5 per cent but never exceeded 6 per cent.

Just as it seemed that the company had surmounted its difficulties the famous Hopkirk fraud, which almost ranks with the Redpath fraud on the Great Northern Railway of England in the 1850s, came to light. The half-yearly report to the shareholders in February 1887 read in part:

> The Directors regret to inform the shareholders that frauds of a serious nature have been committed on the Company by their late book-keeper (now undergoing penal servitude for the offence) and the cashier (lately deceased) amounting in all to £16,616 15s 1d.

Francis John Hopkirk had been in the service for 41 years and was aged 54. About the time of the 1861 amalgamations he was promoted accountant and in 1886 his salary was £360 —a princely sum for those days. With the reorganisation of the board in 1885 the new directors wished to have details of the capital expenditure over the years. A London firm of accountants, Price, Waterhouse & Co, was appointed to examine the books. The principal, Waterhouse, sought precise figures from Collins the engineer, for the renewals of the Londonderry & Coleraine, and discovered a discrepancy of £2,400 between Collins' figures and Hopkirk's. Investigating further, he examined the books for a further period of ten years and discovered defalcations of some £4,800 extending back over at least thirteen years. Hopkirk was also accountant to the Carrickfergus & Larne and the Portstewart Tramway; from the latter he abstracted some £78. He was in addition auditor of the Derry Central and the Draperstown but had no opportunities for peculation.

The problem was, how he obtained the money. Strictly speaking he should not have handled cheques at all; these were all paid through the secretary's office. It appeared that he managed to charge more to expenditure than was actually spent, pocketing the difference. The methods he used were so complex that even Waterhouse was unable to give a precise explanation. Since he was theoretically entrusted with money no security had been sought for him. He was given into the charge of the police.

The deficit of course had to be made good from revenue, and a dividend of $3\frac{1}{2}$ per cent was proposed. But worse was yet to come. In the course of the audit by Waterhouse, Stewart the secretary entered the office of the cashier, Peter Lilley, to seek certain papers there; Lilley had been absent from work since 14 November 1886 owing to ill-health. Stewart was aghast to find defalcations amounting to some £11,170 in Lilley's books: making a total, with Hopkirk's thefts, of £16,616.

On Lilley's appointment security of £500 was obtained, which was of course forfeited; he escaped justice by dying in December. It was thought by some that his death was just a little too fortuitous and that he had fled the country; but Young remarked that it was unlikely an empty coffin had been buried! At the Belfast Quarter Sessions in January 1887 Hopkirk, who pleaded guilty, was sentenced to five years' penal servitude on several counts of frauds of small sums between January and June 1886. In sentencing him the judge said it was almost certain he had been stealing for eleven or thirteen years but definite proof was lacking; had it been to hand he would have had no hesitation in sentencing Hopkirk to fourteen years' imprisonment.

A very heated shareholders' meeting took place on 8 February 1887, only a matter of days after the Lilley frauds had been discovered. As a result the proposed dividend of $3\frac{1}{2}$ per cent was cut to 2 per cent. The affair had thrown commercial Belfast into a panic; the Northern Counties was regarded as one of the most sound of local companies. The board offered to resign but the shareholders did not press this. One shareholder asserted it was all a divine retribution for the running of Sunday trains! Clearly there had been laxity and confusion in the administration of the company; but certainly there was no truth in the rumours whispered about that it was Cotton's fault. It was a terrible grief to him that two of his colleagues of long standing, trusted and in secure positions, were capable of such depravity.

Following this further severe blow to the fortunes, Price, Waterhouse & Co were appointed to make a thorough examination of the finances and report. To replace Hopkirk, Walter Bailey from the South Eastern Railway was appointed—he was later to become celebrated; and a new cashier was found in F. J. W. McGahey. Sir Charles Lanyon, for twenty years vice-chairman, resigned on the grounds of ill-health though one is sure that the happenings affected his position. Following a long illness he died on 31 May 1889. He was replaced as vice-chairman by Henry Hugh McNeile, a veteran director and son of the John McNeile, who, dying in 1855, had been described as 'the father of the railway'.

BRANCHES

We last met with the Belfast Central Railway in Chapter 5. Nearly bankrupt though it might be, it was not devoid of ideas and in 1880 obtained authorisation for a narrow gauge line to the suburbs of Belfast at Ardoyne, a third rail being added to the existing Central line. A year later this was replaced by an ambitious Ballyclare, Ligoneil & Belfast Junction Railway which was to extend from Ardoyne, sweep round eastwards, pass under the B & NC at Templepatrick, and terminate against the Ballymena & Larne's projected branch to Doagh, authorised in 1878 and opened in 1884.

The scheme was furiously opposed by the Great Northern and the Northern Counties and the latter hastily resurrected its own Ballyclare scheme of 1874, which had not been submitted to Parliament. It was said that Cotton 'had long wanted to go to Ballyclare' and the Northern Counties had for a considerable time been subsidising a horse omnibus three times daily to Ballyclare & Doagh station to connect with main line trains. This was always amply filled. Further, the paper mill at Ballyclare offered much traffic. Both the BL & BJ and B & NC Bills were examined simultaneously and both were approved, despite evidence given by Cotton to the Parliamentary Committee against the Belfast Central scheme (which failed to be built).

The B & NC's Act of 22 August 1881 authorised a total of $4\frac{1}{2}$ miles of railway from the main line near Ballynure Road station through Ballyclare to Doagh. A year later the Doagh section was abandoned by Act of 3 July 1882 and $3\frac{1}{4}$ miles of new line to Rashee through Ballygallagh or Springvale were authorised.

By February 1883 the contract for the first $2\frac{1}{4}$ miles had been signed and work was proceeding on the single-line branch. Land for the upper section was proving difficult to obtain and arbitration was necessary. By August 1884, when it was hoped to open to Ballyclare on 1 October, work on the Doagh Valley section had not commenced. In 1886 the decision was taken not to proceed further, so that the branch terminated at Ballyclare, some $3\frac{1}{2}$ miles from the main line; the intermediate halt at Lisnalinchy was not opened until some years later. Provisions were included in the Act to protect the B & L's Doagh branch opened in February 1884. The powers for an extension to Ballygallagh were renewed by the B & NC Act of 22 May 1890 but were not exercised.

The Ballyclare branch was inspected on 29 October 1884 by Major-General Hutchinson who found it generally satisfactory. Unusually, land had only been taken for a single line and there were few engineering works; there was one steep gradient of 1 in 60. Apart from a few very minor details, such as completion of fencing, he certified the line as fit for passenger carriage and he did not propose to delay opening. Opening to Ballyclare was on 3 November 1884; from then Ballyclare & Doagh station was renamed 'Doagh' and Ballynure Road became 'Ballyclare Junction' which was the passenger interchange point, though the actual junction was a mile further west at Kingsbog Junction at which point there was no station.

By now the Belfast Central was in its death throes and had abandoned its high-flown extension schemes. By Act of 6

THE LATE VICTORIAN COMPANY 1880–1899

August 1885 the existing line was sold to the Great Northern with the enthusiastic support of the B & NC, which paid £1,600 per annum for running powers, the C & L bearing a proportion of this sum.

Hardly had the Ballyclare branch begun operation when an accident occurred on 19 May 1885. A special passenger train was entering the station; the driver, assuming that the train was going too fast to stop, having coasted down the heavy gradient approaching the station, contravened orders and, instead of using handbrake only, applied the steam brake violently. In point of fact the train was running quite normally and he only succeeded in skidding the wheels so that the train hit the stopblocks and rebounded 3 or 4 inches; some 35 passengers complained of minor injuries.

When the B & L line was purchased in 1889 there was no connection between its narrow gauge station in Ballyclare and the Northern Counties' broad gauge terminus. Consideration was given to the building of an interchange line but nothing was done and broad and narrow gauge remained separate. The Ballyclare branch was not a profitable venture. It was observed in 1899 that it had cost £30,000 to build while the last half-year's receipts had been only £969.

In 1880 Coleraine station was largely rebuilt to accommodate the newly opened Derry Central. It had long been recognised as a disgrace to the company and every time a new station was opened elsewhere the shareholders made pointed references to it. It was cramped and inconvenient and was hampered by level crossings at either end of the platforms. Before work on the new building could begin a new goods shed had to be provided and the space thus released was used to build new facilities. The new building was a great improvement on the old but still little could be done in the cramped location, though by a costly diversion of certain roads the level crossing at the Belfast end was eradicated. Two through platforms were provided and a bay on the up side especially for DC trains, together with a greatly enlarged goods yard. The new facilities came into use in August 1882.

The Portstewart Tramway ended its independent existence in 1897 when the Courts handed it over to the B & NC. It was in a seriously rundown condition and considerable expense was incurred on it over the next few years. In 1899 a completely new depot was built at Portstewart to the designs of Wise: this beautiful three-storey building in mock-Tudor style with high pointed gables so successfully disguised its function that it was the finest building in Portstewart then and long afterwards.

THE CUSHENDALL LINE

In 1880 the 'High Level Line' at Ballymena was opened to connect the Cushendall and the Ballymena & Larne; it ran alongside the B & NC's main line for most of its length and shared several bridges. It facilitated the transfer of ore but robbed the Northern Counties and C & L of valuable traffic which had been routed via the broad gauge.

The Cushendall was a disappointing line. In the early years it had been extremely profitable but a depression set in in the iron ore trade and despite loans from the Northern Counties totalling £59,500 by 1881 the end was in sight. By the Act of 16 July 1883 the B & NC was authorised to subscribe further; a clause dealing with sale had been deleted by the Lords since no price had been fixed. Finally a second Act was obtained on 14 July 1884 by which amalgamation took place, at a cost to the Northern Counties of some £130,000. The purchase was fiercely resisted by some shareholders who regarded the Cushendall as altogether a worthless investment.

In 1878 the Cushendall had been authorised to construct a number of tramways but nothing had been done and the powers lapsed. By the 1884 Act the B & NC received renewed powers to construct several of these: $2\frac{1}{4}$ miles to Clontrace, $2\frac{1}{4}$ miles to Broughshane, and an extension of the 'main line' $3\frac{1}{4}$ miles from Retreat to Cushendall, always the intended terminus of the line. Power was given to work these lines electrically if desired. But nothing was ever done. In 1885 serious consideration was given to the Broughshane branch and a contract was signed for construction but by 1888 it had formally been abandoned.

But if the extensions did not materialise the Northern Counties had purposes in store for the Cushendall; it traversed fine scenery and so had great tourist potential. Several times the old company had mooted the possibility of passenger working but the expense was prohibitive. In 1885 the B & NC had the line inspected by Maj-Gen C. S. Hutchinson who reported on modifications necessary to fit it for passenger working. Attention first centred on the 8½ mile section out to Knockanally where a new station was erected; there were intermediate stations at Ballycloughan and Rathkenny. Full passenger facilities, though of a simple nature, were provided, with adequate signalling. A programme of relaying was instituted, replacing many of the original rails (which were of poor quality and had seen heavy wear), and sleepers. A set of narrow gauge coaches of unique design known as 'tramcars' was obtained and all was ready for inspection by the Board of Trade, again represented by Hutchinson. A few items caught his eye and when these had been dealt with a passenger service began to Knockanally from Ballymena on 5 April 1886.

Work proceeded on rehabilitating the five miles thence to Parkmore, a new station being built there with intermediate halts at Cross Roads and Cargan. Passenger working over the final section to Retreat was not contemplated due to the heavy gradients and since the extension to Cushendall did not come into being the B & NC contracted with horse-bus operators to maintain a Cushendall—Parkmore service. The work included replacing defective track and the original wooden bridges and it was not until August 1888 that Hutchinson inspected the section. Again he noted defects but passenger working began between Knockanally and Parkmore on 1 September 1888. Parkmore, at 1,000ft above sea level, was the highest railway station in Ireland.

Never again was iron ore to be so important to the line as it had been in the 1870s; the great days were over, though significant tonnages were still carried and in 1890 a new iron trans-shipment gantry replaced the wooden one at Ballymena. Henceforth passengers were the real draw, especially after the acquisition of Glenariff Glen which was served by Parkmore station (see Chapter 9).

THE LARNE LINES AND THE STEAMER

The Ballymena & Larne line was absorbed by the Northern

Counties in 1889 and the broad gauge Carrickfergus & Larne in 1890. Thus the B & NC was in possession of all routes of communication leading to the steamer, and was in a position to provide a better service than ever before. Even before the two acquisitions were complete a new station had been planned for Larne Harbour, and in 1890 the new building was authorised at a cost of £3,000. It was the first to be designed by Wise and was ideally suited to its purpose. It had a double-faced platform, one side serving broad, the other narrow gauge. On the concourse was situated the famous clock which, having two minute hands, showed both English and Irish time, the latter being 25 minutes later than Greenwich Mean Time and at this time used by all Irish railways. At the harbour end of the concourse was a gentle ramp by means of which passengers could step out on to the steamer berth for embarkation.

A change had taken place on the other side. In 1885 the London & North Western, Midland, Caledonian and Glasgow & South Western Railways had formed the Portpatrick & Wigtownshire Joint Committee to operate the Portpatrick Railway. By 1889 the existing steamers were totally inadequate; they were slow and old, despite the alterations made to the *Princess Louise* in 1878 and to the *Princess Beatrice* in 1883. The Steamship Company had no money available—as yet the route could not be regarded as wholly profitable and up to 1885 the loss had been £1,790. The Joint Committee therefore acquired the Steamship Company by paying off all the private owners of shares at 12s 6d (62½p) in the £1—£9,250 of stock was obtained for £5,777. On 1 May 1890 the *Princess Victoria* came into service; it had been built by Denny of Dumbarton and was a paddler of 1,000 tons with a speed of 20 knots, carrying 373 saloon and 630 steerage passengers. On her coming into service *Louise* was sold to David MacBrayne who renamed her *Islay*; she was wrecked in 1902.

On 1 September 1890 the *Victoria* crossed the Channel in the teeth of a tremendous gale to inaugurate an improved service; only 2¼ hours were now taken in crossing. The new service was an immediate success and was much used by businessmen in a hurry. The steamer now docked at Larne Harbour at 8.21am, the boat trains departing at 8.25 and

THE LATE VICTORIAN COMPANY 1880–1899

reaching Belfast at 9.10 and Ballymena (via the narrow gauge) at 9.25. The L & NW and Midland ran sleepers to Stranraer. At long last in 1892 the Postmaster-General agreed to recognise the crossing as a supplementary mail route, Kingstown–Holyhead then being the principal route for mails.

By 1899 the service had been slightly accelerated; the steamer left Stranraer at 6.04am and reached Larne at 7.51; the connecting trains were due in Belfast at 8.40, Portrush at 10.35, and Londonderry at 10.55. In the evening the boat left Larne at 5.50pm on the arrival of the 2.50 ex Londonderry, 3.15 ex Portrush and 5.0 ex Belfast, arriving in Stranraer at 8.23pm. There were consequent alterations on the other side of the Channel.

From 14 July 1891 to deal with the enormously increased traffic (which between 1875 and 1885 had increased 40 per cent)

> during the summer months there is an *Additional Service* worked by one of the Company's swift paddle-steamers, having a morning departure from Larne and an evening departure from Stranraer, with express train connections on both sides of the Channel. By this service passengers are able to leave London, Birmingham, Manchester, Newcastle-upon-Tyne, Aberdeen, Edinburgh, Glasgow, etc., and arrive in Belfast on the same day, and *vice-versa*.

By now the passage occupied rather less than two hours in one direction and slightly over that time in the other; but it was pointed out that the passage time in open sea was only about 80 minutes, the remainder being spent sailing in Loch Ryan.

An indication of the success of the new services was the ordering of a further steamer from Denny, which entered service in 1892. The *Princess May* was a sister of *Victoria* and was the last paddler built for the Irish Sea (it may be mentioned that the shallow approach to Stranraer necessitated the use of paddles until the development of the turbine). With her advent the *Beatrice* became a spare vessel and was disposed of in 1904.

In 1893 another change in management took place. The B & NC had subscribed a large sum in 1890 and received further authorisation in 1895. From 1 July 1893 the working of the steamers was handed over to the Larne & Stranraer Steamship Joint Committee in which the four railways operating the Portpatrick Railway were joined by the Northern Counties. By now the steamer service was a complete and increasing success. With the facilities at Larne greatly improved the terminal at Stranraer appeared in a very bad light, but extensive alterations were undertaken between 1892 and 1897 which brought the Stranraer pier fully up to standard. Cotton remained manager of the service.

BELFAST

A serious fire broke out at York Road in the early hours of 16 September 1885 in the carriage shop, where a number of coaches under construction and repair were destroyed, and spread to the main passenger buildings and offices on the departure platform, which were seriously damaged. Fortunately there was full insurance cover and the buildings were reconstructed in a slightly modified form; the carriage shop and other works buildings affected, which had been of wood, were reconstructed in brick.

By the early 1890s the two platforms at York Road were totally inadequate to deal with the volume of traffic which was offering. Initially the platform lines were cut back a considerable distance from Whitla Street and a clock tower and canopy were added by Wise; this work was completed in 1894. Shortly afterwards tramlines were laid in under the canopy and a special service of tramcars ran to the city centre in connection with the principal passenger trains. Then in 1897 further alterations began. Some of the sidings under the overall roof were removed and a double-faced platform inserted; a short-bay platform was also constructed behind the arrival platform. Five platforms were thus provided, ample for all traffic. A large new concourse was provided, with handsome refreshment rooms, booking offices and bookstalls somewhat in Swiss chalet style. Finally the entire building was wired for electric lighting, introduced into the city in 1895. The alterations to the impressive if somewhat heterogeneous pile was completed in October 1898; a month later the Station Hotel, directly connected with the concourse, opened (*see* Chapter 9).

In 1883 the cartage contract at Belfast was transferred to McCrea & McFarland, whom we have already met with as contractors for the Limavady & Dungiven. Basil McFarland had been a clerk at Londonderry (Waterside) and Cotton, recognising his worth, advised him to set up on his own account as a carter; he chose John McFarland as his partner and they made a formidable pair. They were also responsible for B & NC cartage in Londonderry. In 1883 a telephone was fitted in the goods office at York Road; it must have been one of the first in Belfast and was stated to be of great use. Typewriters were common in all departments by 1898. In 1898 a city office was opened at 12 Royal Avenue with McCrea & McFarland as agents.

Throughout this period constant additions were made to the goods facilities at York Road. In 1895 a new goods shed and crane facilities were provided; this involved the separation of the goods department into 'Inwards' and 'Outwards' divisions with completely separate stores, an arrangement found most convenient. Hydraulic capstans cut the use of locomotives for shunting to a minimum with consequent economy.

The works were also kept fully up to date and additions were made to the buildings and machinery as required. A new engine shed with four roads and a locomotive coal yard were laid out on a new site north-east of the goods yard in 1895 so that the old site immediately adjoining the station could be devoted to other purposes. The new shed provided greatly increased and improved facilities for the ever-expanding locomotive department.

CARRICKFERGUS AND COLERAINE HARBOURS

Carrickfergus Harbour had long been important and clauses to prevent its interfering with the commerce of Belfast had been written into the Belfast & Ballymena's 1845 Act. In 1881 a Bill was promoted which was in the unusual position of being supported by the Northern Counties but opposed by the Carrickfergus & Larne. The Bill was passed on 3 July 1882, incorporating the Carrickfergus Harbour Junction Railway for a line 6 furlongs 15 chains 23 yards long to the new West Pier under construction with a branch 2 furlongs 17 yards to the

Old Pier. The capital was £7,500 of which the Northern Counties was permitted to subscribe up to £5,000 (in the end only £300 was given).

This Act was not implemented and on 6 February 1885 'for reasons of their own' the promoters were granted an Order-in-Council under the Tramways & Public Companies (Ireland) Act of 1883, in the same terms as the 1882 Act but attaching a baronial guarantee to £6,500 of shares.

On 31 March 1886 the contractor, J. Hegarty, began work and on 1 January 1887 the line opened; a portion of its course followed the original B & B line. During the first half year 'there has been but little traffic over the line' owing to the high rates the B & NC was obliged to charge and the toll of 1d per ton levied by the Carrickfergus Harbour Commissioners. But a crane had been erected at the harbour and there was a revival in the rock salt trade.

No marked improvement took place, however, and since a baronial guarantee was involved the County Antrim Grand Jury took possession of the line on 1 January 1889, handing it over to a committee of management. The Northern Counties continued to work and maintain the line; a special signal cabin had been erected at the Harbour Junction which was opened when required.

The circumstances governing the building of Portrush harbour and the railway thereto were detailed in Chapter 5. The Portrush Harbour Company, however, failed to carry out some of its functions and in 1863 the Coleraine merchants were given authority to improve the harbour at Coleraine. By a further Act of 1879 additional finance was made available to dredge the sandbar at the estuary of the Bann, and this was completed and a new harbour opened in 1884. The Coleraine port became increasingly important in the local economy and a passenger service operated to Glasgow. On 31 July 1889 an Act permitted the building of a line to the harbour. It was short—2 furlongs 11 chains—and diverged from the B & NC main line very near the bridge over the Bann. An agreement was signed between harbour and railway authorities on 21 July 1891 and the line opened for traffic in January 1892, providing a valuable supplement to the goods traffic in the Coleraine area.

ENGINEERING

The twenty years under review were an extremely busy period for the engineering department. There was heavy renewal of the permanent way, especially on the newly acquired narrow gauge lines. A new engine shed was provided in Ballymena in 1884 and at the same time a goods shed at Cookstown. Coleraine engine shed was replaced in 1897. Other improvements included the building of new cottages and gatehouses all over the system. The fitting of modern signalling arrangements and the block and tablet systems was an important item; for example as part of the improvement of the Portrush branch in 1891 Portstewart had a loop laid and full signalling provided, and similarly Whitehead in 1894. Goods sheds and similar buildings, and also the stations at Larne Harbour and Portrush built during Wise's time, were mainly of wood with the so-called 'Belfast' roof. This was a type of truss span made of light pieces of timber, easily constructed and erected and needing little maintenance (many are still in use).

The only work of doubling undertaken at this time was on the three mile Carrickfergus—Carrickfergus Junction (Greenisland) section of the Larne line. This had been mooted in 1884 but postponed by reason of economic difficulties and it was not completed until March 1897 at a cost of £28,000.

The outstanding event in the locomotive field was the introduction of Malcolm's celebrated two-cylinder compound locomotives from 1890 onwards. No other railway found such success with this type of engine as the Northern Counties. By 1889 the locomotive department had 53 locomotives to maintain and narrow gauge engines had to be brought to Belfast for such repairs as the shops at Larne were incapable of.

The fitting of the automatic brake after 1882 was another job for the shops. Indeed this was a peak period for the production of new rolling stock and the improvement of old. A number of milestones at this time may be noticed: in 1888 a new class of six-wheeled carriages was introduced which it was stated was modelled on the latest London & North Western pattern. The first bogie coach was built at York Road in 1893 and a few years later a large number were purchased from outside sources. During 1890 the work of cushioning third class compartments began and in 1892 oil gas was adopted as the illuminant in carriages; a plant for its production was built at York Road at a cost of £2,500. A few carriages were experimentally fitted with electric lighting in 1896. In 1894 the first steps in train catering were taken when two saloons with modest kitchen facilities were built; the first dining car was built in 1899. At this time carriage heating was by foot-warmers (introduced in 1896). Finally in 1900 the 'passenger communication' system of the chain connected to the vacuum brake pipes was introduced. A few lines from the *Railway Magazine* in 1897 may be quoted:

> The first and second-class carriages are well upholstered, and a great many of them are provided with lavatory accommodation. The carriages on the Larne boat trains are especially good. A word of praise must be given to the exceedingly comfortable saloon carriages; . . . they are of a special type, something after the pattern of the ordinary Swiss railway carriages, with central corridor and railed platforms at each end, which naturally admit of a better view of the scenery than can be obtained from the interior. The saloons are luxuriously fitted up, and one part is specially reserved for smokers; they are usually run on the Larne boat trains, and on the 9.15am daily (summer) express to Portrush. The wider gauge of the railway enables eight persons to be comfortably seated in each first-class compartment.

Also in the *Railway Magazine*, this time in 1902, a contributor, quoting a menu from the dining car on the 12 noon express to Portrush, asserted that it would have been difficult to surpass in the British Isles: for luncheon, lobster, cold veal and ox tongue, pressed beef, chicken and ham, pigeon and ham pie, roast lamb and mint sauce could be chosen from, at a cost of 2s (10p). Dinner cost 3s (15p).

At this time much attention was focused on the automatic brake and on the block telegraph system. On 30 August 1877 the Board of Trade issued its famous circular extolling the virtues of the automatic continuous brake. This circular the B & NC ignored, nor did they implement the recommendations of a further circular. Stewart wrote to London on 15 July 1880:

The question of brake power has occasioned [the directors'] attention, and having given the matter full consideration, they are of the opinion that the trains running on this line do not require the use of continuous brakes, as from the fact that many of the trains being 'Mixed' they could not be applied. We have steam brakes attached to our engines and tenders, in addition to the ordinary brakes under the control of the guards, and these have been hitherto found quite sufficient for any emergency that has arisen.

Malcolm was much interested in the steam brake, and in the years following his appointment in 1876 had taken out several patents for improvements to this type of brake. At this time some half a million miles per year were being run.

But in June 1882 the decision was taken to adopt the automatic vacuum brake and before the end of the year two engines and nine carriages had been equipped. Over the six months January—June 1883 16,248 miles of passenger working were run using the brake and 282,088 without. At first only the main line stock was equipped but over the next few years all passenger stock and certain goods engines and vehicles occasionally used in passenger trains were fitted. By 1893 90 per cent of the passenger vehicles were fitted and vacuum mileage was 1,074,244—98 per cent of passenger working. The 21,138 miles of non-fitted working was mainly accounted for by the running of mixed trains. The purchase of the Ballymena & Larne in 1889 meant a slight setback since that company had used the Smith non-automatic vacuum brake. By the end of 1892, however, all ex-B & L stock had been refitted with the automatic system. The Board of Trade had set December 1891 as the deadline for completion of fitting the approved brake, under the Regulation of Railways Act, 1889.

By 1883 the line was 86 per cent interlocked; by 1890 94 per cent; by 1894 99.5 per cent. During the 1880s a wide-ranging but gradual programme of building modern signal cabins was undertaken, spreading the load of expense. The date for the completion of interlocking set by the Board of Trade was June 1892. During the 1880s absolute block working was extended to further sections of the line and by the end of 1891—the date stipulated by the Board of Trade—was universal throughout the system, the Ballyclare, Draperstown,

Dungiven and Derry Central branches, the Ballymena & Larne being thus worked from the outset, and the Cushendall line from the beginning of passenger working.

In November 1889 the tablet system was experimentally fitted on the Carrickfergus Junction—Carrickfergus section. Being found successful it was extended during 1890 to the entire Larne line (save the Larne—Larne Harbour section) and from Ballymena to Killagan. During 1891 the Killagan—Castlerock section was fitted and from Castlerock to Eglinton and Coleraine to Portrush in 1892. The final main line section from Eglinton to Londonderry followed in January 1893. It was not until 1901–2 that the system was applied to the Cookstown line and the Limavady branch, and not to the Derry Central until later. In 1899 the Manson tablet snatching system was fitted at main line block posts and also on the Larne line and Portrush branch. When the Cookstown line was re-equipped with tablet instruments, snatchers were placed there also. Despite the gradual adoption of modern methods in the 1880s, the bill to be met under the 1889 Regulation of Railways Act was £21,000.

HOME RULE

Twice in our period serious political upheavals disturbed Ulster and affected the Northern Counties Railway. Ulster as a rule was unaffected by the agrarian troubles associated with the Land War, but the Home Rule Bills of 1886 and 1893 profoundly stirred the Loyalists. The 1886 Bill was marked by a serious outbreak of sectarian rioting in Belfast which almost eliminated the usual crop of Sunday School and other excursions which annually swelled the railway's receipts.

An untoward incident took place on 7 August 1887. The Irish National Foresters, a pro-Home Rule organisation, hired two special trains for a Sunday trip from Belfast to Portrush. On the return journey exuberance exceeded discretion and passing through Ballymena station—Ballymena being a Loyalist stronghold—a number of shots were fired from one train, fortunately without hitting anyone. The Ballymena people were obviously not at all enamoured of the idea of the Foresters passing through their town, for a number of 'obstructions' thoughtfully placed on the rails were removed in the nick of time by the Royal Irish Constabulary, three of whose members were rewarded by the board. The upshot of the affair was a ban on the running of special excursions on Sundays, a ban which was to continue for twenty years and which, apart from its true intent, placated extreme Sabbatarians of whom there were still plenty.

With the repeal of the Party Concessions Act in 1872 it became possible to hold demonstrations on the 'Twelfth of July' and the 'Twelfth of August', providing useful revenue for the railway. The latter day especially—anniversary of the Relief of Londonderry in 1689—brought vast numbers by train to the Maiden City, especially from Belfast.

GILL AND WISE

The old secretary Charles Stewart was seriously affected by the Hopkirk affair and resigned shortly afterwards; he died in 1889 and another link with the old days had gone. To replace him William Robert Gill was appointed. He had been born at Dromore, County Down, in 1843 and joined the Ulster Railway at an early age. He then took a situation in Wales, returning to Ireland as assistant secretary of the Midland Great Western Railway, thence to the Northern Counties.

In 1888 Robert Collins resigned as civil engineer and for a period Bowman Malcolm fulfilled that office in addition to that of locomotive superintendent. Then in October a new and most significant appointment was made—that of Berkeley Deane Wise who was to become as celebrated as Malcolm in his own sphere. Wise had been born in New Ross, County Wexford, in 1853 and joined the Dublin, Wicklow & Wexford Railway as an apprentice engineer. He early showed great promise and in 1877 transferred to the Belfast & County Down Railway as their resident engineer. It was during his time at Queen's Quay that he invented the once famous train staff which bears his name. By the time he came to York Road he was a very eminent civil engineer and also a talented architect —something the B & NC had lacked as a combination since the days of Charles Lanyon, though the architectural styles of the two men could scarcely have differed more. He was to leave his mark upon the buildings of the Northern Counties down to the present day.

By the time Wise came to York Road, renewals of the line with steel rails were well under way; by 1880 half of the mileage was steel and in 1889 70 per cent. Wise might have been described as 'Mr Stone Ballast'; he was a great advocate of stone. The B & NC had never previously been noted for the excellence of its ballast. The standard permanent way specified by Wise was as follows: Rails—steel, bull head 83lb per yd; sleepers—creosoted Baltic redwood; chairs—cast iron, 42lb; keys—compressed oak; fishplates—steel, 39lb per pair; fishbolts—steel, Ibbotson's patent; ballast—broken stone from Whitehead; gravel from local sources. By 1895 the line was 87 per cent steel and by the end of our period hardly any iron rails survived save in sidings.

In the field of signalling Wise introduced the tablet system and the Manson snatcher and gave the Northern Counties the signal which characterises it down to the present day—the 'somersault'. His re-signalling of York Road in connection with the 1897-8 alterations was much admired for its ingenuity and economy in levers, and at the time was the largest installation in Ireland.

Even more important was his work as an architect. The first building he constructed was Larne Harbour station, and one of his major works was Portrush. By 1891 the existing station—that of the Ballymena & Portrush, dating from 1855—was totally inadequate to deal with the heavy summer traffic. A completely new station with three platforms 600ft long was planned—double the length of the single platform of the old station. It was opened in the spring of 1893, having been delayed by a strike of craftsmen employed by the contractors, McLaughlin & Harvey (who did much work for the B & NC). The new building was truly impressive and was certainly one of the most handsome railway buildings in Ireland. The style was 'mock Tudor' in stucco painted black and white on a red brick base. A well-proportioned clock tower rose to a height of fifty feet with four dials each 5ft in diameter. Inside the General Hall, railed off from the platforms, was 100ft long and 60ft wide and provided with all the usual offices splendidly furnished. To one side another wing housed the

'Cafe and Restaurant' in which 250 or 300 could be dined; it was 90ft long and 30ft wide. Outside was a balcony with commanding views of the Atlantic over the recreation ground; these grounds, railway property, were landscaped at this time and a bandstand provided. The station platforms were covered for 200ft of their length by an overall roof of the 'Belfast' type; under the restaurant (sometimes used as a concert hall) were large cellars which were the central stores for liquor for the railway hotels, dining cars and refreshment rooms.

When the work was completed the Northern Counties was provided with a station of which it could be proud, fully capable of dealing with all demands upon it. A goods store for the modest local goods traffic was provided in 1895 at a cost of £800. The entire station with the new track layout and full signalling cost more than £10,000.

During 1893 a new station was erected at Carrickfergus Junction, which was henceforth known as Greenisland. The situation here did not give scope for architectural triumph but Wise provided a fine three-platform station at this important place. Also on the Larne line a new building was required at Carrickfergus in 1895 when the old station was gutted by fire. The new one was an exceptionally fine mock Tudor style erection, with a main and island platform. Two minor stations rebuilt at this time on the Larne line deserve mention—Glynn, a simplified mock Tudor structure, and Trooperslane in the design of which Wise threw restraint to the winds and gave his imagination full rein. The result was a delightful little building on the up platform with high gables, large windows and rich ornamentation.

Wise was also responsible for the alterations at Belfast; the exterior style he used was *à la* Lanyon but the offices inside were and are a sheer delight in the Swiss style (some people say Norwegian), including a bookstall with a fine clock tower mounted atop. He also designed Antrim, Ballymena and Ballymoney stations erected at the turn of the century, and the new depot for the Portstewart Tramway. This is not to speak of his work at Glenariff, Black Head and The Gobbins, mentioned elsewhere.

TRAINS AND TRAFFIC

The 1880s began with depressed conditions prevailing and this was to remain the position for almost ten years. There was a slight increase in 1880 but in the first half of 1881 a fall in receipts of £7,700 was noted. By 1887, however, the receipts were 50 per cent up on the preceding year and thereafter there was a steady improvement. The first half of 1897 was the best period ever for revenue.

A unique phenomenon was noticed for some years in the early 1890s—third class receipts had always been important but now first and second class dropped away sharply. This became serious and from 1 May 1895 a new scale of fares devised by Cotton (who was a firm believer in three classes of carriages, though on the narrow gauge sections only first and third classes were provided), brought into force a sliding arrangement whereby the first and second class fares were lowered for journeys over 40 miles so that first class did not exceed 1½d per mile and second 1¼d; third remained at slightly less than 1d. It was hoped that this new system would lead to more passengers 'enjoying the social comfort and the dignity of travelling in a first class compartment' and such was indeed the case; the new arrangement proved extremely successful.

Third class passengers were not neglected by any means, however. Third class season tickets were first issued in May 1896 and led to a considerable increase in receipts; season ticket travel was of course an important feature on the Larne line especially and in 1900 an early morning workmen's train was put on from Carrickfergus to Belfast with especially low fares.

Goods rates, in common with most other Irish lines, were revised in 1893 and caused a real furore among customers. But since they were enforced by Act of Parliament there was little result from the protest meetings widely organised and largely attended.

For a number of years it had been recognised that the train service provided on the more important lines left much to be desired. In 1889, for example, the fastest train was the 12 noon Saturday express to Portrush which took 2hr 10min for 68 miles—an average of 37mph, including stops; bear in

THE LATE VICTORIAN COMPANY 1880–1899

mind that over half the distance was single line. There was also the tiresome ritual of reversal at Greenisland though by then this had been streamlined: engines of main line trains no longer ran round their trains but the trains were hauled out from Belfast and a second main line engine then 'hooked on' for the journey onwards. Larne boat expresses were not subject to this delay and took 45min to cover the 25 miles, an average speed of some 40mph. On the main line trains ran to Londonderry at 6.30am, 8.30am, 10.15am, 3.30pm and 5.15pm, portions being detached at Coleraine for Portrush. The 8.30 was the Mail and the 10.15 and 3.30 were 'expresses' though they took $3\frac{1}{2}$ hours; almost the same time as in the 1860s. The time lag between the 10.15 and the 3.30 meant that passengers arriving from the steamers missed the 10.15 if their boats were delayed.

In 1893 a complete alteration took place, owing to the altered time of arrival of the English steamers in Belfast. The 8.30 now left at 8am and other trains were run at 9.45am, 12.05pm, 3.30pm and 5.10pm. The 3.30 and 5.10 expresses covered the 95 miles in 2hr 55min, very creditable in view of the two-thirds mileage of single track, the lack of tablet snatchers, and the number of stops. The other main line trains were speeded up also and the expresses maintained an average speed of $33\frac{3}{4}$mph. The Portrush summer expresses now took 2hr and the company's pride was the Saturdays only 'Portrush & Ballycastle Express' which, stopping only at Ballymoney to set down for Ballycastle, took 1hr 40min—an average speed of just over 40mph. The boat trains were expedited to a timing of 40min—an average speed of $36\frac{1}{2}$mph.

A considerable number of new trains were laid on all over the system; the increasing traffic necessitated them. Slip couplings came into use to obviate stops at Ballyclare Junction and other places. On the narrow gauge the best train was the boat express from Ballymena to Larne Harbour in connection with the steamer, taking 1hr for 25 miles—the fastest narrow gauge journey in these islands.

MAGILLIGAN POINT

In Chapter 3 we saw the short life of the railway built by

the Londonderry & Coleraine to Magilligan Point. The route of this line remained the property of the railway after its closure and so it was transferred to the B & NC in 1871; it appears that the rails may have remained *in situ*, at least for a time.

In the 1890s much interest centred on Magilligan Point; at the time trans-Atlantic liners were calling in Lough Foyle and Magilligan was visualised as a second Queenstown, replacing Moville on the Donegal shore which was the point from which tenders put out to the ships. The B & NC also began to evince interest, though their principal reason was the opening up of Inishowen, which had considerable tourist potential; hitherto it had been difficult of access—'locked up', as the chairman said. In 1894 the company proposed to build a line $4\frac{1}{2}$ miles long on the roadbed of the L & C line but slightly longer. Since the majority of the land was already owned the cost was not expected to exceed £7,000 per mile. A pier was to be built at the Point from which steamers would ply to Moville and Greencastle—a matter of two or three miles.

The railway was duly sanctioned by Act of 6 July 1895, the usual period of five years being given for construction. But the clause relating to the pier at the Point had to be withdrawn owing to the concerted opposition of the Admiralty, the Irish Society and the Londonderry Port & Harbour Commissioners. They managed to destroy the real *raison d'être* of the branch and the B & NC rested on its oars. An extension of the time limit was granted for three years by the 1899 Act; interest revived briefly in 1898 when a hotel and golf course were built at the Point and again in 1902 when a military camp opened. But the railway never materialised.

TRAGEDY AT ANTRIM

On 7 August 1897 a very serious accident of a unique nature occurred near Antrim. The train was the 3pm Up Mail from Londonderry which at Ballymena had changed engines, No 58 (formerly No 50), one of Malcolm's very successful 2-4-0 Worsdell-von Borries compounds of 1890 taking over. Behind the tender were nine coaches. The train stopped at Cookstown Junction and everything appeared normal. About 400yd outside Antrim, however, the guard heard a report like thunder and saw dense clouds of steam and smoke emanating from the engine. When he perceived that the train was not slowing to stop at Antrim he applied the automatic vacuum brake and brought it to a stand at the platform.

It was discovered that all was far from well with the engine; on the footplate was the lifeless body of the driver, James Turner, aged 42. Some 400yd outside the station the dead body of fireman Con McAllister, aged 26, was found. Whereas Turner had been scalded to death McAllister had died from a fractured skull sustained in leaping from the engine at speed. At the point where he was found the contents of the cab were strewn about; the fireman's cap was 40yd away in a field and the driver's pipe in a field on the opposite side. Cinders and carbon were scattered about for a distance of 40yd.

Bowman Malcolm arrived by special engine and this engine took forward the Mail from which No 58 was removed. It was obvious that the cause of the accident was the collapse of the firebox, though for no apparent reason. It was presumed that McAllister had been firing at the time and so steam at 160–170lb pressure rushed through the firebox door.

Major F. A. Marindin RE investigated the occurrence for the Board of Trade. The main facts of the case were not in doubt but the reason for the collapse was. Several leading engineers were engaged to examine the boiler when it was taken out of the engine at York Road but no satisfactory cause could be discerned. No 58 was a Belfast engine and worked a heavy roster but had only returned to work in April 1897 following a three month overhaul, since when only 16,880 miles had been run. Under the system then in operation the district foreman thoroughly examined each engine weekly and a boiler inspector periodically certified the boiler—every three or four months. David Turner, locomotive foreman at Belfast and brother of the deceased, had found no faults on his last inspection nor had a workman fitting a new brick arch on 3 August. A leaky stay head in the firebox had been remarked on earlier on 7 August but had caused no special trouble.

On the removal of the firebox it was discovered that of 547 stays 102 were broken, but the fusible plugs were not melted.

It was presumed that at the last inspection the dangerous state of the stays had not been noticed; clearly steam and boiling water had rushed through the holes left by the collapsed stays. But why the firebox should collapse with less than a fifth of the stays gone remained a mystery. Malcolm suggested that at some time the fire had been lit with the boiler empty, though he had caused notices reading 'Boiler empty' to be made for suspension from regulator handles under such circumstances. Marindin for his part considered that the weekly inspection of engines was 'anything but critical' and the system was tightened up; it was arranged that boilers and fireboxes were to be thoroughly examined weekly on shed days. No 58 was rebuilt and continued to work normally thereafter.

OTHER ACCIDENTS

Only four other accidents worthy of note occurred during these years on the Northern Counties' own lines. The first was at Coleraine on 28 September 1887. The 7am up train from Londonderry was derailed just on the Londonderry side of the Bann Bridge so that serious consequences might have resulted. The engine and tender, two passenger vans, a composite, a third, another composite and a guard's van were all derailed but there was little damage to stock and only one passenger complained of injury. The permanent way was old, consisting of 80lb per yd double head rail and Col Rich found the ballast 'of very indifferent quality'. Some 51yd from the bridge a chair had broken—probably under the weight of a previous train—and the rail on the curve spread. The bridgeman going on duty noticed this and set off to stop the train with a flag, but for some reason failed to keep his signal at danger. The driver therefore was running at full normal speed and only shut off steam on seeing the flag; since his train had the automatic brake it stopped in some 70 or 80yd but not before it had passed over the damaged section.

The inspecting officer blamed the quality of the permanent way and also the ganger for his negligence—that morning's inspection had been cursory. He also found fault with the signalling arrangements at the bridge—a distant signal was needed and also timber baulks to prevent trains which might be derailed on the bridge falling into the river. As a result the signalling arrangements were completely revised and some years later a proper signal cabin provided, also controlling the junction with the Coleraine harbour line. The bridge was now over twenty years old and in 1880 a shareholder had enquired as to its safety following the Tay Bridge disaster of the previous year. He was told that constant inspections and renewals took place and a bridgeman was always on duty. Four years later further questions were asked; Collins (who had been familiar with it from its building) said it was stronger than it appeared; wrought iron girders carried the track—'it is the look of it more than anything else that annoys you'. But Rankin the questioner said, 'I thank Providence whenever the train gets over.'

At Castlerock, a quiet seaside station, there was considerable agitation on the morning of 27 February 1892. About 8.25am the 7.0 Londonderry—Belfast passenger was standing at the platform when it was run into in rear by a ballast train from Limavady. There were no injuries and the 7.0 was undamaged, being able to continue its journey after a short delay. Castlerock was being resignalled at this time; the section to Coleraine was worked by tablet but in the Londonderry direction the train staff was still used. The passenger train was 18min late—because of bad steaming owing to the collapse of the brick arch—and it was running on a train ticket. Downhill was a block post to protect the tunnel; the station master there tried to contact Castlerock but got no response since everyone at the latter was examining the engine of the 7.0. The ballast was sent forward; fortunately the fireman of the 7.0 noticed it approaching and slowing to pick up the tablet and took off the brake on his train—so that the impact was lessened and the 7.0 pushed forward only a carriage length. For some reason the distant signal had remained at clear after the arrival of the passenger. The Downhill station master and the Castlerock porter signalman were held to blame by Maj-Gen Hutchinson who also censured Russell, driver of the 7.0, who had known of, but failed to report, the collapse of his engine's brick arch some days previously.

Whitehead was venue of a minor accident on 25 August 1894. The 8.15pm up stopping passenger from Larne Harbour to Belfast was derailed three quarters of a mile on the Belfast side of Whitehead; there were eight vehicles behind the tender and the second, sixth, seventh and eighth left the rails before the train stopped 330yd from the point of derailment. Relaying through the tunnel had been going on and a caution notice had been issued by Cotton, enforcing a speed restriction of 10mph through the area. The gang had left work at midday on Saturday but nothing was left to mark the site of work. The permanent way, being relaid, was in a dangerous condition. Maj-Gen Hutchinson adverted to the possibility of disaster had some of the derailed vehicles hit the walls of the 145yd tunnel through which they were dragged but fortunately all remained upright and no one was injured.

The final accident to be noticed took place also on the Larne line at Larne Town station (broad gauge) on 13 July 1898. The line from Carrickfergus was worked under tablet regulations and thence to Larne Harbour by staff and ticket. A number of specials were being run as it was the day of the Orange demonstrations. The 9.55am Belfast—Larne regular passenger overran Larne down home signal at danger and turned into the sea loop where it collided violently with a train of empty carriages waiting to proceed to Belfast. Both trains were extensively damaged.

The 9.55 was late and the signalman mistook one of the specials which had arrived some time previously for it, reversed the road and pulled off for the empty carriages to proceed; though fortunately they had not yet started. It appeared that Larne distant signal was never lowered and drivers tended to ignore it. Lt-Col G. W. Addison RE, the investigating officer, found the entire circumstances 'quite inexcusable'. He found deplorable the fact that the tablet instrument to Ballycarry was in the station master's office (a common practice then) and so the signalman had no visual record of the position in the section. He also discovered that block working was only enforced from Larne to the Harbour after darkness—otherwise trains proceeded at will (this was not as dangerous as it sounds since the Harbour station could be seen from the Town station). Nevertheless Addison insisted that block working be enforced at all times and shortly afterwards the Town-Harbour section was equipped with tablet instruments and Larne Town was resignalled, the tablet instruments being placed in the signal cabin.

STAFF RELATIONS

From the outset of his management Cotton had set himself to lay the foundations of good staff relations and this early work now bore fruit, sparing the Northern Counties much of the acrimony which attended the development of trades unionism on other Irish lines in the 1890s. Any man with a genuine grievance was always sure of a sympathetic hearing; which is not to say that Cotton was any weakling—both he and Malcolm, the two officers most directly concerned with the men, were stern disciplinarians but never harsh or unjust.

As early as 1861 a Workmen's Provident Society had been set up; it was evidence of the interest Cotton, who was a founder member of the Railway Benevolent Institution in 1858, took in this side of affairs. A clause in the 1890 Act set up a very successful savings bank scheme for the men whereby they could invest in the company. By the 1895 Act power was given to subscribe to the Provident Society and the Pension Fund. The latter had been started in 1894 primarily for the permanent way men whose employment tended to be more seasonal than that of most other grades; in 1888 a superannuation scheme for superior staff had been instituted. From 1 January 1899 a full pension scheme for the entire staff came into being.

Finally, in 1902 a convalescent home was opened at Whitehead under the auspices of the Provident Society, which, as also the Pension Fund, was managed by a committee with representatives of the board and the men sitting side by side in harmony.

TWO JUBILEES

The year 1895 was a momentous one for the company, for it celebrated two jubilees: on 21 July that of its own incorporation fifty years before, and on 29 October the general manager, Edward John Cotton, achieved the fiftieth year of his railway service.

At the 100th half-yearly meeting on 5 August 1895 Young quoted some statistics illustrative of the B & NC's progress over fifty years. The capital had grown from £385,000 to over £2½ million, the number of shareholders from 221 to some 3,400; the mileage from 37½ to 203 with an additional 46 miles worked. The revenue in the first year of operation had been £23,000; in 1894–5 it had been £265,000. The shares at the outset had sold at 22 per cent and now stood at 144 per cent. The dividend for 1848–9 was nil; in 1895 it was 5¾ per cent. Since the instigation of villa tickets nearly 200 had been issued; in 1845 the population of Portrush was about 630, now it was 1,700 or 1,800 in winter and three or four times that in summer. Of the original subscribers only George J. Clarke, chairman from 1867 to 1885, survived; indeed he had been involved in the 1836 proposal.

In commemoration of the company's jubilee the chairman was presented with an oil portrait by the proprietors in August 1896. As was widely remarked at the time, the two jubilees were closely connected. For thirty-eight of the fifty years Cotton had been in control; he had seen the railway expand from its small beginnings to achieve great prosperity and this was in the main due to his able and painstaking management.

On 29 October a meeting was convened in the permanent way carpentry shop in Duncrue Street, near York Road station. The chair was taken by W. R. Gill the secretary, with whom on the platform were representatives from all departments of the B & NC and the railway world generally. They were met, said Gill, to do honour to one of the best known men in the Province of Ulster—to celebrate the railway jubilee of their friend Mr Cotton, who had spent thirty-eight of his fifty years in railway service with the B & NC. The presentation was a portrait, a large one depicting Cotton reading *The Railway News*, and the work of Neil M. Lund RA, a well-known portrait painter. It is of interest that subscriptions were taken only from the officers and staff, many pressing offers from directors and general public being declined.

In reply Cotton said he was proud to have been connected 'from his youth up' with an enterprise which had done more to increase the aggregate of human comfort and happiness and

ROAD TRANSPORT

(*above*) Parkmore—Cushendall mail car, *c* 1890 (*below*) Steam road wagon, 1902

Page 238

GLENARIFF
(*above*) Ess-na-Larach (*below*) Tea House

to give an impetus of the world's industries 'than any other invention of this nineteenth century of ours'. In his early days the third class passenger had been looked upon rather as a necessary evil; his carriages were worse, not better, than cattle wagons. His penny per mile was certainly good value for money if measured in the length of time the journey took. Now they had learned to regard third class traffic as their bread and butter.

He expected to see a continuous growth in Irish passenger traffic, particularly through tourism. 'Ireland is still an unknown country. If the working population of Belfast does not occasionally emerge from the crowded quarters of the city to admire the grand works of nature or to inhale the life-sustaining ozone of the Atlantic Ocean, the blame assuredly cannot be laid at the door of the railway company, which takes people to Portrush for half-a-crown, and to Whitehead for what Mr. Gladstone calls "the comprehensible shilling".'

He went on to recall the offer made in 1869 of a position in India, which he had declined:

> ... My connection with this company was nearly severed a quarter of a century ago, when I had a tempting offer to go abroad. Our present chairman, however, did his best to induce me to stay, and as his persuasion was backed up by the other members of the staff, I declined the offer and continued to sail in the good old ship, the Belfast and Northern Counties Railway ...

Later he was made the recipient of a valuable presentation by the directors. The Rt Hon John Young, in making the presentation, said that 'in the course of his connection with the Northern Counties line their general manager had taken a leading part in all their extensions, purchases and additions over their system, until they now had almost undisputed possession of the north-east corner of Ireland. Mr. Cotton, indeed, had been looked upon by them as being more a managing director than anything else.'

CHAPTER NINE

Tourism

> We will make for Ireland presently
> *Richard II* Act I Scene IV
> This quotation appeared on B & NCR Tourist
> Guides and reflects Cotton's love of Shakespeare.

A VICTORIAN INSTITUTION

One of the most interesting characteristics of the Victorian Age, and one of its most enduring memorials, was the great increase in tourism. Ireland more than anywhere, perhaps, benefited and in the last quarter of the nineteenth century large and ever-increasing numbers made the sea crossing to savour the delights of the scenery of the Emerald Isle.

The Belfast & Northern Counties was excellently placed to serve this traffic for no other railway in Ireland had a system which was so well adapted to carry tourists to such varied attractions. An advertisement in 1902 mentions as draws to visitors, 'Recuperative and Bracing air off the open Atlantic; Good Sea Bathing; Splendid Golf Links; Grand Coast, Glen, Cliff and Mountain Scenery; Prehistoric Settlements, Cromlechs, Tumuli'.

The success which attended the development of the Larne—Stranraer short sea passage may in large measure be attributed to the influx of tourists. The advantages of a 'daylight crossing' in the summer months were not to be minimised, and the ease of communication afforded at Larne Harbour to the north of Ireland with trains running from the steamer berth was also important. The Larne—Stranraer route for these reasons became perhaps the premier tourist route across the Irish Sea. The question may be asked, why railway companies had to expend capital on tourist development. The answer is that until 1898 there were few local authorities in Ireland, and even after that date they were generally penurious. Further, it was to the railways' advantage to encourage tourist traffic.

PLANNING AND PUBLICITY

The tremendous development of tourism in the north of Ireland was not achieved without much thought to planning and a vigorous publicity campaign. There was a general feeling that nothing had been done until the late 1880s. But this was far from the truth; for long before this efforts had been made to draw the attractions of the neighbouring island to the attention of Britons and this net spread farther afield. 'For a considerable time we saw but very little result from our labours, but there is now [1895], I am glad to say, a movement among the dry bones, and for the last year or two we have been deriving a tolerable harvest from the seed which appeared at one time to have fallen on stony ground', said Cotton in an interview in *St Paul's Magazine*.

One of the principal features of the advertisement programme was the commissioning of photographs of places of tourist interest which, besides serving to decorate first class compartments and waiting rooms, were made into pictorial posters and permanently exhibited by the B & NC at Olympia, the Imperial Institute, the Royal Aquarium and in the principal hotels and 'golf clubhouses throughout the United Kingdom. Also included were some 200 public elementary schools; school managers constantly applied for them, Cotton said, since they were found 'to be ornamental as well as useful to school work'.

Illustrated guide books were published and distributed far and wide. They dealt thoroughly with every aspect of the district served by the railway. Each line and branch was systematically described, listing all towns with details of hotels and catering establishments and features of historical interest with precise details of how to reach them. Not the least interesting feature was a special section at the back of the books, consisting of specially-commissioned erudite articles on aspects of the area. Every possible requirement of the tourist was dealt with; these guide books were a pleasure to look at.

The practice of exhibiting photographs spread further afield and it became customary to mount a display at the several international exhibitions held during this period. At the Chicago World's Fair of 1894 a stand was provided jointly with the GNR(I), while at the Antwerp Universal Exhibition of 1895 one was taken by the Northern Counties on its own account; one cannot fail to be struck by the enterprise of a small Irish railway company in spreading its publicity campaign so far afield. One of Cotton's most beneficial moves was in persuading the other Irish companies to join with the B & NC in opening an office at the new Charing Cross Hotel in London in the early 1890s, which facilitated booking to Ireland for the tourist.

EXCURSIONS

The policy instituted early in Cotton's reign of running frequent cheap excursions bore ample reward. Even before his arrival in Belfast, however, cheap travelling facilities were provided; in August 1849 Queen Victoria visited Belfast and it was announced that special trains would be run from Ballymena and intermediate stations. In the same year, day excursion tickets were being issued from Belfast to Randalstown (for Shane's Castle demesne) at fares of 3s 9d (19p) first class, 2s 6d (12½p) second, and 1s 6d (7½p) third, reductions of about one-third on the normal fares.

In 1859 Cotton inserted in the timetable:

> The Belfast and Ballymena Company's line affords great facilities for Excursionists and Pic-Nic Parties. Parties of eight and upwards visiting Shane's Castle, Masserene Park, Toome Bridge, Moyola Park, Castledawson, Dunluce Castle and the Giant's Causeway can obtain Excursion Tickets at reduced fares upon application to Edward J. Cotton, Traffic Manager, York-road Terminus, Belfast.

Shane's Castle and Masserene Park were then open to the public and excursions to there and other places often attracted more than 1,000.

TOURISM 243

Nor was the seaside neglected. Excursion tickets to Portrush and Portstewart at the normal single fares, valid for seven days on the main line with special rates from the Cookstown line, and subscription tickets, were issued. A more ambitious excursionist could obtain tickets available over the Londonderry & Coleraine and Londonderry & Enniskillen line to Omagh, Enniskillen, Lough Erne and Sligo, connection to the two last-mentioned places being by road. A handbill extant from this period, headed 'A GREAT TREAT!', details an excursion from Cookstown to Belfast on 16 September 1857 and it is stated that 'from the Cave Hill the excursionists will have a splendid view of the sea and ships sailing to all parts of the world'.

With the considerable expansion that took place in tourism in the 1880s and 1890s the programme of special attractions was broadened and a glance at the 1899 tourist and excursion guide will illustrate this. An extensive schedule of excursion fares was operated from Belfast, Londonderry, Larne and Portrush and intermediate stations to the seaside resorts and other attractions served by the line, an example being Larne to Ballycastle via broad gauge and Belfast, and Ballyclare to Portrush, outward by broad gauge and returning via Ballymena and the narrow gauge.

The steamer link with Stranraer opened up whole new possibilities and combined rail, steamer and bicycle tickets were issued; the passenger and bicycle were carried to Stranraer, a 'pamphlet descriptive of Twelve Cycling Tours in Galloway can be obtained on application to the Traffic Manager'. Special cyclists' tickets were also issued for travel on the Northern Counties system only. One-day tickets to Stranraer provided a trip to Ayr 'and the Land of Burns'; leaving Belfast at 9.5am, arriving at Ayr at 2.30pm, the return train leaving there at 5.20pm and Belfast being reached at 10pm. Coach tours by char-a-banc were made available from Stranraer station to Loch Glentoul, Murray's Monument, the Vale of Glenapp and Portpatrick for parties of six or more; and two-day or weekend hotel, train and steamer tickets to the Galloway Arms Hotel, Newton Stewart, and a weekend excursion to the Gatehouse-of-Fleet. A series of six circular tours of the Scottish Highlands, based on Glasgow, was also offered.

Nor was this programme confined to Scotland. The English

Lake District was served by two arrangements, one offering through tickets to Harrogate, Scarborough and Buxton, the other a circular tour 'enabling holders to travel via Carlisle and Penrith to Keswick, and thence by Coach through Grasmere and Ambleside to Windermere (L & NW Station) returning by Rail from Windermere via Oxenholme to Larne and Belfast'.

Within Ireland the Cork International Exhibition was held in 1899 and through tickets from Portrush, Coleraine, Ballymoney, Ballymena, Kilrea, Maghera, Magherafelt, Randalstown and Larne were issued, valid over the B & NC, GNR(I) and GS & WR. Through bookings were also available to many stations on the Donegal Railway, opening up the beauties of that county, and a circular tour encompassing the Giant's Causeway, Londonderry, the Donegal Highlands and Lough Erne was run, entitling passengers to travel from Belfast and other stations to Portrush, then by electric tramway to the Causeway and back to Portrush, thence by train to Londonderry and on via Strabane and Stranorlar to Donegal. Coaches carried the passengers through the Highlands to Bundoran, whence they returned to Belfast (Great Victoria Street) via Enniskillen and Lough Erne.

Besides the very many special tickets issued to Portrush and the other resorts Saturday excursions were run to Portrush especially for golfers, these being naturally of first class standard. Through fares were offered from points as far distant as Dublin and Enniskillen, in co-operation with the other railways, to Portrush links. Then there were the combined railway and hotel tickets to the Northern Counties Hotel, Portrush, to Ballycastle (Antrim Arms and Marine Hotels) and Larne Harbour (Olderfleet Hotel).

The picnic party tickets were still being issued to Masserene Park and Lough Neagh ('Pic-Nics may be held in the Deer Park Cottage' [Shane's Castle]). Larger parties could have special reductions on even the excursion fares 'provided that it is exclusively a Pleasure Party'. An interesting trip was available by steamer and train; leaving Londonderry by rail the tripper could join the *Melmore*, one of the Earl of Leitrim's steamers, at Portrush, returning by it to Londonderry. The same steamer also plied in Mulroy Bay in Donegal.

Again for the golfing enthusiast, G. B. Baillie was at this

time operating his celebrated golfing excursions to Portrush and Newcastle which for £3.75 included first class train fare, green fees, and accommodation at the Northern Counties Hotel or the B & CD's Slieve Donard Hotel in Newcastle, for five days. A similar tour embraced the Donegal links at Rosapenna, Portsalon and Lisfannon; 'these tickets are not confined to golfers' and included rail fares over the B & NC and Lough Swilly Railways, hotels, green fees and steamer and char-a-banc trips.

We have to remember that every effort was being made (and with great success) to attract cross-Channel tourists and through fares were available from all over Great Britain. Not only was there the London office, but certain travel agents in the principal centres also issued tickets. Naturally most of these attractions were run in summer only—but the Northern Counties' enterprising spirit did not confine itself to the warmer period of the year. In 1894–5, when Lough Neagh was largely frozen over for six weeks, 'skating specials' were run at cheap fares and Antrim Bay was illuminated by a number of 'Well's patent lights'.

Besides these excursions organised by the railway company itself there was the heavy summer programme of special trains operated on behalf of outside organisations, especially Sunday Schools and other church bodies, and works trips to the seaside and the country. Saturday was the most popular day for these outings—Sunday being a *dies non* in Northern Ireland and Sunday specials being withdrawn after the incident in 1887 mentioned in Chapter 8. On a typical Sunday, 17 June 1899, probably not less than 10,000 persons were on the move on the B & NC in special parties—taking no account of ordinary travellers. This was no small order to a railway owning only slightly more than 200 carriages with a seating capacity not far in excess of 12,000, and also having to maintain its regular summer Saturday service.

Nor must we neglect the large number of special trains chartered by the Loyalist organisations around the 'Twelfth of July' and the 'Twelfth of August', the latter event being concentrated on Londonderry; and the trains required from time to time, especially in the years after 1886, to carry those politically minded (and there were few in Ulster who were not at this time) to important political meetings and rallies, often held in the demesnes of landowners.

Whatever the source excursion traffic was a most valuable agent in the augmentation of the revenue. Certain sections of this traffic were recurring—the Sunday School trips, for example, scarcely ever varied in their destination, one preferring Portrush, another Whitehead, and so on. But the cross-Channel tourist traffic was largely governed by considerations of weather, and it was only a slight exaggeration to write, as did a contributor to *The Railway Magazine* in 1897, that 'a wet season and unfavourable weather may make the half-yearly report very unpleasant reading for the shareholders'.

SPECIAL ATTRACTIONS

Cotton once said, 'I am credibly informed by a regular trans-Atlantic traveller that the average American tourist when he visits this country inquires for two places only—the Lakes of Killarney and the Giant's Causeway. Our good friends the Great Southern & Western Company and the Cork & Bandon company are in possession of the communications to Killarney, and we are equally fortunate in regard to the Causeway.' This is by no means an exaggeration even today. The interest of tourists in the strange volcanic headlands and rock formations east of Portrush may seem inordinate to the Ulsterman but whatever the reason they come in their thousands to ogle at the polygonal vertical rock formations.

In the early days of the railway, passengers had to be conveyed the seven miles from Portrush station to the Causeway in jaunting or side-cars. In 1883 the Giant's Causeway, Portrush & Bush Valley Electric Tramway began operations to Bushmills and in 1887 reached the Causeway; since the line began outside the railway station in Portrush the journey became much quicker and easier, besides being an attraction in itself, since the tramway was the first hydro-electric railway in the world.

Golf was a sport which had a remarkable expansion in the closing years of the last century. The first course in Ireland dated from 1881; shortly afterwards a small course was laid out at Portrush by a number of enthusiasts; in the spring of

1888 the County Club was opened at Portrush. This, a nine-hole course, was adjacent to the railway station and was promoted by local golfers with the assistance of the B & NCR. A clubhouse was erected in 1891; the railway lent £200 free of interest to help build it. In 1892 the first Irish Open Amateur Championship was played here. In the same year it was granted the prefix 'Royal' when it came under the patronage of HRH the Duke of York. By 1889 the original nine holes had been increased to eighteen.

One of Ulster's most celebrated tourist attractions is the famous Antrim Coast Road stretching from Larne to Ballycastle and Portrush, engineered in the years after 1832. Just as famous are the 'Nine Glens of Antrim' which may be seen from the Road—Glentow, Glenshesk, Glendun, Glencorp, Glenaan, Glenballyemon, Glenariff, Glencoy and Glenarm. All are very beautiful but the largest and finest is Glenariff, sometimes called 'The Queen of Glens'—'Switzerland in miniature', Thackeray termed it—stretching from Parkmore down to the sea. When the Cushendall line was bought and opened to passengers whole new possibilities of tourism were opened up. Glenariff was leased from the landlords, Conway R. Dobbs (of the C & L) and Robert Hassard, and Wise laid out a series of paths and bridges through it so as to make it easily accessible to the tourists who were brought down from Parkmore station in jaunting cars. It was opened to the public in July 1889.

Glenariff derives its name from the Gaelic *Glynn Aircomb* ('Valley of the Numbers'), probably an allusion to the number of waterfalls it contains. Three are famous: the Hermit's Fall, the stupendous *Ess-na-Larach* ('Fall of the Battlefield') and *Ess-na-Crub* ('The Mare's Fall').

In 1891 a 'Tea House' was opened at the lower end of the Glen, which besides providing refreshments incorporated a darkroom for photographers.

The walk through the Glen occupied about an hour, in places the path cantilevered from sheer rock faces, at others clutching for support only a few feet above the roaring waters. Rustic shelters were built at strategic points, including the famous one below *Ess-na-Larach* from which the great fall could be observed through coloured glass with wonderful effect. Special arrangements were made with a number of carmen to

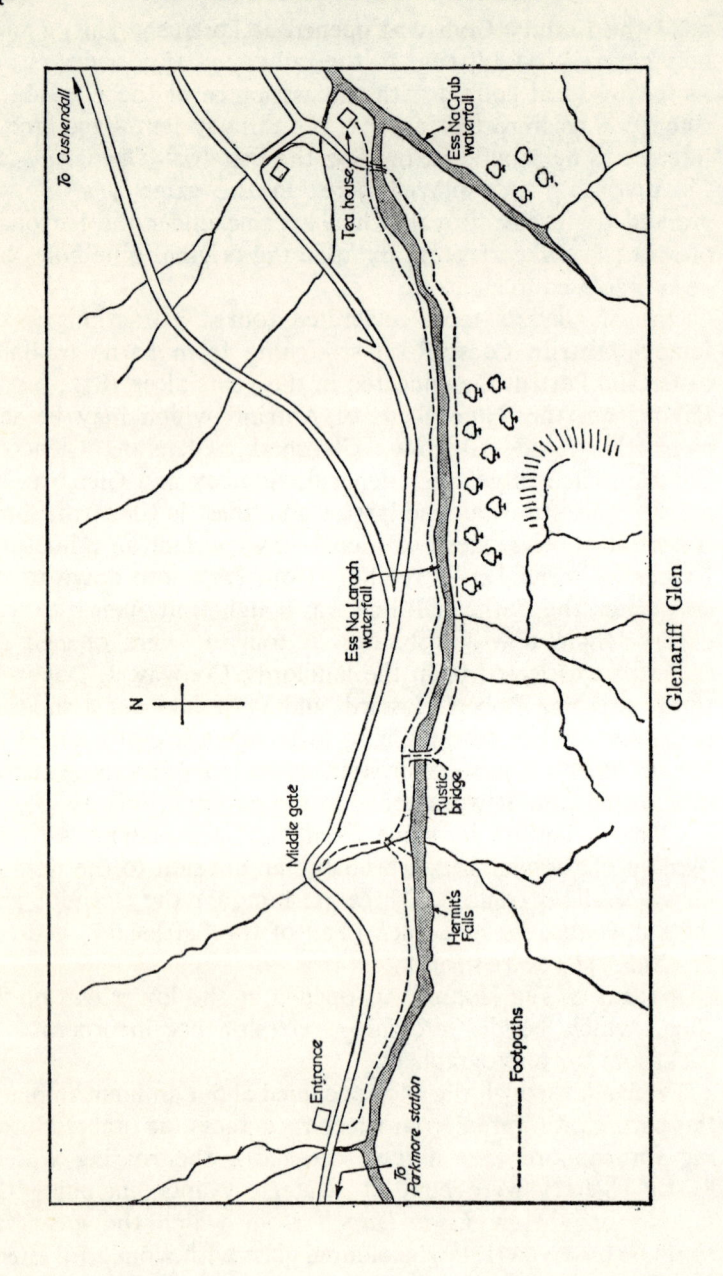

Glenariff Glen

attend at Parkmore station to convey passengers to Glenariff:

> Passengers are warned not to listen to any proposals regarding conveyances at Parkmore that may be made to them by Persons in the Train, and are respectfully requested to call the attention of the Guard to any case of annoyance caused by such persons . . . To avoid excessive demands visitors should engage only Cars bearing the names of the Owners enumerated above . . .

The lease of the Glen was continued until the 1930s when the NCC purchased the wayleaves outright, thus preserving the beauties of Glenariff forever. In 1967, under the reorganisation of public transport in Northern Ireland, the Glen was transferred to the keeping of the Ministry of Agriculture for Northern Ireland, which body has considerably improved it. There are few of Wise's rustic structures left now, but their replacements are just as pleasing.

There is also much fine scenery of a different kind in the Islandmagee area—the peninsula extending northwards from Whitehead and cutting off a long inlet of the sea known as Larne Lough. Here is to be found much of interest in natural history and geology as well as many traces of man's habitation in former eras. North of Whitehead town is the promontory known as Black Head. Here the Carrickfergus & Larne had already made some provisions for tourists, noted in Chapter 6. With the Northern Counties in control, Wise decided to make further improvements and in 1892 he engineered a cliff path stretching $1\frac{1}{4}$ miles out from Whitehead, its lower stretches bordering the shore, but blasting and cantilevering out from the upper cliff faces as necessary. The path was circular at its northern end, the upper path topping Black Head, and including McCartney's and The Swallow caves.

The little town of Whitehead was growing by leaps and bounds, largely thanks to the villa tickets, the B & NC fulfilling many of the functions of a local authority. The 1899 Act gave the B & NC authority to build a promenade and landing stage at Whitehead and an agreement was signed with the Board of Trade on 21 January 1901 assigning the railway portion of the foreshore. The promenade, some half a mile in length, bore tribute to its owners, since it was largely built of railway sleepers and lit by typical railway-type oil lamps. It gave the town a real tourist attraction and was the source of much pride to the company. The landing stage enabled pleasure boats to tie up.

It was also necessary to provide a beach, which was lacking. To overcome this deficiency Wise, with his usual enterprise, imported sand by special train from Portrush, and to protect the new strand groynes of old sleepers were built! A bandstand was built on the promenade ('Marine Parade' was its official title) and here on Waterloo Night four or five bands provided the music and there was a display of what the Victorians called pyrotechnics. Ladies' and gents' bathing places, with the usual boxes, completed the new facilities. To improve train running a loop was opened in 1902 at the Briggs Point, between Whitehead and Kilroot.

The railway was fulfilling the functions of a local authority. A local effort about 1895 to set up a development company met with very little success.

Further north of Whitehead on the eastern coast of Islandmagee lies the region of high basaltic cliffs known as The Gobbins. They reach a height of 250ft and were then approachable only by water. Erosion has worn them into fantastic shapes and features.

> To the active spirit of enterprise of the engineer who had already accomplished so much, these cliffs soon revealed another source from which, with but little expenditure, could be derived an almost endless source of pleasure . . .

Wise set to work to build a path which for long stretches was quarried out of solid basalt only a few feet above the sea. Steps were cut to reach the various levels and across ravines bridges were thrown; at one point two bridges connected a spectacular feature, the 'Man o' War's Stack', to the main path, one of these tubular bridges being 70ft long. These and the other bridges were built at Belfast, then hauled out from Whitehead on barges and laboriously lifted into place.

The first section was completed in August 1902 in time for the visit to Belfast of the British Association. On 20 August a special train carried the members, who had elected Wise chairman for the visit, and the Northern Counties directors

TOURISM 251

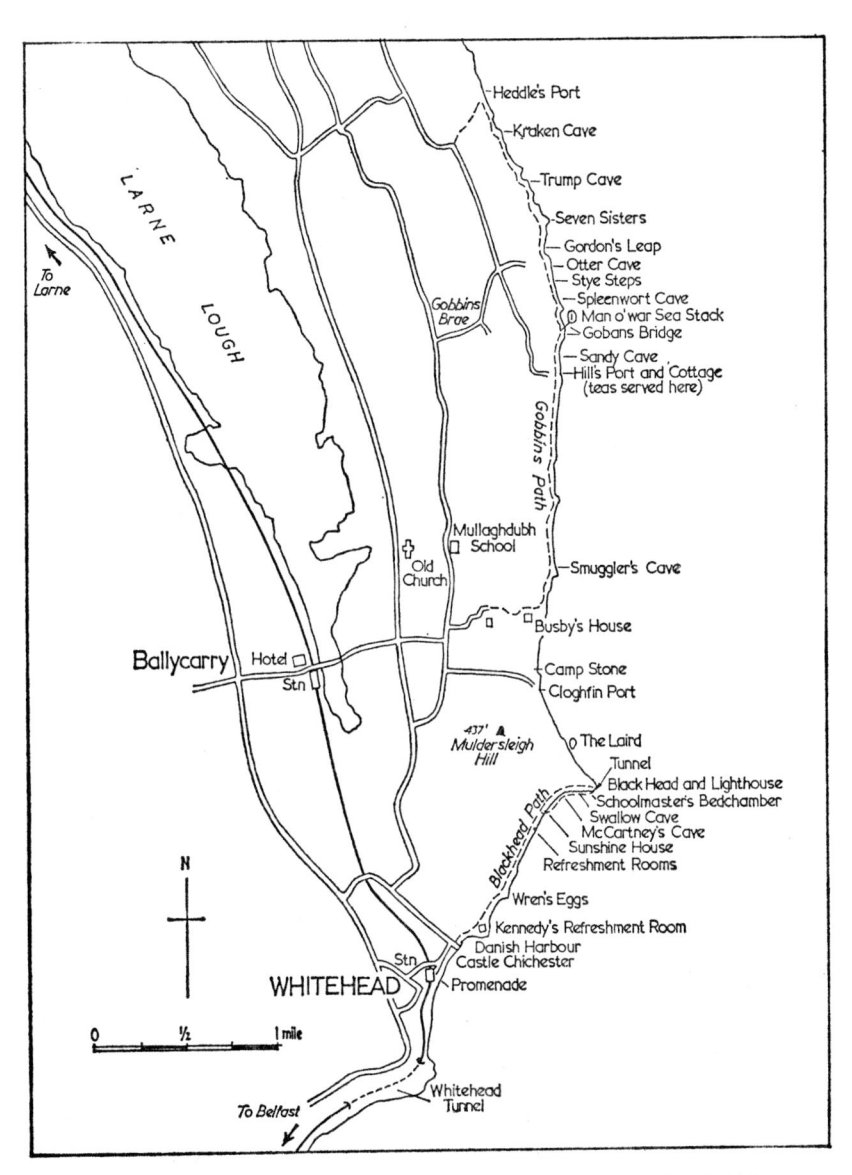

Whitehead and Islandmagee with Black Head Path and The Gobbins Path as originally planned

to Ballycarry, and thence they were led over the path by the engineer 'whose skill . . . has added so much to the success of the Northern Counties Railway'. In his honour two of the promontories were named 'Deane's Head' and 'Berkeley's Point', while the small tunnel entrance became 'Wise's Eye' to the locals.

A contemporary B & NC advertisement proudly proclaimed:

> The New Cliff Path along the base of the Gobbins Cliffs, Ballycarry, with its ravines, bone caves, natural aquariums, &c., has no parallel in Europe as a Marine Cliff Walk.

The Gobbins Cliffs formed part of the Islandmagee estate and on 24 March 1902 the B & NC had signed a lease with the trustees, paying £50 per annum.

Wise had planned to complete the path over a distance of $3\frac{1}{4}$ miles to Heddle's Port. Extensions were opened in 1906; but then Wise fell ill and it was Malcolm who reported in August 1906 to the new Northern Counties Committee that if the path were to be completed to Heddle's Port a double suspension bridge, a tubular bridge and a single span girder bridge would be required, costing £750, plus the cost of a tea house at Heddle's Port; maintenance of the existing portion was estimated at £209 per annum. He was authorised to proceed to a point past 'the seven caves' and to postpone any further work. This final extension, opened in 1908, opened up perhaps the most spectacular section of the path, where the mouths of six of the caves known as 'The Seven Sisters' were bridged by a 250ft suspension bridge and a considerable tunnel through the basalt was blasted. Thereafter the path was maintained for so far as it went; but it would have been a grievous disappointment to Wise to know that it ended as a 'cul de sac', no northern exit ever being opened, and visitors had to return to 'Wise's Eye'. Instead of stretching $3\frac{1}{4}$ miles it never exceeded two; nevertheless it was a prodigious undertaking.

The path required constant maintenance, being in an extremely exposed position and prey to all the fury of winter storms. During the second world war the staff to carry out maintenance were not available and in 1940 it was closed, remaining so until 1951. Arrears of maintenance affected it mortally and over the next few years landslips carried much of it away. It was officially closed in November 1961 and today the sea grasps hungrily for the twisted remains of the railings and even the words 'The Gobbins', proudly engraved in the rock beside the entrance at 'Wise's Eye', have been obliterated with concrete.

It all seems a rather inglorious end to Wise's work; but all may not yet be lost, since it is understood certain public bodies have expressed interest in seeing the path restored and reopened to make it again the tourist attraction it once was.

THE HOTELS

The standard of hotel accommodation in the Ireland of the last century was, with a few notable exceptions, not high. Railway companies were obviously directly interested in such matters, yet few in Ireland took much initiative until comparatively late in their history. The exceptions were the Belfast & Northern Counties and the Great Southern & Western. By the B & NC's 1881 Act authority was given to subscribe to or erect hotels at Portrush and the Giant's Causeway. The latter place was not given railway hotel accommodation but on 7 February 1881 the shareholders agreed to the spending of up to £20,000 on purchasing a share of a lease of the Antrim Arms Hotel in Portrush, an establishment of long standing and excellent reputation, where HRH the Duke of Connaught had been entertained in 1869.

It was not until 1883 that anything was done; then a separate limited liability company, 'The Northern Counties Hotel Company Ltd', was formed, the hotel, which had been managed under a temporary arrangement for some time previous, being renamed accordingly. An excellent manager in the person of Franz Koenigs was installed; on his departure to GS & W service he was replaced by G. O'B. Hamilton who in time became manager of the Lancashire & Yorkshire's hotels and was succeeded at Portrush by Frank Cox.

The hotel was primarily intended for the accommodation of high-class tourists proceeding to the Causeway; it contained more than one hundred bedrooms and splendid public apartments which afforded vistas of the Atlantic Ocean both at front and rear. Opposite it were pleasant gardens where in summer minstrel shows were held and tennis courts constructed. Though not entirely convenient to the railway station, hotel porters attended all trains and horse conveyances were provided.

The 1884 Act gave authority for the spending of an additional £11,000 and this was used to enlarge and improve the facilities. At this time an American tourist told Clarke the chairman that it was the finest hotel in Ireland. The Northern Counties held practically all the shares which were estimated to produce about $4\frac{1}{2}$ per cent and it was described as 'one of the best spokes in our wheel'. The 1891 Act gave the B & NC authority to purchase the hotel outright and amalgamate it with the undertaking as a whole, and this was effected. During 1891 many guests had to be turned away and further accommodation, planned by John Lanyon, was completed in 1892. In 1894 a new steam laundry was erected at a cost of £1,700, and hot and cold sea water baths, of which the company was very proud, at a cost of £6,000; the architect in this case was Wise. By now, also, 'An experienced London Hair-Dresser is on the Hotel Staff'. The *salon* was opened from 7.30am to noon and 3.30pm to 8pm and, unusually, from 8am until noon on Sundays.

In 1902 the lease of the hotel, which had some thirty years to run, was purchased from the Earl of Antrim outright in perpetuity so that the hotel was entirely the company's freehold property. Further additions were made at the turn of the century and it was estimated that $6\frac{1}{2}$ or 7 per cent was being earned on capital. To encourage business for the hotel in winter when tourists were thin on the ground, combined railway and hotel tickets were issued from various points on the railway, for periods of two days, three days or a week.

It was considered desirable to have a hotel in Belfast and as part of the reconstruction a hotel building was erected to Wise's designs in Whitla Street, directly connected to the station. It was opened in November 1898 and was the last great scheme carried through under Cotton's management and one of which he was justifiably proud. Retrospective authority for its construction was obtained in the 1899 Act. The new hotel, a fine three-storeyed building, was rather prosaically styled the 'Station Hotel', later the 'Midland'; it cost some

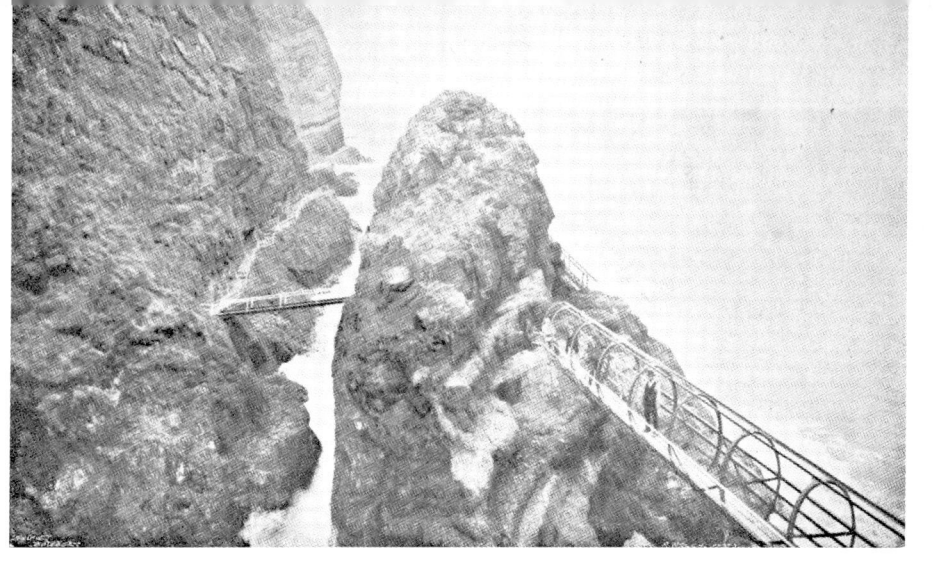

Page 255
THE GOBBINS
ove) Overall view of typical length of path with Man o' War seastack and tubular bridge
(*below*) Suspension bridge at Seven Sisters Caves

Page 256
RAILWAYANA

(*above left*) Milepost 24 near Larne Harbour (*above right*) Trespass board (*below*) B & crest on roof girders, York Road

£16,000. Though on a more modest scale than the Northern Counties, it had the same high standards—'the arrangements combine the artistic refinement of the French Cuisine with the homely comforts of the best English Hotels'. It was placed under a manageress.

The Belfast hotel was the only one in the city under railway management and as such was of inestimable benefit to the Northern Counties. The smokeroom on the first floor was used twice a year for shareholders' meetings; also on this floor were the drawing and reading rooms with the dining and coffee rooms on the ground floor. Understandably the first receipts were not large, though they were considered satisfactory since the hotel was entirely new. It was pointed out to a shareholder in 1900 that 'the hotel at Belfast terminus was not opened solely on the ground that it should be a profitable speculation'. It was opened for the purpose of accommodating long-distance travellers, and it had the advantage of being convenient to the cross-Channel steamer berths.

In the 1890s arrangements were made with the Olderfleet Hotel at Larne Harbour, and the Antrim Arms and Marine Hotels in Ballycastle, for the issue of combined hotel and railway tickets. No financial stake was held in these establishments by the Northern Counties, however.

On the opening of the original line in 1848 refreshment rooms were opened at Belfast, Carrickfergus and Ballymena. In due course the Larne line's opening added rooms at Whitehead and Larne. Later, rooms were opened at Londonderry, Coleraine and Portrush, and at Parkmore and Glenariff Glen (in summer only). Ballymoney was thus equipped with the opening of the new station. All these refreshment rooms and dining cars, introduced between 1894 and 1899, came under the superintendence of the hotels manager who had his office in the Northern Counties Hotel.

THE HOLDEN TRAIN

Something new in Irish tourism was instituted in 1903 just before the end of the Northern Counties' independent career.

In 1902 A. W. Holden, who had for a number of years previously owned the Laharna Hotel in Larne and hired a train from the railway for his summer tours of Ulster, approached the Northern Counties to provide him with a special train. The construction was undertaken by Malcolm at York Road and the saloon carriages, all of first class, were the last word in Edwardian luxury. Three of the coaches were of centre-corridor type, the fourth a dining saloon with large kitchen. All were bogie vehicles with corridor connections and two six-wheeled passenger vans received connections to work with the trains. As turned out the entire train was an eloquent tribute to the craftsmen of York Road. 'All the coaches had the lower panels finished in match-boarding; the end doors at the vestibule ends were recessed [in the Pullman manner] . . . The interior finishing was very grand, with Lincrusta-decorated roof-panelling, and all doors finished with poker-work; the upholstery was an embossed leaf pattern in old gold, and was of such good quality that it lasted the life of the coaches.'

'Holden's Popular Tour', using the Laharna Hotel as base, embraced 400 miles of railway travel and a further forty miles by road. Places visited included Belfast, Larne, Portrush, the Giant's Causeway, The Gobbins, Ballymoney, Ballycastle, Carrick-a-Rede (the Rope Bridge), Parkmore and Glenariff, the Coast Road, Whitehead. All this, together with full accommodation at the Laharna and meals on the train for six days, cost £2 7s 6d (£2.37½)! The tours continued until the outbreak of the first world war, being operated by the railway itself after the takeover of the Laharna Hotel (to be dealt with in Volume II), but were not resumed after the peace.

CHAPTER TEN

Into The New Century

THE DEATH OF COTTON

Almost on the threshold of the new century the hand of fate rested heavily upon the Northern Counties Railway when after a short illness Edward John Cotton died on the morning of 14 June 1899. The regret at his passing was universal and widespread and at the funeral many members of the board and employees and representatives of all the large railway companies in the British Isles were present; he who 45 years before had been the youngest manager of them all, was now the doyen of his kind. He had certainly given the lie to a statement he had made to Joseph Tatlow—'they don't think much on the other side of Irish railways or Irish railwaymen', certainly insofar as his railway and himself were concerned.

The work of the railway had to go on and a new manager was appointed almost immediately in the person of James Cowie, a Belfast man born in 1855 who had joined the B & NC in 1869 as an apprentice in the manager's office. In 1885 he became Cotton's principal assistant. He was a capable manager and was to have a long reign, but he lacked the sparkle that had been Cotton's and it might truthfully be asserted that after the old man's passing never was anything quite the same for the Northern Counties Railway. In order to lighten the new manager's tasks it was decided that Young the chairman should assume additional responsibility especially in external matters —relations with the Board of Trade, Post Office and so on. It was remarked that both he and Cowie were well acquainted with 'Mr Cotton's views'. Joseph Martin became assistant manager.

The board and shareholders felt a deep sense of loss as well as being fully aware of Cotton's unique contribution to the railway's welfare over nearly half a century. At the August 1899 half-yearly meeting eloquent tributes were paid and the unusual step was taken of voting £1,500 to certain of Cotton's relatives. 'It had been one of Mr Cotton's fads to induce people to come from North, South, East and West to visit the Northern Counties Railway', it was remarked.

The magnitude of Cotton's achievement can hardly be overestimated. His interest in the Irish Railway Clearing House and in the parent institution in London, together with his attendance at railway conferences everywhere, made him a well-known figure throughout railway circles. To him was owed much of the popularity the Northern Counties enjoyed among the travelling public; it was remarked that on the departure or arrival of an important train at York Road he was always on the platform, ready to listen to a complaint. To him also the railway owed the excellent staff relations which prevailed at a time of militant trades unionism.

He was chairman of the Irish Railway Managers' Conference from 1864 until his death; he was closely associated with the Railway Benevolent Institution. Ireland in him had a firm friend. He was appointed by the government as a general investigator under the Congested Districts Board for Connaught and it was largely due to him that the so-called 'Balfour Lines' in these areas were constructed. No one owed more to him than the third class passenger and the tourist; of the welfare of both he was always most solicitous.

In literary circles throughout Ulster he was well known as an interpreter of Shakespeare and himself featured as a character in one of the remarkable novels of Mrs Amanda McKittrick Ros, *Delina Delaney*, in which he was portrayed as 'The Father of Steamy Enterprise'. An impressively sincere tribute from Joseph Tatlow, a young man whom Cotton assisted to become manager of the Belfast & County Down Railway and later of the Midland Great Western Railway, may be quoted:

> In railway circles throughout England, Scotland and Ireland he was widely known. He attended all railway conferences, for he loved travel and movement. Shrewd and well-informed, his knowledge was acquired not from books or study but from

close observation of passing events and free and friendly intercourse with all whom he met. His railway was very popular and he and it were held in high esteem. Easily accessible to all, courteous and reasonable ever, he was in many respects a model railway manager...

It is not too much to say that his staff loved him; certainly they all admired him. He was the readiest man I ever met to acknowledge generously the worth of those who served him, and whenever possible he took the occasion to do so in public...

His coat may not have been a Lincoln Bennett, or his neck-tie a product of Burlington Arcade, but who could wear a tall white hat with a back band, with the least little rakish tilt, and a light grey frock coat with a rose in the buttonhole, with such an air and grace as he? He appreciated keenly all the good things that life can give and loved his fellow men. *Pax vobiscum*, kind, warm-hearted Edward John! You were an ornament to the railway world, and always my friend.

THE 1899 ACT

Almost the last event of Cotton's reign was the preparation of an important Parliamentary measure which became law on 13 July 1899. The new Act was principally concerned with the Larne line and authorised the doubling of the Carrickfergus—Larne Town section. At Whitehead permission was given for the construction of 'a pier and sea road or embankment' (the latter being a promenade). Certain additional lands were to be acquired. The purchase of the Portstewart Tramway in 1897 was confirmed as was the building and operation of the Station Hotel, Belfast.

Perhaps most significant of all the company

> ... may provide own work and use coaches motor cars and other vehicles to be drawn or moved by animal power electricity or any mechanical power for the conveyance of passengers luggage parcels and goods in connection with or in extension of their railway system and may enter into contracts or agreements with any company or person with reference to the supply and working of such coaches motor cars and other vehicles and may apply their corporate funds to the purposes aforesaid or any of them.

Additional capital of £100,000 was authorised. Unfortunately the full provisions of the Act were not exercised at this time; the doubling of the Larne line did not take place for another thirty years. The work at Whitehead, however, was carried out.

ROAD TRANSPORT EXPERIMENTS

In road transport, as in so much else, the Northern Counties Railway was an outstanding pioneer. The 1899 Act had given authority to run passenger and goods services by road, but in fact experiments had already begun.

During 1898 the board authorised the purchase of a Milnes-Daimler 6hp petrol-engined van and this was delivered in February 1899. This vehicle was used for parcels deliveries in Ballymena and later it was transferred to Belfast. There is evidence that at one time it was fitted with passenger seats but few details of this survive now. This van continued in service until 1910 when it was withdrawn and scrapped.

The B & NC already had horse buses plying on the Shore Road in Belfast, serving the Whiteabbey—Greenisland—Seaview Road, in connection with the trains at Whiteabbey and Greenisland stations. The company decided to replace these and in August 1901 the shareholders were told of plans to order two motor buses. These were in fact 24hp Thorneycroft steam buses, fitted with 14-seat bodies. In March 1902 one of them made a trial run between the Automobile Club in Whitehall Court, London, and Hampton Court Palace. It was then delivered to Belfast where it joined the other which had been delivered earlier and had been on trial. Both entered service on the Shore Road in April 1902. This was the first mechanised railway-owned omnibus service in the British Isles. The buses were withdrawn in 1913 but the service continued until 1925 with replacement vehicles.

At the February 1902 half-yearly meeting the chairman announced that the company had been approached by several country areas regarding the construction of branch lines. Young declared that, while the board could not entertain the building of branch lines which could not possibly be remunerative, it was felt that the answer lay in road transport. He alluded to the planned Shore Road service. It was decided to purchase a further road vehicle, this time a Thorneycroft steam wagon of three tons' capacity, hauling a trailer of two tons' capacity. It was placed in service in November 1902 at Moneymore station on the Cookstown line for use in conveying goods to and from the adjoining village of Coagh. Young reported that the buses and wagon had cost £2,218 and were giving every satisfaction in service, and bringing valuable traffic to the railway which could not otherwise be tapped. But he reckoned without the roads. Complaints soon arose that the roads were being damaged, both from Antrim and Londonderry County Councils and eventually the latter body succeeded in forcing the withdrawal of the steam wagon from Moneymore in 1906.

These were pioneer efforts; it was a revolutionary concept to break into road transport using mechanised vehicles and another 'first' for the Northern Counties Railway. But perhaps the most interesting aspect of these experiments was the fact that the company realised there was no future in further expansion of the railway—not that there was any thought of contracting it. Instead any extensions would be made by road. This was significant, though not even the most prescient person could have seen an augury of the future when road transport would sweep large portions of the railway away.

PURCHASE OF THE DERRY CENTRAL

The story of the Derry Central Railway was told in Chapter 7. The Bill for amalgamation might have been expected to have a relatively easy passage through Parliament, despite a petition offered against it by the DC directors (who were in no position to offer successful opposition) and similar opposition from the Londonderry County Council. But T. M. Healy, Irish Nationalist MP for North Lough, 'the bitterest tongue that ever wagged in Ireland', seeing in the position a chance to blackguard the Conservative government, alleged that the Northern Counties had tried to 'force the Derry Central into the corner' by refusing to renew the working agreement. The position was made worse when Hanbury of the Treasury, who, it will be remembered, was one of the principal instigators of the sale, agreed

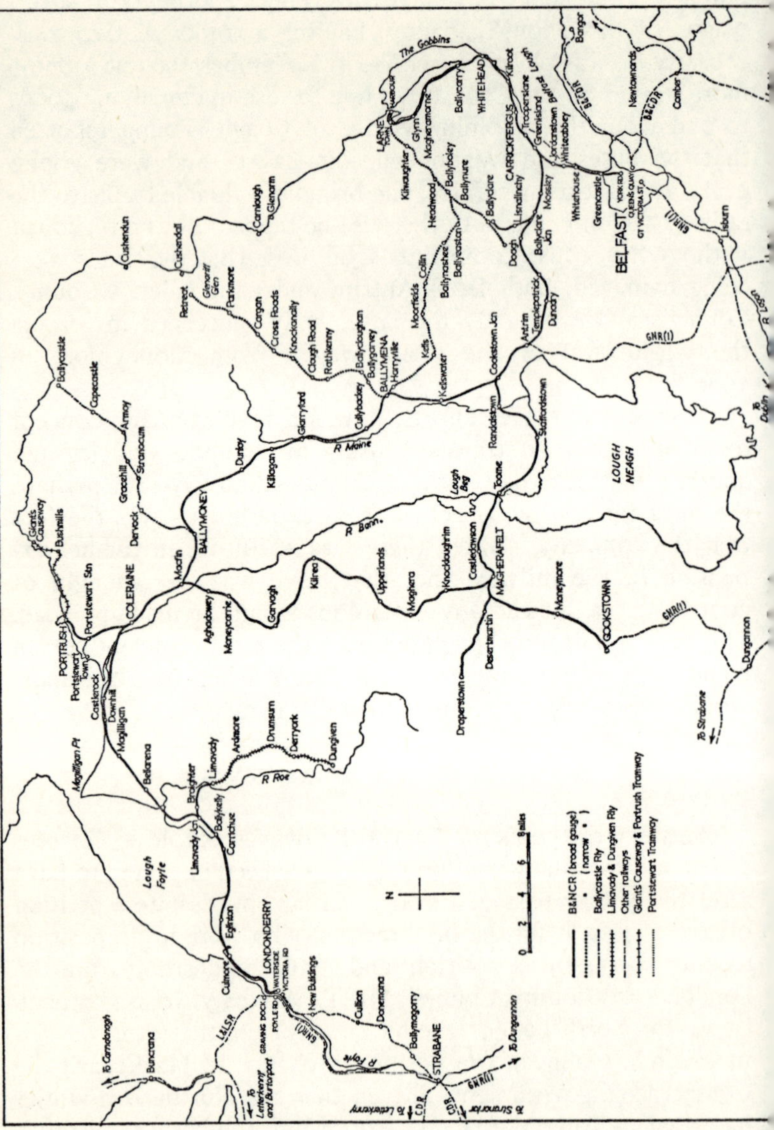

The Gobbins
LARNE
Glynn
Magheramorne
Ballycarry
WHITEHEAD
Kilroot
CARRICKFERGUS
Trooperslane
Greenisland
Jordanstown
Whiteabbey
Whitehouse
Greencastle
BELFAST
YORK RD
QUEEN'S QUAY
GT VICTORIA ST
Bangor
Newtownards
Comber
B&CDR
GNR(I)
Lisburn
Kilwaughter
Headwood
Ballyboley
Ballynure
Ballyclare
Lisnalinchy
Mossley
Ballyclare Jcn
Doagh
Ballyrobert
Ballynashee
Ballyeaston
Collin
Moorfields
Templepatrick
Dunadry
Antrim
Cookstown Jcn
Kells
Kellswater
Randalstown
Staffordstown
Toome
Lough Beg
LOUGH NEAGH
R Lagan
To Dublin
Carnlough
Glenarm
Cushendall
Cushendun
Retreat
Glenariff Glen
Parkmore
Cargan
Cross Roads
Knockanally
Clough Road
Rathkenny
Ballycloughan
Ballygarvey
BALLYMENA
Harryville
Cullybackey
Glarryford
R Maine
Dunloy
Killagan
BALLYMONEY
Ballycastle
Capecastle
Armoy
Stranocum
Gracehill
Dervock
Giant's Causeway
Bushmills
Portstewart Stn
COLERAINE
Macfin
PORTRUSH
Portstewart Town
Castlerock
Downhill
Magilligan
Magilligan Pt
Bellarena
R Bann
Knockloughrim
Castledawson
MAGHERAFELT
Moneymore
COOKSTOWN
Dungannon
Desertmartin
Draperstown
Kilrea
Upperlands
Maghera
Garvagh
Aghadowey
Moneycarrie
Limavady
Broighter
Ardmore
Drumsurn
Derryork
Dungiven
R Roe
Ballykelly
Limavady Jcn
Carrichue
Lough Foyle
Eglinton
Culmore
LONDONDERRY
WATERSIDE
VICTORIA RD
GRAVING DOCK
FOYLE RD
New Buildings
Cullion
Donemana
Ballymagorry
STRABANE
R Foyle
To Dungannon
To Strabane
To Stranorlar
To Letterkenny
C.D.R.
L&LSR
Buncrana
To Carndonagh
To Letterkenny and Burtonport
N
0 2 4 6 8 Miles
B&NCR (broad gauge)
" (narrow ")
Ballycastle Rly
Limavady & Dungiven Rly
Other railways
Giant's Causeway & Portrush Tramway
Portstewart Tramway

with Healy who further alleged that the DC had been 'starved' by the B & NC.

Eventually, however, the Bill made its passage and received Royal Assent on 17 August 1901. Young strongly resented Healy's allegations and was at pains to tell the half-yearly meeting in August 1901 the steps by which the Northern Counties had almost been forced into acquiring the DC. He repeated that the crux of the matter was the DC's intention to seek running powers over the NC line. As to the 'starvation': the Northern Counties had subscribed £10,000 in shares in the Derry Central and had spent between £15,000 and £20,000 in extensive rebuilding at Coleraine. They had *not* wished to possess the line; now that they *had* obtained it—largely to keep it out of other hands—it would need 'all the resources of the management' to make the DC pay. It was found by 1903 that it was only paying its way and had required heavy expenditure.

ACCIDENTS

On 10 October 1900 the 4pm train from Kilrea to Coleraine left the rails 2,000 yards east of Coleraine station. No 22 engine of 1878 was running tender-first hauling four six-wheelers and a four-wheeled horse box. All the vehicles were derailed but again no one complained of injury. Major J. W. Pringle RE, investigating, found that the cause was excessive speed over old iron rails; further, No 22 was double-framed and so rode more rigidly over the road, which had been in place since 1875. He strongly urged the completion of the relaying programme, and this was put in hand forthwith.

In the early hours of 25 September 1902 an accident occurred between Trooperslane and Carrickfergus which might well have had more serious consequences. A special troop train was being run from Ballincollig, County Cork, to Larne Harbour; the train ran over the GS & W to Dublin where it was handed over to the GNR(I) and run to Antrim where B & NC engine No 3 took over. The train was made up of three six-wheeled carriages, one goods brake van and 24 cattle wagons, all GS & W property. Aboard were some 50 or 60 officers and men and about 140 cavalry horses. The vacuum brake was not in operation throughout the train; the carriages were behind the non-braked wagons.

Descending Mossley bank steam had been shut off and it was here that Major Pringle reckoned the train divided. Steam was not again put on until passing Greenisland down advanced starting signal; the front portion drew away rapidly down the 1 in 130 gradient. Passing Trooperslane the train was slowed while the rear portion ran faster down the 1 in 98 incline. Both portions collided violently, destroying four vehicles completely and seriously damaging many others. Three horses were killed but miraculously there were no other injuries.

Pringle was unable to attach blame to any one person but felt that the enginemen had not been sufficiently vigilant in keeping a sharp lookout; William Getty, assistant traffic inspector, had been on the footplate. Pringle was also censorious of the fact that the GS & W, GNR(I) and B & NC had all treated the train as a goods or cattle—with the passenger vehicles behind the wagons as normally placed for drovers—and this, he felt, was a contravention of the Regulation of Railways Act, 1889.

CONTINUING IMPROVEMENTS

The principal civil engineering task at this time was the construction of the Gobbins Marine Cliff Path, already dealt with in Chapter 9. During 1901 and 1902 work was also in progress on the construction of handsome new station buildings at Antrim and Ballymoney. These buildings, basically of the same design, were the work of Wise, and since Antrim was a joint station the GN bore part of the cost of rebuilding. Fortunately for its finances the alterations at Ballymoney scarcely affected the Ballycastle. Also in 1901-2 a completely new station and block post was constructed and opened to traffic at Staffordstown, dividing the Randalstown—Toome section of the Cookstown line; and in 1903 work began on the long-mooted Ballymena station, at a cost in excess of £15,000.

The permanent way department was heavily involved in relaying the remaining stretches of iron rail and stone ballasting was being carried out; the permanent way was described as 'the finest in the country' by the chairman. The Manson tablet-snatching apparatus was adopted in 1899 on the main, Cookstown and Portrush lines and in 1901–2 £1,300 was spent on extending the tablet system to the Cookstown line.

The locomotive and carriage shops were also fully extended in building Malcolm's latest design of compound locomotives, a new corridor carriage set for the boat train, the Holden train, and a set of refrigerator wagons. For some years Malcolm had had in service some 30 ton bogie and 16 ton six wheeled wagons; he was a pioneer of large capacity stock and now designed a new class of four-wheeled 20 ton wagons for the carriage of coal, manure and the like.

THE MIDLAND IN ULSTER

The Midland Railway had for some time been engaged in constructing a completely new harbour at Heysham which would be accessible at all states of the tide with the intention of transferring to it from Barrow, the cross-Channel steamer service to Belfast. The new dock was about two miles west of Morecambe, and the work involved the construction of $3\frac{1}{2}$ miles of new railway. Heysham was to be equipped and provided with the usual facilities and before the work was completed and the new service opened on 1 September 1904, more than three millions of Midland capital having been expended.

Having thus committed itself to the expenditure of such a huge sum, the Midland was naturally anxious that its influence in Ulster should not end at Donegall Quay in Belfast. The best method of extending its activities into Ireland was by the purchase of an interest in or complete control of a large Irish railway.

Such a proposal was not new. The L & NW had control of the Dundalk, Newry & Greenore line in connection with its Greenore—Holyhead steamers; the Great Western had a large financial interest in the Fishguard & Rosslare Railways & Harbours Company which was engaged in building up yet another cross-Channel service from Fishguard to Rosslare in County Wexford and constructing a connecting line to Cork with the support of the Great Southern & Western. Another proposal which came to naught was that the L & NW should purchase the Midland Great Western, third largest railway in Ireland.

But for the Midland's purposes the Belfast & Northern Counties filled the bill. It was admirably situated; not only did it connect the two largest cities of Ulster but it had direct links with Donegal and north-west Ireland. This was the foothold the Midland sought; here would be a valuable adjunct to the great new steamer service, a gateway to Ulster. Here was a railway efficient even by Ulster standards, well equipped, ably directed and managed, with an enviable record of prosperity.

So an approach was made to the Northern Counties, the initial negotiations taking place between the Midland chairman, Sir Ernest Paget Bt, and the B & NC's chairman, the Rt Hon John Young. The matter was then laid before the board and the terms ascertained. They were too tempting to be lightly refused and may be summarised as under:

(1) Each £100 of B & NC 4 per cent debenture stock to be exchanged for £160 of Midland 2½ per cent debenture stock

(2) Each £100 of B & NC 3 per cent preference stock to be exchanged for £120 of Midland 2½ per cent preference stock

(3) Each £100 of B & NC 4 per cent preference stock to be exchanged for £160 of Midland 2½ per cent preference stock

(4) Each £100 of B & NC ordinary stock to be exchanged for £220 of Midland 2½ per cent preference stock

The directors were disposed to accept and decided to advise the shareholders to do likewise.

The 115th half-yearly meeting was held in the Station Hotel at York Road on Friday 13 February 1903. As usual a satisfactory report was presented; the purchase of the DC had been completed; despite a heavy expenditure in completing the relaying with steel rails there was an increase in the balance of £1,532 and the dividend of the ordinary shares was increased to 5½ per cent. Immediately afterwards a special general meeting was convened. The purpose of this, as stated in the advertisement, was 'the . . . considering, and, if thought fit, of approving of a Bill proposed to be introduced into Parliament in the present Session entitled "A Bill to provide for the Vesting of the Undertaking of the Belfast and Northern Counties Railway in the Midland Railway Company" '.

Making the opening speech in support of the motion the veteran chairman, John Young, who had been a director for 44 years and chairman for eighteen, said:

> Some months ago I was personally approached by the chairman of the Midland Railway Company and this matter was fully and thoroughly discussed between us. When I was satisfied in my own mind of the desirability of the proposition and that it would be for the benefit of the shareholders, I laid it before the Board, and I may say that the Board were entirely unanimous in approval of the proposition before them, and considered it to be manifestly and largely for the interest of the Company.

He pointed out that the Midland offer would increase the value of the Northern Counties debentures by £36,000, the 4 per cent preference by £34,000, and the 3 per cent by £3,000, while the ordinary shares would be increased in value by £150,000. 'The transaction that involves such a fine premium is certainly one that cannot well be refused.' The Midland preference shares would produce a dividend of $5\frac{1}{2}$ per cent and while this figure had often been realised by the B & NC in the past, he prophesied that they need not expect a higher figure in the future whereas the Midland $5\frac{1}{2}$ per cent stocks were more dependable.

Young went on to say that the Northern Counties had always done everything possible to encourage industries and to promote the interests of the districts it served. He mentioned the completion of the magnificent new Gobbins Path. They had 'always been characterised by commendable enterprise and an earnest desire to serve the public'. But the Midland, with its infinitely greater resources, could do more; though their own company was prosperous, there was a limit to what they could do.

The venerable vice-chairman H. H. McNeile, whose connection with the company stretched back to 1855, spoke in seconding the motion, stressing its favourable character. Indeed the only dissident voice at the meeting was that of the Rev

John Fawcett—the latest and last in that series of objectors at half-yearly meetings. He asserted now, citing his experience as a Midland shareholder in the 1870s, that the Midland was floated on 'twenty-nine millions of bogus capital' and forecast that in ten years' time 'they would not get a penny of dividend'. He tried to propose an amendment but Young declined to receive it, since it was 'a direct negative'. On the motion being put to the meeting it was carried by acclamation, Fawcett alone loudly expressing his disagreement. It transpired that Fawcett, although entitled to attend the meeting and express his views, owned less than £250 of shares and so could not vote; therefore the motion was carried unanimously.

Steps were already in progress to obtain the Act necessary for amalgamation. The Nationalist MP Jeremiah McVeigh stated his intention of lodging a petition against the Bill since the Northern Counties had been one of the few progressive Irish companies and he felt that its acquisition by the Midland would end all this. An assurance from the Midland that rates would not be altered caused him to withdraw his opposition (a clause was inserted in the Act enforcing this) and the second reading passed. Into the Bill were incorporated safeguards for Larne Harbour, the North Eastern, London & North Western, Lancashire & Yorkshire, Great Northern of England, Great Central, Great Western and Caledonian Railways. Stores on hand were to be paid for separately and the officers of the company were to be remunerated at at least the same rate as hitherto.

The date of vesting was fixed for 1 July 1903 and on 21 July 1903 the Bill passed into law. The Midland shareholders had already given their consent to the purchase and in recommending it to them their chairman adverted to the excellent condition of the B & NC generally. So high a reputation did the Northern Counties enjoy in England, that 'not a single question was asked, nor any criticism offered' by the Midland proprietors.

THE END

The vesting on 1 July 1903 was not of course the end of the B & NC as a *company*. The 116th meeting of shareholders took place on 3 August. Only two matters of importance were raised: on 27 February a serious storm had inundated one mile of the main line between Coleraine and Londonderry, and the long-planned new station at Ballymena was under construction with the agreement of the Midland.

Young recalled that a total of 58 directors had served the company; each as far as possible represented an area served by the railway. A balance of £40,000 was available and from it £3,500 was voted for the present board. A further £4,500 was allocated for distribution among the six principal officers and £500 to the Workmen's Provident Society. An interim dividend of $4\frac{1}{2}$ per cent was declared on the preceding half-year. A last meeting was called on 16 October 1903. This was an extraordinary general meeting for the winding up of the company's affairs. A final dividend of $7\frac{5}{8}$ per cent was declared.

And so, with votes of thanks to the directors and officials, the history of the Belfast & Northern Counties Railway Company drew to a close, its undertaking already under other control. The secretary's department remained open for a short time thereafter, to supervise the liquidation of the remaining business.

CHAPTER ELEVEN

Conclusion

BIG NANCY COMING RUNNING

So ended the separate existence of the Belfast and Northern Counties Railway. It was a very minor railway in terms of size by British standards; indeed in Ireland, as fourth largest with 200 broad gauge track miles and 49 narrow gauge, it was little more than half as large as its nearest rival, and paled beside the 1,000 miles of the Great Southern & Western.

Yet it was respected and admired out of all proportion to its size. Its enterprise was remarkable; it had a long list of innovations and successful experiments of which many a far larger concern might well be jealous and proud. Of more immediate importance to the public, over its fifty-five years of continuous service it acquired a justifiable reputation for efficiency and reliability, its officials from the traffic manager downwards courteous and ever willing to assist. It produced a remarkable crop of first-class railwaymen: we remember Malcolm and Wise, Bailey and Quirey and the rest. We remember the inestimable contribution made to the success of the company by its manager for over forty years, Edward John Cotton. To the Northern Counties he brought talents rarely encountered on a great English railway, still less on an Irish line; his policy of accommodating his railway to the public needs, and not vice-versa, paid off handsomely.

For many years the company was one of the most prosperous railways in the British Isles and certainly Ireland's most lucrative—Northern Counties shares were regarded as first-rate investments. This prosperity did not appear overnight; the first years were lean and it was only by the careful attentions of directors and officials that happier days came.

The company was never loath to advance capital on some project which offered little return in the short term but which appeared to be advantageous in time. Born on the newly founded commercial prosperity of Belfast, it advanced concomitantly and commensurately with the increasing wealth of that city. Its effect upon the countryside it traversed was prodigious and beneficial. It made available easy access to places hitherto remote and difficult of access; its contribution to tourism in Ireland was very considerable and continues even to the present day.

These were some of the characteristics which caused the Midland Railway to turn its eyes towards the Northern Counties; and so the entire spectrum of railways in North East Ulster was immeasurably altered—for the better. Certainly, the prosperity of the old company would not have survived the first world war. Those connected with the Belfast & Northern Counties Railway had every reason to be satisfied, proud even, with the undertaking they handed over to the Midland in July 1903. Their railway had secured for itself a place in Irish railway history that will never be superseded. A significant sentence uttered by the Rt Hon John Young at the February 1900 half-yearly shareholders' meeting is illustrative of the principle which underlay the operation of the railway :

> The first duty of a Board of Directors is to see to the safety of the passengers and of their own rolling stock.

This indeed characterised the Northern Counties Railway's attitude to its public.

R

Appendices

APPENDIX 1: ACTS OF PARLIAMENT

Of necessity there is some cross-referencing between Acts

BELFAST & BALLYMENA/BELFAST & NORTHERN COUNTIES

1845	8 & 9 Vic Ch lxxxi	Incorporation
1853	16 & 17 Vic Ch lxxxi	Extension to Cookstown
1858	21 & 22 Vic Ch liii	Purchase of Ballymena & Portrush
1860	23 & 24 Vic Ch xlvi	Alteration in title; additional capital; purchase of Coleraine Junction
1864	27 & 28 Ch cvi	Portrush Tramway; additional capital
1871	34 & 35 Vic Ch clxviii	Purchase of Londonderry & Coleraine; additional capital
1874	37 & 38 Vic Ch lxxiii	Additional lands and capital
1877	40 & 41 Vic Ch cxii	Subscription to Derry Central; additional capital
1878	41 & 42 Vic Ch cxviii	Loop line; additional lands and capital
1881	44 & 45 Vic Ch ccxvii	Branches; additional capital; hotels
1882	45 & 46 Vic Ch xv	Subscription to Limavady & Dungiven
1882	45 & 46 Vic Ch lxxvi	Alteration to 1881 Act; additional capital
1883	46 & 47 Vic Ch cxxvii	Subscription to Limavady & Dungiven
1884	47 & 48 Vic Ch cxxviii	Tramways; hotels; additional capital; purchase of Cushendall
1889	52 & 53 Vic Ch xcvii	Purchase of Ballymena & Larne
1890	53 & 54 Vic Ch xxiii	New railways; additional lands and capital; purchase of Carrickfergus & Larne

APPENDICES

1895	58 & 59 Vic Ch civ	New railways; additional capital; purchase of Draperstown
1899	62 & 63 Vic Ch lxiv	Widening of Larne line; additional lands and capital; Whitehead; purchase of Portstewart Tramway
1901	1 Edw VII Ch cclix	Purchase of Derry Central
1903	3 Edw VII Ch cxxvii	Purchase by Midland Railway

LONDONDERRY & COLERAINE

1845	8 & 9 Vic Ch clxxxvii	Incorporation
1848	11 & 12 Vic Ch cxvii	New share capital; deviation
1850	13 Vic Ch xvii	Additional time for land purchase
1852	15 Vic Ch xliii	Dissolution and reincorporation
1853	16 & 17 Vic Ch lxxix	Extension to Castledawson; additional capital
1855	18 & 19 Vic Ch clxvii	Power to lease
1859	22 & 23 Vic Ch cxxxi	Issue of debentures
1862	25 & 26 Vic Ch clxx	Issue of debentures
1871	34 & 35 Vic Ch clxviii	Sale to Belfast & Northern Counties

BALLYMENA, BALLYMONEY, COLERAINE & PORTRUSH JUNCTION

1853	16 & 17 Vic Ch lxxx	Incorporation
1858	21 & 22 Vic Ch liii	Sale to Belfast & Ballymena
1859	22 Vic Ch xxi	Bann Bridge at Coleraine
1860	23 & 24 Vic Ch xlvi	Sale of Bann Bridge

CARRICKFERGUS & LARNE

| 1860 | 23 & 24 Vic Ch liv | Incorporation |
| 1890 | 58 & 59 Vic Ch xxiii | Purchase by Belfast & Northern Counties |

BALLYMENA, CUSHENDALL & RED BAY

1872	35 & 36 Vic Ch lxxxv	Incorporation
1878	41 & 42 Vic Ch cxvii	Extension tramways
1880	43 & 44 Vic Ch cv	Application of capital
1883	46 & 47 Vic Ch cxxvii	Power for B & NC to appoint director

1883	46 & 47 Vic Ch cxxviii	Additional capital	
1884	47 & 48 Vic Ch cxxviii	Purchase by Belfast & Northern Counties	

BALLYMENA & LARNE

1873	36 & 37 Vic Ch ccxl	Incorporation of Larne & Ballyclare
1874	37 & 38 Vic Ch cc	Repeal of above; incorporation of Ballymena & Larne
1878	41 & 42 Vic Ch ccxxvii	Link line at Ballymena
1879	42 & 43 Vic Ch clxxiv	Extensions
1885	48 & 49 Vic Ch lxxv	Issue of preference stock
1889	52 & 53 Vic Ch xcvii	Purchase by Belfast & Northern Counties

BALLYCASTLE

1878	41 & 42 Vic Ch cxcv	Incorporation
1925	15 & 16 Geo V (NI) Ch iii	Sale to LMS (NCC)

DERRY CENTRAL

1875	38 & 39 Vic Ch ccx	Incorporation
1877	40 & 41 Vic Ch cxii	Power for B & NCR to subscribe
1901	1 Edw VII Ch cclix	Purchase by Belfast & Northern Counties

LIMAVADY & DUNGIVEN

1878	41 & 42 Vic Ch cxxxix	Incorporation
1882	45 & 46 Vic Ch xv	Additional subscription from B & NCR
1883	46 & 47 Vic Ch cxxvii	Additional subscription from B & NCR
1907	7 Edw VII ch cxxx	Purchase by Midland Railway

DRAPERSTOWN

1878	41 & 42 Vic Ch clxxviii	Incorporation
1895	58 & 59 Vic Ch civ	Purchase by Belfast & Northern Counties

PORTSTEWART TRAMWAY

1880	26 April	Irish Privy Council Order of Incorporation
1899	62 & 63 Vic Ch lxiv	Purchase by B & NCR

APPENDIX 2: DIRECTORS AND OFFICIALS
BELFAST & BALLYMENA/BELFAST & NORTHERN COUNTIES

Chairmen
1845–1867 Hon George Handcock
1867–1885 George J. Clarke
1885–1903 Rt Hon John Young

Vice-chairmen
1845–1855 John McNeile
1855–1857 John Harrison
1857–1867 Robert Grimshaw
1867–1887 Sir Charles Lanyon Kt
1887–1903 Henry Hugh McNeile

Managers
1848–1857 Thomas H. Higgin
1857–1899 Edward John Cotton
1899–1903 James Cowie

Secretaries
1845–1851 John Wilson
1851–1857 Thomas H. Higgin
1857–1887 Charles Stewart
1887–1903 William R. Gill

Engineers
1845–1860 Sir Charles Lanyon Kt
1860–1865 Arthur Forde
1865–1867 George Orson
1867–1873 Phineas Howell
1873–1888 Robert Collins
1888–1903 Berkeley Deane Wise

Locomotive Engineers
1847–1849 Ellis Rowland
1849–1868 Alexander Yorston
1868–1875 Edward Leigh
1875–1876 Robert Finlay
1876–1903 Bowman Malcolm

Accountants
1861–1886 Francis J. Hopkirk
1887–1903 Walter Bailey

LONDONDERRY & COLERAINE

It is very difficult, and in some cases impossible, to be precise as to the date of appointment of some of the directors and staff of this company.

Chairmen
1845   J. L. Ricardo MP
1845–1849 J. G. Frith
1849–1857 Capt Daniel Warren
1857–1861? Mr Serjeant John Cross
1863?–1865 Henry Laver
1865–1867 Timothy Tyrrell
1867–1871 John Robert Hall

Vice-chairmen
1845–1849 Capt Daniel Warren
1849–?   George Henry Vandeput
1856–1857 Mr Serjeant John Cross
1857–1861 Henry Laver

APPENDICES

Managers
1852–1854 W. R. Boyle
1854–1855 John S. Sinclair
1855–1861 Peter Roe

Engineers
1844–1847 Charles Lanyon
1847–1849 R. Hassard
1849–1853 Edward Preston
1853–1857 Arthur W. Forde
1857–1871 Robert Collins

Secretaries
1845–1855 Frederick H. Hemming
1855–1861 James K. Arthur
1861–1871 Henry Laver (honorary)

Locomotive Engineers
1852–1853 Robert Dods
1853–1854 Robert Fairlie
1854–1855 John S. Sinclair
1855–1861 Edward Leigh

BALLYMENA, BALLYMONEY, COLERAINE & PORTRUSH JUNCTION

Chairmen
1853–1855 Earl of Antrim
1855–1856 William Wilson Campbell
1856–1861 John McGildowny

Vice-chairmen
1853–1855 John McGildowny
1855–1861 Robert Young

Managers
1855–1857 Thomas H. Higgin
1857–1861 William Parsons

Secretaries
1853–1861 James Tompson

Engineer
1853–1860 Sir Charles Lanyon Kt

CARRICKFERGUS & LARNE

Chairmen
1859–1864 Conway R. Dobbs
1864–1887 Viscount Templeton
1887–1890 John Macauley

Managers
1860–1890 Edward John Cotton

Engineers
1859–1860 Sir Charles Lanyon Kt
1860–1865 Arthur Forde
1865–1867 George Orson
1867–1873 Phineas Howell
1873–1888 Robert Collins
1888–1890 Berkeley Deane Wise

Vice-chairmen
1859–1864 James Agnew
1864–1873 Henry Hugh McNeile
1873–1887 Sir Edward Coey
1887–1890 Sir Thomas Dixon

Secretaries
1859–1866 Samuel Vance
1866–1889 Charles Stewart
1889–1890 Cecil B. Stewart

DERRY CENTRAL RAILWAY

Chairman
1875–1901 Rt Hon Sir Henry Hervey Bruce Bt

Vice-chairmen
1875–1880 J. J. Clarke MP
1880–1884 James Adams
1884–1901 Col H. S. B. Bruce

APPENDICES 281

Managers
1880–1899 Edward John Cotton
1899–1901 James Cowie

Secretaries
1875–1895 James Blair Stirling
1895–1901 Frederick Dawson

Engineers
1875–1880 James Barton (consulting engineer 1880–1901)
1880–1888 Robert Collins
1888–1901 Berkeley Deane Wise

LIMAVADY & DUNGIVEN

Chairmen
1880–1885 Archibald Frederick Paul
1885–1886 Samuel Alexander
1886–1907 Samuel M. Macrory

Vice-chairmen
1880–1885 Samuel M. Alexander
1885–1886 Samuel M. Macrory
1886–1902 George L. Young
1902–1907 John ff. Young

Managers
1883–1899 Edward John Cotton
1899–1907 James Cowie

Secretaries
1880–1905 David Hamilton
1905–1907 Henry Cowie

Engineers
1880–1883 John Lanyon
1883–1888 Robert Collins
1888–1906 Berkeley Deane Wise
1906–1907 Bowman Malcolm

DRAPERSTOWN

Chairman
1880–1895 Hon Robert Torrens O'Neill MP

Secretaries
1880–1889 Charles Stewart
1889–1892 Cecil B. Stewart
1892–1895 William R. Gill

Manager
1883–1895 Edward John Cotton

Engineers
1880–1883 John Lanyon
1883–1888 Robert Collins
1888–1895 Berkeley Deane Wise

BALLYMENA, CUSHENDALL & RED BAY

Chairmen
1872–1873 William Valentine
1873–1876 John Skelly
1876–1884 Thomas Valentine

Engineers
1874–1884 Robert Collins

Managers
1875–1884 Edward John Cotton

Secretaries
1872–1884 Silas Evans

Locomotive Engineers
?1872–1884 James Donaghey

BALLYMENA & LARNE

Chairmen
1873–1885 James Chaine MP
1885–1890 Ogilvie Blair Graham

Managers
1877–1886 Frederick W. Rew
1886–1890 J. D. Nott

S

Secretaries
1873–1874 W. R. Anketell
1874–1876 Charles H. Brett
1876–1878 George Brett
1878–1886 F. W. Rew
1886–1890 J. D. Nott

Engineers
1876–? William Lewis
1886–1889 ? Horner

Locomotive Engineers
1877–1886 William Pinkerton
1886–1889 ? Horner

BALLYCASTLE

Chairmen
1878 Rev Sir Frederick Boyd Bt
1878–1900 John Casement
1900–1901 R. M. Douglas
1901–1923 Hugh McGildowny
1923–1925 R. P. Woodside

Secretaries
1878–1885 Silas Evans
1885–1886 T. B. Hamilton
1886–1925 Hamilton McAllen

Managers
1880–1885 Silas Evans
1885–1899 Edward John Cotton
1899–1925 Hamilton McAllen

Engineers
1877–1905 James F. McKinnon

Locomotive Engineers
1880–1923 George Bradshaw
1923–1924 James A. Q. Bradshaw

PORTSTEWART TRAMWAY

Chairmen
1880–1892 James Hay

Secretaries
1880–1892 James Lyle

Locomotive Engineer
1882–1897 Bowman Malcolm

Manager
1882–1892 Edward John Cotton

Engineers
1880–1888 Robert Collins
1888–1897 Berkeley Deane Wise

Receiver & Manager
1892–1897 Samuel R. Henry

APPENDIX 3: DIVIDENDS PAID ON ORDINARY SHARES

BELFAST & BALLYMENA/BELFAST & NORTHERN COUNTIES RAILWAY

1849*	0.9%	1870	5%	1891	$5\frac{1}{2}$%
1850	$2\frac{1}{2}$	1871	$6\frac{1}{2}$	1892	$5\frac{1}{4}$
1851	$2\frac{1}{10}$	1872	$7\frac{1}{4}$	1893	5
1852	$3\frac{3}{8}$	1873	$7\frac{1}{2}$	1894	$5\frac{1}{4}$
1853	$4\frac{1}{8}$	1874	$7\frac{1}{4}$	1895	$5\frac{3}{4}$
1854	$4\frac{1}{8}$	1875	$7\frac{1}{4}$	1896	6
1855	$4\frac{1}{2}$	1876	$7\frac{1}{2}$	1897	6
1856	$6\frac{1}{4}$	1877	$7\frac{1}{2}$	1898	$5\frac{1}{2}$
1857	5	1878	$6\frac{1}{4}$	1899	$5\frac{3}{4}$
1858	$4\frac{1}{2}$	1879	$4\frac{1}{4}$	1900	$5\frac{1}{4}$
1859	$4\frac{1}{2}$	1880	$4\frac{1}{8}$	1901	5
1860	$4\frac{1}{2}$	1881	3	1902	5
1861	$4\frac{1}{2}$	1882	4	1903	5
1862	$4\frac{1}{2}$	1883	$3\frac{3}{4}$		
1863	4	1884	3		
1864	$3\frac{1}{2}$	1885	$2\frac{3}{4}$		
1865	$4\frac{1}{4}$	1886	2		
1866	$4\frac{1}{2}$	1887	$3\frac{1}{2}$		
1867	5	1888	$4\frac{1}{2}$		
1868	5	1889	$5\frac{1}{4}$		
1869	5	1890	$5\frac{1}{4}$		

This dividend for 1903 does not include the final dividend of $7\frac{5}{8}$% declared 16 October 1903

* half year only

APPENDIX 4: BELFAST & NORTHERN COUNTIES RAILWAY SHARE CAPITAL

as at 30 June 1902

A—STOCK AND SHARE CAPITAL

Description	Amount created	Amount received	Nominal addition to capital by Consolidation of Preference Stocks under 1890 Act	Total
Ordinary Stock	£933,652	£933,652	—	£933,652
Consolidated Preference Stock 4 pc	993,025	937,450	£55,575	933,025
Preference Stock 3 pc	128,540	128,540	—	128,540
Ordinary or Preferred Stock	98,621	—	—	—
	£2,153,838	£1,999,642	£55,575	£2,055,217

B—CAPITAL AUTHORISED TO BE RAISED BY LOANS & DEBENTURES

Amount authorised to be raised	Amount raised by issue of 4 pc Debenture Stock	Available borrowing powers
£962,119	£837,552	£91,267
less £33,300 not yet available		
£928,819		

Amount issued: £98,621 / £98,621

APPENDIX 5: B & NCR STATISTICS, 1861–1903

These statistics include those of lines worked or leased, from opening until absorption

Year	Miles open	Passengers First	Passengers Second	Passengers Third	Total	General Merchandise & Minerals Tons	Total receipts £	Average receipts per mile £	Total working expenses £	Operating Ratio %
1861	136	116,114	205,935	663,224	965,273	198,605	103,883	763	45,994	44
1862	151	111,449	192,401	656,882	960,732	216,631	107,457	711	52,859	49
1863	151	128,747	184,287	761,174	1,074,208	241,779	110,556	732	64,829	59
1864	151	120,730	188,258	778,231	1,087,219	244,063	113,948	754	58,481	51
1865	151	117,617	202,343	871,222	1,191,182	235,859	126,694	839	66,343	52
1866	151	124,129	210,607	945,788	1,280,524	269,505	134,214	888	71,762	53
1867	151	130,515	221,571	1,004,028	1,356,114	318,320	143,966	953	79,855	55
1868	151	125,316	212,982	962,722	1,301,020	308,361	143,643	951	79,325	55
1869	151	123,110	214,685	995,409	1,333,204	294,997	140,869	932	78,602	56
1870	151	129,117	220,163	1,055,861	1,405,141		148,957	986	82,907	56
1871	151	135,027	226,381	1,102,942	1,464,350	369,925	165,111	1,094	81,803	49
1872	151	132,036	225,738	1,161,560	1,519,334	363,974	173,528	1,151	92,554	53
1873	151	139,629	236,982	1,196,381	1,572,992	386,960	186,893	1,237	114,554	61
1874	151	144,072	233,458	1,229,728	1,607,258	398,074	186,880	1,237	111,909	60
1875	151	140,895	244,050	1,320,027	1,704,972	447,077	198,140	1,312	109,304	55
1876	151	136,999	257,541	1,366,219	1,760,759	495,233	206,031	1,373	110,075	53
1877	151	139,689	256,224	1,397,052	1,792,965	540,725	213,334	1,412	123,923	58
1878	151	141,874	268,020	1,411,103	1,820,997	490,391	201,281	1,333	113,343	56
1879	151	128,171	250,912	1,306,369	1,685,452	541,037	191,850	1,270	106,629	56
1880	180	137,356	278,189	1,446,243	1,861,788	554,682	198,321	1,102	113,942	57
1881	180	130,600	277,702	1,492,026	1,900,328	525,777	190,799	1,058	113,621	60
1882	180	129,249	280,904	1,584,457	1,994,610	558,893	202,130	1,123	115,095	57
1883	197	135,819	293,193	1,694,909	2,123,921	547,073	203,685	1,034	118,619	58
1884	217	137,182	302,536	1,759,632	2,199,350	545,021	207,597	957	123,919	60

APPENDICES

Year	Miles open	Passengers First	Passengers Second	Passengers Third	Total	General Merchandise & Minerals Tons	Total receipts £	Average receipts per mile £	Total working expenses £	Operating Ratio %
1885	217	136,683	292,734	1,691,539	2,120,168	504,943	199,897	921	114,867	57
1886	217	121,326	278,519	1,636,323	2,036,956	494,376	203,377	937	117,995	58
1887	217	122,176	293,755	1,746,169	2,162,100	553,194	214,175	988	114,019	53
1888	217	119,738	288,313	1,768,539	2,176,590	568,985	219,661	1,012	116,183	53
1889	249	124,612	306,880	2,074,121	2,505,613	729,360	248,910	999	129,853	52
1890	249	119,652	282,541	2,102,566	2,504,759	670,745	253,645	1,018	137,442	54
1891	249	110,231	249,241	2,139,994	2,499,466	637,515	261,497	1,050	144,429	55
1892	249	111,247	220,202	2,188,788	2,520,317	625,486	261,765	1,051	152,046	58
1893	249	106,762	202,106	2,262,799	2,571,667	593,186	265,048	1,064	150,703	57
1894	249	101,791	189,894	2,386,103	2,677,788	633,684	276,709	1,111	158,441	57
1895	249	113,239	183,934	2,508,634	2,805,807	639,022	288,964	1,160	162,924	56
1896	249	114,014	170,363	2,567,923	2,852,300	688,324	292,278	1,173	164,429	56
1897	249	107,968	162,647	2,583,488	2,854,103	689,910	295,982	1,189	171,393	58
1898	249	107,202	163,395	2,685,676	2,956,273	724,506	304,004	1,221	186,304	61
1899	249	108,036	164,125	2,835,274	3,107,435	722,342	312,299	1,254	192,162	63
1900	249	106,579	166,359	2,953,916	3,226,854	717,619	318,918	1,280	201,564	63
1901	249	105,287	164,985	2,937,711	3,207,983	733,713	348,883	1,401	241,558	69
1902	249	104,806	162,705	2,996,096	3,263,607	714,766	354,910	1,425	221,293	62
1903	249	108,853	166,359	3,089,399	3,364,611	752,193	365,547	1,468	227,906	62

NOTES

(1) Season ticket issues not included in passenger returns
(2) 'Workmen's ticket' issues included in third class passenger returns
(3) Receipts of Portstewart Tramway not included
(4) Receipts of Hotels & Refreshment Dept not included

APPENDIX 6: MILEAGE AND ROLLING STOCK, 1903

Mileage

	Broad gauge	Narrow gauge
Main line: Belfast—Londonderry	95	
Cookstown Junction—Cookstown	29	
Coleraine—Portrush	$6\frac{1}{2}$	
Greenisland—Larne Harbour	$17\frac{1}{2}$	
Kingsbog Junction—Ballyclare	$3\frac{1}{2}$	
Draperstown Junction—Draperstown	$6\frac{1}{2}$	
Limavady Junction—Limavady	$3\frac{1}{4}$	
Limavady—Dungiven (*worked only*)	$10\frac{1}{4}$	
Derry Central: Magherafelt—Macfin	$29\frac{1}{4}$	
Cushendall: Ballymena—Retreat		$16\frac{1}{4}$
Ballymena—Larne Harbour		$25\frac{1}{4}$
Ballyboley—Doagh		$5\frac{3}{4}$
Portstewart Tramway		$1\frac{3}{4}$
	$200\frac{3}{4}$	49

Total of first track	$249\frac{3}{4}$
Double track	36
Sidings and miscellaneous track	$49\frac{1}{4}$
Total	335

Rolling Stock

Locomotives

Broad gauge	62
Narrow gauge	11
Tramway	3
	76

Passenger Vehicles
    Broad gauge   322
    Narrow gauge   33
         355

This total includes 141 non-passenger vehicles of various types, suitable for attachment to passenger trains

Goods Vehicles
    Capital stock   2,294
    Includes brake vans, etc
    Departmental stock   64
         2,358

Index

Where appropriate the following abbreviations
are used in index entries:

BR	Ballycastle Railway
BBC & PJR	Ballymena, Ballymoney, Coleraine & Portrush Junction Railway
BC & RBR	Ballymena, Cushendall & Red Bay Railway
B & LR	Ballymena & Larne Railway
B & BR	Belfast & Ballymena Railway
B & NCR	Belfast & Northern Counties Railway
C & LR	Carrickfergus & Larne Railway
DCR	Derry Central Railway
DR	Draperstown Railway
L & CR	Londonderry & Coleraine Railway
L & DR	Limavady & Dungiven Railway
PT	Portstewart Tramway

Accidents: Antrim (1897), 230-2; Ballyclare (1885), 213; Ballymena (1863), 124; Belfast: (1857), 61, (1873), 123; Bellarena (1856), 79; Carrickfergus: (1878), 125, (1882), 151-2; Carrickfergus Jct (1868), 124; Castlerock (1892), 233; Coleraine: (1875), 124-5, (1887), 232-3, (1900), 265; Cookstown Jct (1876), 125; Garvagh (1893), 180-1; Larne: (1878), 151, (1898), 234-5; Macfin (1880), 174-5; Magilligan (1858), 179; Moylena (1876), 126-8; Rosses Bay (1855), 79; Trooperslane (1902), 265-6; Whitehead (1894), 233-4

Acts of Parliament: BR: (1878), 162, (1925), 165; BBC & PJR: (1853), 88-9, 90, (1858), 62, 97, 104, (1859), 62, 98, (1860), 103, 104; BC & RBR: (1872), 156, (1884), 158, 214; B & LR: (1873), 159, (1874), 159, (1878), 160, (1885), 161, (1889), 161; B & BR: (1845), 35-6, 131, (1853), 53-4, (1858), 62, 97, (1860), 62-3; B & NCR: (1860), 62-3, 103, 104, (1864), 114-15, (1871), 86, 122, (1874), 115, 131, (1877), 171-2, (1878), 129, (1881), 129, 212, 253, (1882), 191, (1882), 212, (1883), 193, 214, (1884), 158, 254, (1889), 161, (1890), 155, 212, (1895), 203, 217, 230, (1899), 206, 230, 249, 254, 261-2, (1901), 189, 265, (1903), 270; C & LR: (1860), 136, (1890), 155; DCR: (1875), 166-8, (1877), 171-2, (1901), 189, 265; DR: (1878), 198, (1895), 203; L & CR: (1845), 67, (1848), 70, (1850), 71, (1852), 72, (1853), 77-8, (1855), 81, (1859), 83, (1862), 84, (1871), 86, 122; L & DR: (1878), 189-90, (1882), 191, (1883), 193, (1907), 197; PT: (1880), 204, (1899), 206; Miscellaneous Acts: Belfast Central Rly: (1865), 114, (1885), 212-13; Carrickfergus Harbour Jct Rly:

INDEX

(1882), 219-20; Coleraine Harbour, 220; Dublin, Belfast & Coleraine Jct Rly: (1846), 31; Dungannon & Cookstown Rly: (1874), 112; Gauges (Ireland): 1846), 20; Ulster Rly: (1836), 18; see also Regulation of Railways Act (1889); Appendix 1, pp 275-8
Addison, Lt-Col G. W., 234
Agnew, James, 136
Agricultural & Commercial Bank, 27
Alexander, S. M., 190
Amalgamations: with B & NCR, of BBC & PJR, 103-4; of BC & RBR, 158, 214; of B & LR, 161-2, 215-16; of C & LR, 154-5; of DCR, 186-9, 263-5; of DR, 202-3; of L & CR, 83-6, 121-3; of L & DR, 196-7; of PT, 205-6, 213-14; of B & NCR with Midland Railway, 267-71
Andrews, James, 111
Antrim, 20, 28, 38, 111-12; new station, 227, 266
Antrim, Earl of, 78, 88, 89, 92, 95, 156
Armagh, Tyrone & Londonderry Rly, 26
Automatic vacuum brake, 129, 222-3

Bailey, Walter, 211
Bald, William, 24
Ballycastle, 112-14; Ballycastle Rly, 162-5
Ballycastle Rly: 1863-4 proposal, 112-14; 1878 scheme, 162-5; amalgamation with NCC, 164-5
Ballyclare broad gauge branch, 211-13
Ballymena, 20, 24, 32, 50, 57, 91; and narrow gauge lines, 155-62; new station, 227, 271; opening of B & BR, 45, of BBC & PJ, 95; 1887 incident, 224-5
Ballymena, Ballymoney, Coleraine & Portrush Jct Rly, 53, 57, 60, 62; incorporation and construction, 89-90; and Dargan, 91-4, 96; inspection and opening, 96; 1858 Act, 97; Bann Bridge, 97-103; sale to B & NC, 103-6

Ballymena, Cushendall & Red Bay Rly, 156-8, 208, 214-15
Ballymena & Larne Rly, 158-62, 215-16
Ballymoney, 32, 88, 89, 91; and Ballycastle Rly, 162-5; new station, 227, 266
Bann Bridges: *Coleraine*, 62, 83, 96, 97-103, 232-3; *Macfin*, 172-3, 174, 175, 176, 180
Barton, James, 150, 168, 173, 174, 178, 198
Belfast: early development of city, 17-19, 24, 28, 104; York Road station, 40, 59, 108, 123-4, 218-19, 227
Belfast & Ballymena Rly; prospectus, 30-1; traffic table, 30-1; 1845 Act, 34-6; first directors, 36; sod cutting, 37-8; contract, 36-7; stations, 40; Board of Trade inspection, 41-3; opening, 43-6; statistics, 48, 63; Cookstown extension, 53-4; opening, 55-7, 58; appointment of Cotton, 59-61; and 1860 Act, 62-3; and BBC & PJR, 91, 97, 103-6; and C & LR, 136
Belfast Central Rly, 114, 211-12, 213
Belfast & County Down Rly, 114, 209, 225, 244, 245, 261
Belfast & Northern Counties Rly: and automatic brake, 129, 221, 223-4; Ballyclare broad gauge branch, 211-13; and BC & RBR, 158, 214, passenger working, 215; and B & LR, 161-2, 215-16; and Belfast Central Rly, 114, 211-12; block system, 128, 222-4; capital, 284; and C & LR, 109-10, 138, 141, 144, 147-8, 150-2, amalgamation, 154-5; coaching stock, 221-2; competitors, 109, 111-12; death of Cotton, 259-61; and DCR, 171-2, 175ff, 180, 182ff, amalgamation, 186-9, 263-5; dividends, 283; doubling of line, 109, 125-6, 221; and DR, 198-9, 200, amalgamation, 202-3; economics, 131-2; engineering, 116-18, 221-4, 266-7; formation of company, 63, 103-6; harbour lines, 115, 219-20; Hopkirk fraud, 209-11; 1895 jubilees,

INDEX

235-9; and L & DR, 189-90, 193ff, amalgamation, 196-7; leasing and purchase of L & CR, 83-6, 121-3; loop line, 128-9; Magilligan, 229-30; negotiations and amalgamation with Midland Rly, 267-71; new works, 107-8; officers, 279; political considerations, 224-5; and PT, 205-6, 213-14; road transport, 261-3; and 'Short Sea Passage', 216-18; staff relations, 235: statistics, 285-6, 287-8; third class traffic, 110-11; tourism, 240ff; train services, 228-9; Wise's work, 226-7; York Road, 123-4, 218-19; *see also entries under constituent companies*
Black, Samuel, 198
Black Head paths, 152-3, 249
Block working, 128, 222-4
Boyle, W. R., 75
Bromhead & Hemming, 67, 70
Bruce, Sir Hervey H., 76, 166, 181-2, 184, 185, 186, 187
Bruce, Col H. S. B., 166, 167, 178

Caledonian Rly, 216, 270
Campbell, W. W., 92
Carlisle, Earl of, 57
Carlyle, 71
Carrickfergus, 20, 26, 104, 135; harbour line, 219-20; new station, 227; opening of B & BR, 45, of C & LR, 140-1
Carrickfergus Harbour Jct Rly, 219-20
Carrickfergus & Larne Rly, 109; incorporated, 155-7; opening, 140; and B & NCR, 138, 144, 147-8, 150, 152, amalgamation with, 154-5, 216; and B & LR, 148-9; Black Head paths, 152-3; and 'Short Sea Passage', 133-5, 138-9, 140-2, 145-6, 154; and Whitehead, 142-3, 152-3
Castledawson, 77
Chaine, James, 145, 148-9, 153
Chaine, William, 36, 39
Clarke, G. J., 29, 130, 191, 208
Clarke, J. J., 168, 171, 178
Coleraine, 50, 64, 73, 77-8, 88, 90; Bann Bridge, 100, 232-3; harbour line, 220; new station, 172, 213; opening of BBC & PJR, 95, of L & CR, 73
Collins, Robert, 76, 128, 130, 149, 150, 209, 225, 233
Cookstown, 50, 112; opening of extension to, 56-7
Cork & Bandon Rly, 69, 246
Cotton, E. J.; early career and appointment, 59-60, 107, 121, 128, 130, 138-9, 142, 145-6, 154, 157, 163, 164, 174, 175, 176, 178, 179, 180, 195, 202, 204, 211, 218, 235; jubilee, 235-9, 241, 242; death, 259-61, 272
County Donegal Rlys, 116
Cowie, Henry, 196
Cowie, James, 259
Cox, Frank, 253
Cromie, Mr, 90, 91
Cushendall line; *see* Ballymena, Cushendall & Red Bay Rly

Dargan, William, 36-41, 54, 89ff, 96-8, 100, 103, 107, 129, 137
Davison, Richard, 24, 27-9, 32, 36, 38
Dawson, Frederick, 181
Derry Central Rly: inception, 166-73; inspection and opening, 174-5; working, 175ff; and Board of Works, 182-9; and B & NCR, 171-2, 175, 180, 182-3, 184; amalgamation, 185-9, 263-5
Devonshire Commission, 82
Dining cars, 222
Dobbs, Conway R., 136, 144, 147
Dods, Robert, 74
Donaghadee, 133
Downhill tunnels, 66, 67, 68, 69
Drapers' Company, 198
Draperstown Rly: inception, 197-9; construction, 199-200; opening, 200; and Board of Works, 200-3; and B & NCR, 198-9, sale to, 202-3
Dublin & Antrim Jct Rly, 111-12
Dublin, Belfast & Coleraine Jct Rly, 31-2, 88
Dublin & Kingstown Rly, 19, 132
Dundalk, Newry & Greenore Rly, 267
Dungannon & Cookstown Rly, 112

INDEX

Edwards Bros, 137, 141, 146
Employees, number of: B & BR, 50; BBC & PJR, 95; L & CR, 122

Fairlie, Robert, 75
Finlay, Robert, 131
Fishguard & Rosslare Rlys & Harbours Co, 267
Forde, A. W., 76, 107, 118, 130, 141
Frith, J. G., 67

Giant's Causeway, 79, 162-3, 246
Gill, W. R., 155, 201, 225, 236
Glasgow & South Western Rly, 216
Glenariff Glen, 215, 247-9
Glenariff Iron Ore & Harbour Co, 156
Gobbins Cliff path, The, 250-3
Golf, 244-5, 246-7
Grainger, J. & W., 199
Great Central Rly, 270
Great Northern Rly (England), 270
Great Northern Rly (Ireland), 66, 112, 182, 185, 211, 213, 244
Great Southern & Western Rly, 130, 244, 246, 253, 267
Great Western Rly, 267-70
Grimshaw, Robert, 55, 88
Gunning-Moore, J. B., 178, 182, 198

Hamilton, David, 190, 196
Hamilton, G. O'B., 253
Handcock, Hon George, 36, 47, 49-50, 107, 130
Harrison, Hugh, 36
Hassard, R., 70, 71, 76
Hemming, Frederick, 66, 67, 81
Heysham steamer service, 267
Higgin, T. H.: appointment, 43, 45, 54; retirement, 59, 65
Holden, A. W., 257-8
Holland, C. M., 172-3, 177, 178, 182, 187
Hopkirk, F. J., 198; fraud, 178, 209-11
Howell, Phineas, 76, 130, 143, 147
Hutchinson, Maj-Gen C. S., 175, 180, 193, 200, 212, 215, 233-4

Irish North Western Rly, 66, 111

Irish Society, 86
Ironmongers' Company, 171

Jordanstown, 108

Koenigs, Franz, 253

Laffan, Capt R. H., 41-3, 45-6
Lancashire & Yorkshire Rly, 270
Lanyon, Sir Charles, 28-9, 31-2, 36, 38-40, 42-3, 46, 48, 53, 56, 58, 62, 66, 70, 89-92, 94, 107-8, 130, 136ff, 141, 150, 153, 158, 171, 178, 191, 211, 225
Lanyon, John, 122, 143, 190-1, 198-200, 201, 203, 254
Larne (and Larne Harbour), 26, 133-5; narrow gauge lines, 159-62; new station, 149, 216; opening of C & LR, 140; *see also* 'Short Sea Passage'
Larne & Antrim Rly, 148, 158; *see also* Ballymena & Larne Rly
Larne & Ballyclare Rly, 148, 159; *see also* Ballymena & Larne Rly
Larne & Stranraer Steamboat Co, 145-6, 216
Larne & Stranraer Steamship Joint Committee, 217-18
Leigh, Edward, 75, 130-1
Lilley, Peter, 210
Limavady, 64, 70, 72, 73, 104; opening of L & CR, 73, of L & DR, 193
Limavady & Dungiven Rly: inception, 189-91; opening, 193; working, 193-6; and Board of Works, 190, 194, 195, 196-7; and B & NCR, 189-90, 193ff, sale to NCC, 196-7
London Livery Companies: Drapers, 198; Ironmongers, 171; Mercers, 171; Salters, 198; Skinners, 190-1, 194, 197, 198
London & North Western Rly, 131, 132, 138, 139, 145, 216, 217, 221, 244, 266-7, 270
Londonderry, 64, 73, 104; harbour tramway, 115-16; new station and goods yard, 122-3; opening of L & CR, 73
Londonderry & Coleraine Rly, 53,

58, 89, 99-103; 1845 Act, 66-7; contract, 67; 1848 Act, 70; 1852 Act, 72; opening, 73-4; stations, 74; officials, 75-6; expenditure, 76; Magilligan branch, 76-7; Castledawson extension, 77-8; land reclamation, 64-6, 69-72, 80, 86; leasing of line, 80-6; sale to B & NCR, 86-7, 104-6, 121-3
Londonderry & Enniskillen Rly, 64, 66, 67, 72, 75, 81, 109, 115
Londonderry & Lough Swilly Rly, 71, 116, 181

Macauley, John, 155
McCormick, William, 71-2, 78, 80, 81-3, 85, 104
McCrea & McFarland, 190, 192, 194, 219
McGahey, F. J. W., 211
McGildowny, John, 92
McNeile, H. H., 211, 269
McNeile, John, 28, 36, 55
Macneill, Sir John, 29
McQuillan, Patrick, 38-9
Macrory, S. M., 196
Magilligan, 66, 70, 76-7, 79; 1895 proposal, 229-30
Malcolm, Bowman: early career and appointment, 131, 180, 204, 230-1, 235, 252, 258, 266
Marindin, Maj F. A., 230-1
Martin, Joseph, 259
Massereene, Lord, 29, 30, 37, 57, 129
Maunder, Joseph, 46-7
Mercers' Company, 171
Midland Rly, 216; Heysham steamer service, 267; negotiations with B & NCR, 267-70; take-over, 270-1
Midland Great Western Rly, 81, 82, 225, 268
Moylena accident (1876), 126-8

Narrow gauge lines, 155-65; *see also* Ballycastle Rly; Ballymena, Cushendall & Red Bay Rly; Ballymena & Larne Rly; Portstewart Tramway
Newcastle & Carlisle Rly, 239
North British Rly, 139
North Eastern Rly (of Ireland), 24-7

Northern Counties Hotel, Portrush, 208, 244, 253-4
Northern Counties Rly; *see* Belfast & Northern Counties Rly

O'Neill, Hon R. T., 198
Orson, George, 130

Paget, Sir Ernest, 268, 269
Parsons, William, 103
Pasley, Maj-Gen, 19-20
Permanent way, 56, 58, 75, 86, 94, 110-16, 226
Portadown, Dungannon & Omagh Rly, 109
Portpatrick, 133
Portpatrick Rly, 138, 139
Portpatrick & Wigtownshire Jt Committee, 216
Portrush, 57, 60, 88, 104; harbour line, 115; new station, 226-7; Northern Counties Hotel, 208, 253-4; opening of BBC & PJR, 95
Portstewart, 90
Portstewart Tramway, 203-6, 213-14, 261
Preston, Edward, 71, 76
Price, Waterhouse & Co, 209-11
Pringle, Major J. W., 265, 266
Provident Society, 235
Public Works Loan Commissioners, 76, 81-2, 84, 86

Randalstown, 32, 50
Refreshment rooms, 118, 257
Regulation of Railways Act (1889), 179, 180, 195, 201-2, 223-4
Ricardo, J. L., 67
Rich, Col F. H., 127, 140, 159, 174, 232
Road transport, 261, 262-3
Roe, Peter, 81-2
Ross, Capt, 80
Rowland, Ellis, 43, 107

Salters' Company, 198
Seals, 22-3
'Short Sea Passage', 133-5, 138-9, 140-2, 145-6, 216-18, 240-1
Sinclair, J. S., 75
Skinners' Company, 190-1, 194, 197, 198

Station Hotel, Belfast, 218, 254-7
Steamers: *Briton*, 139, 140, 142; *Princess Beatrice*, 154, 216, 217; *Princess Louise*, 145-6, 216; *Princess May*, 217; *Princess Victoria*, 216-17
Stephenson, Robert, 66, 67
Stewart, C. B., 201
Stewart, Charles, 59, 107, 146-7, 198, 201, 210, 225
Stirling, J. B., 168, 176, 177, 180, 181
Stranraer, 133-5, 138, 218; *see also* 'Short Sea Passage'
Stranraer & Girvan Rly, 145, 154

Tablet working, 224
Templeton, Viscount, 144
Thomson, James, 89, 94, 95
Torrens, James, 32, 38, 53, 136
Trade, Board of, 35, 66, 128, 222-3; inspections: BR, 163; Ballyclare broad gauge branch, 212; B & BR, 41-3, 56; B & LR, 159, 160; BBC & PJ, 94, 95; C & LR, 140; Cushendall, 215; DCR, 200; L & DR, 193; dall, 215; DCR, 174; DR, 200; L & CR, 73; L & DR, 193; *see also* Accidents; Regulation of Railways Act (1889)
Traffic table, 30-1
Trollope, Anthony, 82
Tyler, Capt H. W., 56, 100

Ulster Rly, 19-20, 27, 40, 109, 111, 112, 114

Vance, Samuel, 136, 146
Villa tickets, 50, 108, 142-3

Warren, Capt Daniel, 72
Webb, Edward, 69, 71
Whiteabbey, 121
Whitehead, 142-3, 147; Black Head paths, 152-3, 249; Convalescent home, 235; The Gobbins path, 250-3; promenade, 249-50
Wilson, John, 36, 54
Wise, B. D., 180, 214, 216, 218; early career and appointment, 225; work, 226-7; and Glenariff, 247-9; Black Head, 249; Whitehead, 249-50, 254, 266; The Gobbins, 250-3
Woodhouse, T. J., 24, 26-7
Workmen's Pension Fund, 235
Works, Irish Board of: and BR, 163; and DCR, 173-4, 176, 177, 178, 179, 182-9; and L & DR, 190, 191, 194, 196-7; and DR, 200-1, 202
Wynne, Lt-Col George, 61, 73, 94

Yorston, Alexander, 107, 118, 130
Young, Rt Hon John, 92, 155, 186, 197; becomes chairman of B & NCR, 209, 236, 237, 259, 265, 268, 269, 271, 273
Young, Robert, 28, 38-9